PUSHMONDON

FREDERICK SHAMLIAN

TABLE OF CONTENTS

i

left: Dad's sister Nevrig with son John; and my parents, Vahan and Sophia with me and Warren, my little brother.

Much to my regret, our Father never taught his children to speak, read or write the Armenian language. It would have brought us closer to the culture he left behind when he came to America.

Knowing how badly we fractured the word when we tried to say it, Dad took the Armenian word for sloppy and careless, and changed it to 'Pushmondon.' As the years progressed, the word took on additional meanings such as clumsy, dirty and stupid. In my youth, to be called Pushmondon was next to being the lowest form of life.

The following chapters recall my early years and the impact of that word.

Frederick Shamlian

The Sisters of Mercy founded Misericordia Hospital in 1918. Seven years later at 7a.m., I arrived in West Philadelphia two months early, and not yet two pounds.

CHAPTER 1

WEDNESDAY'S CHILD

Chemicals, they are nothing but chemicals, she thought, as she read the slip of paper in her hand. The late July air was stifling. She loosened the blanket around the infant to cool him. How small he is, so weak, so fragile. She leaned back, tired and distraught. The monotonous rhythm of the car lulled her into a sleepy reverie recalling the doctor's words.

"Mrs. Shamlian, we've done everything we can for your child. This formula may help, but we can't give you much hope."

A bump in the road awakened her. She looked at her son and tearfully whispered, "You will not be fed chemicals. You will live to grow big and strong."

She held the formula out of the car window and the wind whisked it away, possibly to lie in the gutter and be washed into the sewer. Or maybe the wind carried it to a place to lie hidden and preserved for thousands of years, only to be found and pondered over like some ancient hieroglyphic.

At home, while the children gawked at their new baby brother, their mother went into the kitchen. From the cupboard, she took barley grain, from a drawer a piece of cheesecloth. The barley was put to boil, and the cloth was sterilized over the boiling water. She worked, not thinking of the heat and steam, which engulfed the kitchen like some primeval forest. When the broth reached the proper consistency, it was strained through the cheesecloth. She waited until it cooled, then carried the broth to the infant's room. The babe was laid across her lap, and with an eyedropper, she fed him the broth, drop by drop by drop. This ritual was repeated nine or ten times a day.

The doctors at Misericordia Hospital were amazed that I survived, for I came into the world two months ahead of schedule on July 15, 1925 at seven o'clock in the morning, weighing less than two pounds.

MILLION ARMENIANS KILLED OR IN EXILE

American Committee on Relief Says Victims of Turks Are Steadily Increasing.

POLICY OF EXTERMINATION

More Atrocities Detailed in Support of Charge That Turkey Is Acting Deliberately.

From a 1915 New York Times article.

At age 12, in the farming village of Yozgat, Turkey, my father watched his family murdered in their fields by Turks with long knives. Roughly 1.5 million Armenians lost their lives in the Genocide.

CHAPTER 2

MASSACRE

Across the alley, behind Scanlon's Saloon, was the small room Dad had converted into a pressing shop. It was just a few steps from our kitchen door. Dad was alone when I walked in. He continued to press suits, handing me each finished piece to hang. It was September 1943 and America was at war. Tomorrow I would leave for the Navy.

For a long time, Dad didn't say anything. Then he turned and said, "You think your sailor suit will make all the girls ask you to their beds, and you can drink all the liquor you want?"

Girls? Beds? Liquor? What's he talking about? I never heard him say anything about girls. The closest I came to a girl was the one who kissed me in the drug store in full view of nearly every citizen in Bryn Mawr. The only liquor I ever had was the teaspoon of Armenian Raki he gave each of us one New Year's Day.

"I will tell you what that uniform means," he said, looking at me with a terrible intensity. "It was a day in summer. Our family was up early, ready to work the fields and prepare food. We did not see the Turks until they came over the hills, waving their long knives and guns. They came too fast for everyone to hide. I jumped out of the window, ran behind some bushes and watched.

"The Turks drove their knives into my father and mother...into my sister and brothers... into their wives and husbands. I watched my family murdered, one by one. They dragged my sister out of the house. She was with child. The Turks held her on the ground and placed bets if the baby was a boy or a girl. Then they cut open her belly to see who won. I was twelve. I still hear her screams today.

"They took what they wanted from our home, killed the animals, trampled the fields, then rode away laughing and shouting, waving knives dripping with the blood of my family.

"You wear the uniform for every Armenian in America who escaped the Turks. You should get on your knees and thank God each day you wake up in America. You are an American and an Armenian, and no Armenian should disgrace himself or this country. Don't turn that uniform into a drunken whoremaster's suit. Walk straight, with respect and honor. Be a man. Don't be a Pushmondon!"

It was the first time Dad spoke of the massacre, and the first time he ever addressed me like a man. That night, lying in bed with eyes open wide, I tried to push the images of slaughter from my head.

The next morning, Mother and Dad accompanied me to the station. The train arrived moments later.

"Don't worry, Mother. I'll be back, eating you out of house and home before you know it."

I gave her a bear hug and a kiss. Dad hugged me and kissed me on the cheek – the only time I remember being kissed by him. As I waved goodbye from the train, there were tears in their eyes.

CHAPTER 3

ESCAPE

After the Turks rode away, my father emerged from the bushes to face the bodies of his family. Vahan could still hear the hatchet as it smashed into his mother's back, and his sister's screams as they cut her open. Other family members lay dead in the fields. His three-year old sister, Nevrig, had been stabbed with a pitchfork and left for dead. She was lying in a pool of her own blood, but still alive. Dad wrapped his shirt around her to stop the bleeding and carried her away. He left her in the care of friends, knowing that if he stayed, the Turks would surely be back and kill them both.

After leaving his village of Yozgat, Vahan moved from farm to farm, city to city, always in mortal fear of the Turks. He traveled on foot through Greece, Persia, Iraq, Lebanon and Arabia. In Egypt, he took an apprenticeship with a tailor. Dad described it like this:

"A miserable sweatshop. I began work at sunrise, and worked late into the night by oil lamp. Sometimes I worked all night. When I finally left Egypt, I could make a suit, every stitch by hand, that any Sultan would be proud to wear."

Dad still made clothes by hand.

Dad journeyed back to Yozgat to search for surviving members of his family. A few days after he returned, the Turkish police arrested him on suspicion of being Armenian. In fluent Turkish, he told them he was a Turk, but still they held him. The police were clever, and tried many tactics to make him speak Armenian, without success. After hours of relentless interrogation, he was released.

"The Armenians can't escape us," the officer said as he removed Vahan's chains. "Someday we will wipe them from the face of the earth, and their God won't raise a hand to help them."

Vahan walked away from the jail thanking "his God."

One evening not long after, on his way home from the coffeehouse, Vahan heard a woman's voice whispering his name.

"Vahan! Vahan, up here!"

He looked up. On a balcony was a woman he did not recognize, beckoning to him. He hesitated, and then started to walk away.

"Vahan, please, come up. Your life is in danger!"

Cautiously, he climbed the stairs, ready to bolt. She was waiting just inside the door. She grabbed him, pulled him inside with unexpected strength, and quickly shut the door.

"Do you remember me, Vahan? Your parents were kind to my family. The Turks know you are Armenian and are going to kill you. Don't ask how I know, just stay here. Tomorrow I will help you escape."

He slept fitfully, one eye open. The next morning, she handed him a bundle of clothes. "Here, put these on."

The clothes were old and dirty, the type worn by dockworkers. She told him the number of a pier and the name of a ship.

"Go to the pier. There, you will join others carrying coal into the ship. Once you deposit the coal, instead of exiting with the rest, walk in the opposite direction to another hold. There will be other men there. You won't know them, but they will know you. Don't speak. You must stay in there all day, possibly all night, until the ship leaves."

"I felt just like a Turk the minute I put on the clothes," Dad recalled. "They were filthy." With his grimy clothes, unshaven face, a fez, and few loud Turkish swear words, he eluded the police searching for escaping Armenians. He carried the coal up the gangplank and down into the hot, foul-smelling hold of the ship. After depositing the coal, he lingered long enough to let the others leave before him, and then turned in the opposite direction.

It was nearly pitch black in the hold. Someone lit a match and motioned to Vahan to sit on the deck against the bulkhead. No one spoke. Tired, hungry and confused, he soon fell asleep, and slept through the rumble of the engines and the rocking of the ship bound for France. He was awakened by someone gently shaking his arm.

"Wake up Vahan, wake up! You are free!"

Man wearing a Fez

"Want to sell your hat for twenty-five cents?"
the immigration officer asked my father.
Vahan, now legally "Victor," walked through
the gate at Ellis Island a free man, minus
the Fez he had worn to escape the Turks.

CHAPTER 4

THE EMIGRANT

The ship rocked in the violent Atlantic storm. Hatches were sealed against the thundering seas crashing over the deck. Deep in the bowels of the ship, known as steerage, huddled the frightened emigrants. Steerage reeked of the foods of many nations – and of seasickness.

How did so many people who spoke such a kaleidoscope of languages, ate different foods, wore different peasant clothes, and prayed to different Gods get along together? The emigrants might have answered, "Do not forget, soon we will be in America, where we will become citizens, and speak, dress and live just like Americans."

Vahan was part of the great migration to America during the early 1900s. He could not speak English. He had very little money. But he did crave freedom.

Finally, the storm passed, the hatches were opened and all were permitted on deck. What a blessing to breathe fresh air, and see the blue sky and calm sea. Seagulls soared in a welcoming ballet. All faces looked westward; America was close. Words were spoken in hushed tones of great expectations. As the Statue of Liberty rose from the horizon, old men and women openly wept. Couples held hands in silent hope, and children were held high to see the Lady of Freedom. Vahan prayed that God would let him become an American.

To the immigration officials, a boatload of foreigners was just the daily routine. Their job was to check papers, ask questions by the book, and go home. There was no time to listen to their tales of horrors, hopes and dreams.

Vahan's turn came. He handed his papers to the seated official, who looked up at the thin man with the funny hat. Through an interpreter, the interrogation began.

"How do you say your name?" "Vahan Shamlian."

"Vahan? Never heard of it. From now on, your name is Victor," and with a flourish wrote Victor on the papers.

"Do you have a trade?"

"I am a fine tailor."

The official looked at the health certificate, then at Vahan. "You look pale. Are you sick?"

"No, I had some sea sickness. I am fine now." "Do you have any money?"

Vahan produced a small amount of currency. The official counted it and handed it back. Vahan waited for the judgment that would either make him an American or send him back to tyranny.

With a loud thump, the official stamped his document. "You are clear to pass."

Vahan looked at the official and repeated over and over in Armenian, "Thank you, thank you." At the gate, the guard pointed to Vahan's hat. "Want to sell your hat for twenty-five cents?" The guard reached into his pocket, held up a quarter and again pointed to the hat.

"Twenty-five cents, yes?"

Vahan finally understood. "Yes, twenty-five cents," he said, smiling proudly.

His first words as an American! He took off his hat and handed it to the guard, who happily escorted him through the gate.

Truly, it was a miracle. He was an American and could speak four words in English! Vahan walked through the gate a free man, minus the Fez he had worn to escape the Turks.

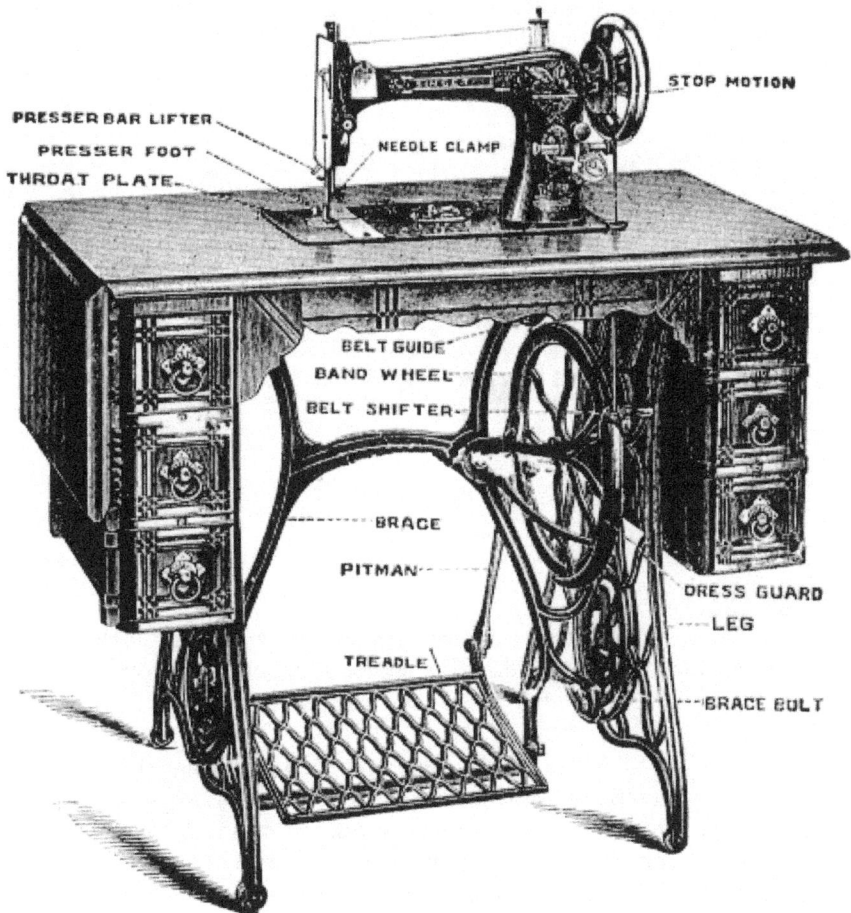

PRESSER BAR LIFTER

PRESSER FOOT

THROAT PLATE

NEEDLE CLAMP

STOP MOTION

BELT GUIDE
BAND WHEEL
BELT SHIFTER

BRACE

PITMAN

DRESS GUARD

LEG

TREADLE

BRACE BOLT

Vahan's Tailor Shop in the Bronx had a Singer treadle sewing machine, a second hand steam press, a fitting room with a tall mirror, and tapestries from the old world.

CHAPTER 5

GRAND OPENING

Vahan stood behind the counter, watching people pass by. No one even looked in his window. He began pacing back and forth. In his small shop, he did not have to take many steps.

The shop had a little counter with a wooden shelf where he kept his chalk, tape measure and pins. An empty cigar box served as his cash box. Behind the counter was a small worktable neatly arrayed with needles, threads, buttons and shears. There was a canvas-covered pressing board, sponge, bowl and iron. In front of the counter was a chair for customers. In the window, between two potted plants, was a one-word sign: TAILOR.

It took more than a year to save enough money to rent the store and buy the fixtures. Vahan worked six days a week, pressing pants from seven in the morning until seven at night. On Sundays, he would meet with the Armenians who had befriended him. They shared stories of the old country and the tragedies that befell their families. It was a brotherhood of survivors.

One Sunday, Vahan was asked, "Why do you not open your own store? A fine tailor like you could make a good living. Why slave as a pants presser?"

The seed was sown. Those words gnawed at Vahan as he worked, and as he lay awake in bed late into the night.

"In America, anything is possible. I will do it. I will become a merchant tailor," he thought. "Someday I will have a large shop and a tall mirror," he thought to himself as he straightened his tie and adjusted his suit coat in the mirror for the hundredth time.

He continued watching the crowds pass by until he became too tired to pace. He sat down, put his hands on his knees, and said a few silent prayers.

About mid-morning, Vahan stood to greet his first customer, smiling as he took the suit from the man who had not stopped talking since he entered the store. Vahan, who only understood a few words, nodded his head and said, "Yes."

When the customer left, Vahan took the suit, sewed the loose seams, fixed a loose cuff, tightened a dangling button, mended a frayed buttonhole, then carefully sponged and ironed the suit.

It was late when the customer returned. Vahan took the suit from the rack, proudly pointing to everything he'd done. The more he pointed to his expert tailoring, the redder the customer's face became. The customer began to wave his arms and speak in a loud voice. When he stopped to take a breath, Vahan said,

"Twenty-five cents."

"Twenty-five cents?" asked the astonished customer.

"Yes, twenty-five cents." They were the American words Vahan could speak clearly.

The man paid Vahan and fled the store with his newly reconstructed suit. Vahan lifted the lid of the cigar box and dropped in the coin.

There were no more customers that day.

Behind the shop was the tiny apartment where Vahan dined alone. He tore off a chunk of French bread and filled it with Armenian string cheese. After each bite, he ate a few grapes. This very meal was to become an occasional summer lunch as we grew up. Then, in a small brass pot, he made Turkish coffee.

After dinner, he took his water pipe from the shelf and filled the glass bowl with fresh water.

From a box, he took sheets of tobacco about four inches square, which he crumbled to fill the small bowl. Connected to the neck of the pipe was a long hose with an ornate woven cover, capped with an ivory pipe. Vahan lit the tobacco and began to puff slowly, in silent meditation, until there was only ash in the bowl.

He lay in bed as doubts and fears twisted like a knot in his stomach. "I cannot speak American, yet I open a store. What a fool am I." It was a long time before he fell asleep.

The next morning, more customers brought their clothes for the miracle twenty-five cent treatment. After a week, he had many customers, but little money. He went to his friends and shared his problem.

"We were wondering when the twenty-five cent tailor would come," they teased.

They laughed because, not too long ago, they had faced a similar problem. They sat with Vahan and taught him how to charge for his work. It took him a long time to learn to speak, read and write English.

Despite his new prices, he kept many customers and gained new ones each week. He bought new equipment for the store, and opened a savings account towards a larger store. After months of work, he'd built a reputation as a fine tailor and had sold his first handmade suit.

Vahan still had much to learn about his America. Some of his neighbors called him Greek, some called him Jew. Others called him

Italian or Arab. Many of the shopkeepers in his neighborhood would close their stores on their old-world holidays. When they closed, Vahan closed too.

One day, a customer asked, "Vahan, why do you close so often?" "I do so to respect the other merchants who close."

"That is wrong," said the customer. "In America there are just a few days a year, other than Sundays, when businesses close. Here, let me write them down." Vahan took the list, and said as he read it, "There is so much to learn about America."

One day Vahan checked his savings. "It is time," he thought.

His new store had a secondhand Hoffman steam press, a Singer treadle sewing machine, and a fitting room with a tall mirror. At the front of the store stood an three-panel oak framed mirror. There were wicker chairs, potted plants, and tapestries from the old world. In the windows, easel-backed cards featured the latest fashions for ladies and men.

Vahan stepped out of the store to admire the windows. "Today, I am an American merchant tailor," he thought proudly. Painted in small gold leaf letters were the words, VICTOR SHAMLIAN, TAILOR.

My parents, Sophia Ginsburg and Vahan Shamlian.

My mother, Sophia Ginsburg, grew up on Manhattan's fashionable Riverside Drive. Her father, a maker of custom furniture, visited his clients in top hat and tailcoat. After her mother died, Sophia lived with her Aunt in the Bronx, not far from dad's shop. The moment she first entered at age 15, Victor (right) was smitten.

CHAPTER 6

SOPHIA AND VICTOR

With her ear pressed against the wall, Sophia listened to a young girl in the next apartment taking singing lessons. As the girl sang the scales, Sophia would repeat them. Sophia loved singing, especially opera, and sang along and memorized arias from La Traviata, La Boheme, Aida, Norma and others. As she listened, her hands were clenched. If only Daddy understood how much I want to sing.

Sophia's mother died when she was twelve. By the time she was fourteen, she had developed a beautiful coloratura soprano voice, and could sing "The Bell Song" from Lakme with a crystal bell C above high C. But despite her pleas, her father's old world beliefs remained steadfast: "Decent young ladies do not go on the stage." Her pent-up emotions would break forth in aria after aria. Years later, she would sing these same arias to her children – her long lost audience.

Sophia's father brought his family to New York from Bucharest, Romania. She was born shortly after their arrival, on October 23, 1900. Her father opened a manufacturing company specializing in custom-designed furniture. Wearing his formal morning suit and top hat, he would call on a prospect and measure the rooms for which the furniture was intended. He then designed the furnishings for each room. Each approved design was handcrafted under his strict supervision. His business prospered, and the family lived in a large apartment on New York's fashionable Riverside Drive.

America in the early 1900s was a nation of immigrants escaping war, famine and genocide. Many Europeans came to "pick the gold lining the streets." Our young nation was emerging from the industrial revolution as the land of great inventions, with the world's highest standard of living.

Many immigrants who did not wish to work in the mills, mines or factories chose to carry on their trade, and opened small shops. They married and adopted many of the American ways, yet retained some of their customs. Some refused to change and ran their homes with old- world parental authority and prejudices. Sophia's father was among the latter.

Sophia, at age 15, was the youngest. Though her brothers and sisters sympathized with her, they dared not ask their father to allow Sophia to sing. The tension between father and daughter heightened when he remarried. Sophia and her stepmother instantly disliked each other, increasing Sophia's loneliness. Her aunt suggested that Sophia live with her.

During those months of working to set roots in "his America," Victor (now using the American name they gave him at Ellis Island) absorbed the sights and sounds of a free people. Gone were the days of walking the streets looking over his shoulder for the enemy. But Victor was lonely. Many evenings were spent with his Armenian friends, but they were married, with families to care for. What good is making a success of yourself without someone to share it with? Victor yearned to find a wife to make a home with children.

One day, a beautiful woman entered Victor's shop. The young lady's companion, no doubt her mother, discussed the tailoring to be done. She would be back in a few days for the clothes.

When they left, Victor thought only of the lovely slim girl with the chestnut brown hair, hazel eyes and beautiful smile. Will she return with the lady? Oh God, let it be.

Long days passed before the young lady and her companion returned. Though his friends had taught him English, Victor's heavy accent made him self-conscious, and he spoke very little. As the older woman checked the alterations, Victor stole glances at the young lady, but a gentleman does not stare. He had spent longer than usual on the tailoring; he wanted to please these ladies the most.

The older lady was delighted with the alterations and continued to bring work to his shop. After many visits, Victor learned that the girl's name was Sophia, and her companion was her Aunt. Following the old-world customs of the time, a young lady of virtue could not venture the streets alone. Wherever Sophia went, so did her chaperone.

As their visits continued, the conversations between Victor and the Aunt grew friendlier. He was no longer conscious of his accent. Victor learned that Sophia had older brothers and sisters. He also discovered that she was fond of opera. One morning, the ladies came to the shop with clothes that needed to be altered in a rush.

"I will fix them at once."

"I'll call for them this afternoon," said the Aunt.

"I will gladly bring them to your home," said Victor, looking at Sophia.

"It's too much to ask."

"It's no trouble," replied Victor, looking at Sophia again.

The Aunt looked at Victor, then at Sophia. "I would very much appreciate it if you would bring the clothes to me." She wrote an address on a slip of paper, which Victor carefully put in his breast pocket.

A maid opened the door. The apartment was spacious and beautifully furnished. From inside, Victor heard an aria being sung. It was the most beautiful voice he had ever heard.

When the Aunt came into the room, Victor asked, "Who is singing?"

"That's Sophia."

"Such a beautiful voice. She has been blessed."

He had hoped to see Sophia, but she continued to sing in the next room. That evening Victor lay awake thinking. Is it wrong to ask them to the opera? Surely they are quite wealthy. He fell asleep with his troubled thoughts.

From then on, Victor delivered the clothes to Sophia's apartment. One day, he said to the Aunt, "May I have the pleasure of taking you and Sophia to the opera?"

Sophia did not answer, but the Aunt replied without hesitation: "We would be pleased to go." At the Metropolitan Opera, custom dictated that the Aunt sit between Sophia and Victor. As Victor watched the joy in Sophia's eyes, her Aunt was keenly aware that the glances were one-sided.

More evenings at the opera ensued. On one occasion, the Aunt announced that she had mislaid her playbill. "Victor, would you see Sophia to her seat while I go for another program?"

From then on, Victor sat next to Sophia.

During the opera, Sophia glanced at Victor and thought, what am I doing next to this man? He doesn't even speak English well. Yet something in him spoke of decency and honesty. His eyes were caring. Sophia had never known love from any man. As the months passed, she felt drawn towards Victor and became more animated. The three enjoyed their dinners after the opera.

Victor was deeply in love. His life and work took on a new meaning. He would build his business to produce enough income for a large apartment and fine furniture. The Aunt noticed the change in Sophia. She smiled more and no longer seemed distant. It would not be long before Victor asked for her hand in marriage. But Victor was full of doubts. Am I the man for Sophia?

She's so well educated. Will her father let me call on her at home?

As Victor feared, her father was appalled at the thought of Sophia being courted by an uneducated clothes mender. She must find a husband from a fine, wealthy family – someone learned, from her church.

Though ashamed of his meager schooling, Victor had become a wise man. During the years of running from the Turks, traveling across the Middle East and the Mediterranean, he observed nations in upheaval and noted the subtle changes in world diplomacy. He worked side-by-side with Greeks, Arabs, Persians, Armenians, Jews and Italians. Victor could correctly describe a person's character and predict, with great accuracy, political events about to happen.

Her father's objections drew Sophia closer to Victor with each visit. One day, Victor expressed his love to Sophia and asked her to be his wife. They were married with Sophia's aunt, brothers and sisters, and Victor's friends in attendance.

Sophia's father refused to attend. That very day, he disowned her.

CHAPTER 7

LOVE AND SACRIFICE

For the first weeks of their marriage, Sophia and Victor dined in the little restaurant on the ground floor of their apartment building. One morning Sophia said, "Victor, today I will make our breakfast. I must learn. We cannot continue to dine out."

Victor sat down and watched his seventeen year-old bride as she poured the coffee. Her eyes sparkled with pride. He did his best not to show concern as he watched her pour the milky substance with brown specks into his cup. Surely this is not coffee, he thought. He took a sip. Yes, it is coffee. He let the grounds settle to the bottom, and drank it. As he ate her very first breakfast, Sophia sat across from him, beaming. Her smile was infectious.

The next morning, Victor awoke early. Sophia was already in the kitchen, beginning to prepare breakfast.

"Let us make breakfast together," said Victor. "I will make the coffee."

He took the coffee pot, removed the basket, filled the pot with water and placed it on the stove to boil. Sophia watched as he measured spoonfuls of coffee into the basket and replaced the lid.

She made sure to remember what Victor did. When the coffee began to percolate, Victor said, "I do not allow this to boil for more than five minutes." The next morning, Sophia made the coffee just as she had seen Victor do. Sophia worked hard to become a good cook, learning much from Victor.

They were married just a few months when Victor announced he was bringing a friend home to dinner. That night, Sophia set before them a large roast, dishes of potatoes and vegetables, and warm rolls. There was even a special dessert with coffee. After dinner, as the men walked into the parlor to smoke, the guest said, "Victor, you are fortunate to have a beautiful wife who can cook."

After the guest departed, Victor said, "Sophia, our dinner was fit for a Sultan. How did you know to do it so well?"

"Victor, I have a confession to make. I did not cook the dinner. I had the restaurant send it upon the dumbwaiter."

Victor looked at Sophia and laughed. "That will be our delicious secret."

On May 1, 1919, Victor rushed Sophia to the Manhattan Square Sanitarium, where Newert Victoria was born. Translated from the Armenian, Newert means "new rose."

Sophia became a dedicated mother, but longed for the affections of her family, which was denied because she had married "beneath" her. Victor took notice. Alone in his store, he thought of ways to ease her pain.

One evening, Victor said, "Sophia, I would like to leave New York and open a business in Philadelphia."

"Philadelphia? Your shop is prospering. You have hired a presser and a seamstress. Is something wrong?"

How could he say to her, "Each day I see the hurt in your eyes because you miss your family. I cannot stand by and see you suffer because your father will not love you...because of me?"

Victor just said, "Philadelphia needs good tailors. I feel I can be more successful there."

In the spring of 1920, Victor, Sophia and their infant daughter left New York to begin a new life in Philadelphia.

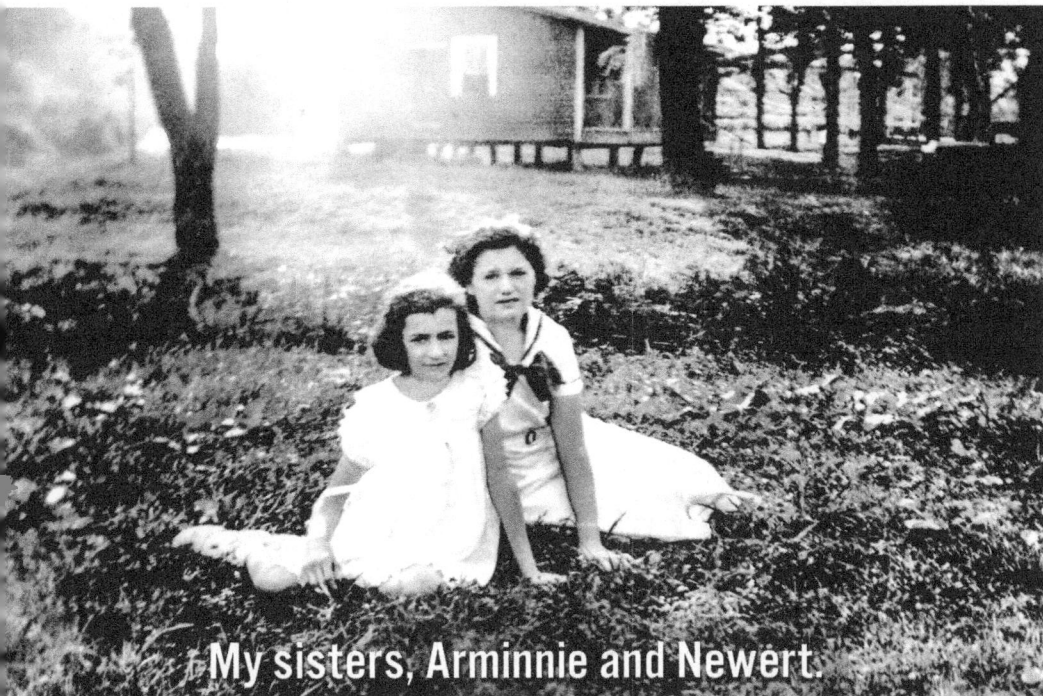
My sisters, Arminnie and Newert.

Victor's family grew faster than his savings.
That's me at 15, Minnie at 18, and Warren, 12.

CHAPTER 8

PHILADELPHIA

Dad rented a store with an upstairs apartment at 7037 Woodland Avenue, at the western edge of the city. Mother prayed that when the people of Philadelphia saw Victor's fine tailoring, his business would flourish once more, and he could again hire a presser and seamstress to keep up with the work.

If fine tailors were needed, it certainly was not in this section of Philadelphia. Just earning enough to feed his family was a daily struggle. With a second child due soon, Dad took a part-time job with a tailor in Bryn Mawr, then returned home to work on what little business came in that day.

Unable to afford a hospital, Dad engaged an Armenian woman doctor to come to the apartment. On Thursday, December 16, 1920, she helped bring their son John into the world.

Each week, Victor put aside a small sum for a new store in a new location. His family grew faster than his savings. Arminnie was born on Labor Day, September 4, 1922. Three years later, I came along on a Wednesday, July 15, 1925. Warren followed on a Tuesday, August 16, 1927.

Sometime between 1922 and 1925, we moved to 7016 Woodland Avenue. Dad's Record of Family Births in our Bible does not give a reason for the move.

The winter of 1927-28 was so cold, Dad bought a portable oil heater. Warren, only a few months old, was in his crib in the kitchen, the warmest place in the apartment. Newert, John, Min and I had the mumps. Towels were wrapped around our heads and tied under our chins to keep our swollen jowls warm.

Any contagious disease meant being quarantined for twenty-one days. Once the doctor notified the Health Inspector, he came almost at once and pasted a large yellow paper on the door.

Printed in large black letters was the word QUARANTINE, along with the type of disease and the dates of the quarantine period – a stern warning to visitors. Only the Health Inspector could remove the paper at the end of the quarantine.

Restless from our days of confinement, we were running from room to room when Minnie accidentally knocked over the oil heater. Flaming oil seared her arm and started a small blaze. Firemen came almost at once, and contained the fire to a small portion of one room. When the firemen saw Minnie's badly burnt arm, they wrapped her in a blanket and carried her to the fire truck. One fireman held her in his arms while the other raced, with bells clanging and sirens screaming, to Misericordia Hospital. Teachers from Stowe Elementary School across the street came to offer assistance, as did neighbors and nuns from the nearby Catholic school.

Newert, John and I sat at the kitchen table in our babushkas, crying. Even Warren, who had been asleep until the fire, added to the wailing chorus. Despite Mother's calming words, she was frightened for Minnie. She should be with her, she thought. We were very subdued when Dad brought Minnie home. Her arm was bandaged and set in a sling. Our parents put her in one of the bedrooms and gave her some broth to help her sleep. We too were sent to bed, with orders to be very quiet.

A few days later, the Doctor came to remove the bandages and examine Minnie's arm.

Newert was horrified to see the skin hanging loose. "Oh God, please let Minnie's arm be well again," she prayed. Her prayers were answered. By the time Minnie grew into a young woman, there was hardly a sign of a burn.

In the fall of 1928, Dad moved us to 1029 County Line Road in Bryn Mawr, the first and only house my family ever lived in. Newert and John attended a one-room schoolhouse in Garrett Hill, Delaware County. Dad opened his store at the corner of Lancaster Pike and Roberts Road.

One year later, in October, 1929, the stock market crashed.

The Great Depression hurt everyone. Dad couldn't pay two rents, so we moved into the apartment above the store, which meant we were now living in Montgomery County. John and Newert transferred to the Bryn Mawr Grammar School. It was in this apartment and store that the memories of my youth begin.

In the Navy – a lowly Seaman at Boot Camp.

CHAPTER 9

THE NAVY
NEWPORT, RHODE ISLAND

He was short and lean, with a thin mustache that added an air of authority to his slight stature. The stripes and insignia on his sleeves impressed me, though I didn't know what they meant. With his feet astride and his hands at his sides, he glared at us.

"Now hear this!" he bellowed. "From this moment on, you will obey all orders, salute everything that moves, and you will call me 'SIR!' Now get your gear off the deck and put it against the bulkhead."

I wished I knew what he was saying. I just stood there. He walked towards me, stopped about three inches from my face and roared, "You deaf, Boot?"

He pointed towards my string-tied valise, the floor and the wall.

"That's your gear, that's the deck and that's the bulkhead. NOW GET YOUR GEAR OFF THE DECK AND PUT IT AGAINST THE BULKHEAD. ON THE DOUBLE!"

I grabbed my bag and flew to the bulkhead, praying that my hearing wasn't impaired for life. Before leaving the hall, he asked, "Any questions?"

I raised my hand. "Sir, where is the men's room?"

He called to another sailor, "Boats, show this Boot to the head." Oh my God, what did I do wrong?

The next morning, we marched to the dispensary for a physical. I was worried sick about the eye test. As I stood in line waiting my turn, I memorized the eye chart backward and forward.

After the test, the optometrist examined my thick lenses and said, "The Navy means a lot to you, doesn't it, son?"

"Yes sir, it does."

With a smile, he stamped the paper. "You passed."

The last doctor I saw that day asked me questions such as, "Do you love your mother?" "Yes."

"Do you love your father?" "Yes."

"Do you like girls?" "Yes."

"Would you rather go out with girls or be with boys?" "I like to date girls and play baseball with my buddies."

After many questions, he told me to turn around, and with a swab of iodine, put a mark on my back. A petty officer looked at the mark and told me to join a group of about twenty Boots. There was another, smaller group of Boots across the room. After the physicals, we never saw them again.

Boot Camp was located in Newport, Rhode Island, on Coddington Point. Across the bay was the Naval War College. Moored in front of the college was the frigate, U.S.S. Constellation. I was assigned to Company 584. We were billeted in large, corrugated steel Quonset huts. Our bunks were lined up beneath the windows on each side of the hut. In the center was a potbelly stove.

Each Boot had to stand watch, feed the stove from the coal bucket, and watch for fires caused by overheating.

Being the youngest, I was made the messenger. Three times a day, every day, I had to double-time to the Mess Hall, report to the Mess Chief that "Company 584 is ready for chow, Sir", receive his nod, double-time back, and then double-time the entire company to chow – in cadence.

One night about eleven o'clock (twenty-three hundred hours, Navy time), I was awakened by Company Commander, Ohanian, with orders to report to the Battalion Commander, on the double.

I saluted and stood at attention. The Commander just sat there and looked me over like something not of this world.

"Shamlian, your Company Commander says that you're doing a good job, but answer me one thing. Do you always salute with your left hand?"

Sure enough, I had saluted with my left hand.

"I try not to, sir."

"See that you don't. You're excused."

Couldn't I have been told that in the morning?

We were nearing the end of a ten-mile march with a full pack and a dummy Springfield '03 rifle. About a mile from camp, we stopped for a ten-minute rest. Hot, dirty and tired, I leaned against a rock, being careful not to let my rifle fall.

Company Commander Ohanian approached me. "Shamlian, tomorrow is graduation day. I want you to know that you took everything we threw at you. You've done a great job."

As he turned to leave, he added with a smile, "This Armenian is proud of you."

Believe me, I marched that last mile proud and tall. Mother and Dad, your Pushmondon came through!

Dad, mother and Minnie

Sophia expressed her emotions in her singing,
and her love in her cooking.

In 1934, my mother fed a family of seven
on $3 a week. We all loved her meatloaf and
roast lamb, and every Sunday mother made
dad's favorite – homemade chicken soup.

CHAPTER 10

ON LEAVE
BRYN MAWR, PA

We had an hour before our train arrived in New York City. Five of us went to a saloon across from the Pennsylvania Station.

"Whadaya guys wanna drink?" asked the bartender.

"Scotch and soda for me."

"Rye with a chaser." "Whiskey and water."

"Double rye with a beer chaser."

All during this litany, I fretted. I didn't know what to order, much less how to drink it. "Whad about you," the barkeeper growled.

"Give him the same as me," someone said.

Placed before me was a lethal-looking double rye and beer chaser. I 'downed-the-hatch' with the rest, and didn't remember much after that.

As we exited the train at Philadelphia's 30th Street Station, the porter said to me, "Mister, you sho has a nice singing voice."

"Me? I didn't do any singing," I said.

"That must have been sum party," he said, laughing. "You sang to all the ladies on the train. You sho has got a nice singing voice. Yes sir, it'll do." I rushed to catch the Paoli Local with his laughter fading in the distance.

It was late when I arrived home. "Look how thin you are," mother cried as she hugged me. I didn't lose any weight at Boot Camp. The Navy just shifted it to its proper places. Before I had finished greeting my family, mother had enough food spread to feed the U.S. Navy.

1008 Lancaster Avenue was a three-story clapboard house with a store on the first floor. I remember the health inspector telling my parents that the place could not be rented. Due to the sorry conditions left by the previous tenant, a baker, it was going to be condemned.

"Just give us two weeks, "said Dad.

The Inspector yielded, and returned in two weeks as promised. No other place in history endured a more thorough inspection. Afterwards, shaking his head incredulously, he asked my parents, "How did you do it? I was sure it couldn't be done."

Heck, I wasn't worried at all. Mother was a fanatic about cleanliness. While other kids had trouble keeping clean, we had to sneak out to get dirty. Who ever heard of five kids all wearing white linen at a picnic?

My younger brother, Warren, and I shared a room on the third floor. My parents had the room beside ours, and my sisters, Newert and Arminnie, shared the room next to theirs. The third floor was laid out like an "L" with a small center hallway. The winding stairs reminded me of a passageway in an old castle. My older brother John was lucky. He had his own room on the second floor – and he didn't have to wear gloves to bed in the winter.

When the house was originally built, I'm pretty sure that there was no inside plumbing or electricity. Old gas lamp pipes, now sealed, protruded from the walls. We used them to hang pictures. Across the hall from John's room was the bathroom and tub, wedged under the stairs at an angle so acute, you risked brain damage to take a bath. Beside the bathroom door was another tiny door once used for storage. When they built the bathroom, the tiny door remained. You could open it and see the person taking a bath.

The parlor took up the entire front of the second floor. Its cleanliness was sacrosanct. No one dared desecrate it, not even with dirty socks. We spent most of our time in the first floor dining room and kitchen, behind the store. With the only radio in the house, the dining room was where we did our homework, entertained friends, and shared The Lone Ranger, Lux Radio Theater, and all the radio programs of the time.

With its potbelly stove, our kitchen was the best place of all. In winter, we would flee our deep-freeze bedrooms and frost-caked windows, and rush downstairs to dress by the warmth of the stove.

This morning, as always, Dad was up when I entered the kitchen. He enjoyed his first cup of coffee alone, listening to the news.

"How do you like the Navy?" he asked.

"I'd like it better if I knew what they were talking about. The Navy has a language of its own." "You will learn the good Navy language if you try. What are the other sailors like?" "They're much older than me, dad. They're always talking about their girls, their ex-wives, and drinking."

His face grew hard. "Is that what you want to learn? You don't need the Navy to teach you that. Go next door to the saloon. Every bum needs company. Don't be a Pushmondon. Don't cheapen yourself for anyone."

Just then, mother came in to make breakfast. As we drank our coffee, I told them about boot camp. They absorbed every word.

After breakfast, I walked to the drugstore. Lulu was wiping down the back bar of the soda fountain. I crept up behind her, locked my arms about her waist, and kissed her on the cheek. She twisted in my arms and was about to send a hay-maker to the jaw when she recognized me. "Still trying to be the great lover with all us pretty girls?"

Lulu must have been in her fifties. I don't think she knew what "a day of rest" meant. Her graying hair was always neat, and her blue eyes sparkled when she became excited or mad – which happened quite often when I was around. I sat at the fountain and told Lulu about the dumbest sailor in the Navy. I kept looking towards the door.

"She ain't coming." She said it low and soft, almost as an apology.

"When you left for the Navy, she stopped coming. You know, you ain't no Don Juan, and there's still some good-looking guys around. By the way, go see Doc. He's pretty sick."

Doc Martin was one of the finest men I ever worked for. He looked like a kindly Karl Malden with glasses and a mustache. Mrs. Martin took me to Doc. He was sitting in the living room.

"Hi Doc," I said, smiling. He looked at me as if I was behind a screen. Finally he asked, "How do you like the Navy?" His words came slowly. "I like it a lot."

"How do you like the Navy?" he asked again. And then again. He never heard a word I said.

I left the room to join his wife on the porch. She said Doc had a brain tumor and it was just a matter of weeks. I left that house on Summit Grove Avenue in tears, and never saw Doc again.

I continued down Bryn Mawr Avenue past my old grammar school, across the P&W trestle, pass the Wister home, and into open country. The winding, high-crested two-lane road was lined with wildflowers. Not far from Sproul Road, by the stone bridge, was a springhouse with a solitary willow tree. I climbed the fence and sat under the tree. My brother John and I were to do this a number of times after the war. I thought about Doc, and I thought about her.

She came in everyday around noon. With her golden-brown hair and brown eyes, she looked like Olivia DeHaviland. I remember working at the drugstore after passing my Navy physical.

Customers were two-deep at the fountain. She was seated at the end of the counter. "Did you take your physical today?" she asked.

"Yep," I said, trying to sound like Gary Cooper. "Are you in the Army?"

"Nope," said Gary Cooper.

"I'm sorry," she said. "Did they tell you why?" "Yep." I had a great way with words.

"Why?" she asked.

"Because I'm in the Navy." She reached across the counter, put her arms around my neck and gave me a big kiss on the lips. I was redder than an overripe tomato. And I was never prouder or happier than at that moment.

"Just because you're a sailor now, ain't no reason to act like one here," Lulu said to the delight of the customers. She had me wait on every customer at the counter alone. There were nearly twenty-five dollars in tips. Bless you, Lulu.

I thought about that kiss, how pretty she looked, how clean she smelled, and then laughed loud enough to startle a sheep grazing nearby. This city slicker sailor-boy lover didn't even know her name.

A drugstore soda fountain, circa 1930s.
I learned the art of soda fountain showmanship
and called myself the 'Fizzician.'

CHAPTER 11

THE "FIZZICIAN"

Sandwiched between the Bryn Mawr Trust Company and Tapper's Service Station, where Warren worked after school and on weekends, was Liggett's Drug Store. I had heard that they were looking for a soda jerk, and went there before the store opened.

"The store doesn't open until nine." Behind me, wearing glasses and a mustache, was the friendliest smile I ever saw.

"I know. I'm waiting to see the manager."

"Some special reason?" he asked.

"I hear there's a soda fountain job."

"Ever work in a drugstore before?"

"I work a couple of days a week at Prickett's, on Prospect Avenue."

"Well, let's go in before the others get here and you can show me what you know. I'm Ben Martin, the manager. What's your name?

45

"Fred Shamlian."

"How old are you?"

"I'm 16, sir."

We went in and Doc Martin handed me an apron. I mixed a black and white milkshake, a strawberry ice cream soda, and a bromo. Then I had to explain how to make various sundaes and a banana split.

"All the employees at Liggett's are bonded," he said. "If you're caught stealing, you'll never get another job. You must be clean, and wear a white shirt and black bow tie at all times. I do not tolerate dirty jokes or disrespect to customers, even though some may deserve it. The hours are six to eleven p.m. Monday through Friday, eight hours on Saturday, then Sunday morning from nine to one, and again from six to nine at night. We pay fourteen dollars a week."

"Fourteen dollars a week! You mean I have the job?"

"Yes. How soon can you start?"

"I'll start right now!"

He smiled. "Go home first, tell your parents, and come back with your birth certificate. Enjoy your soda first."

That morning I broke the two-minute mile.

"Fourteen dollars a week!" said Mother. "What are the hours?"

"What about your homework?" asked Dad.

"Nights, Saturdays and Sundays. Don't worry, I'll do my homework." Mother made me put on a clean shirt. The one I'd put on an hour ago had wrinkled. No son of hers was going to disgrace the family starting a new job with a wrinkled shirt.

"Fix your shirt. Stand up straight. And don't do half a job. Don't be a Pushmondon."

"I won't, Dad," I said, and ran back to the drugstore with my birth certificate. I had made it to the big time.

Lulu was chopping celery when Doc introduced me. Her blue eyes looked right through me.

She greeted me warmly with, "Don't stand there gawking. Put on an apron and get to work!"

In those days, Bryn Mawr was a busy town on Saturdays. People came in from the farms and country estates, and chauffeurs in big limousines were seen everywhere. The fountain was busy. Lulu didn't let up. "Wipe the counter! Clean the glasses! You didn't give the lady a glass of water and a napkin! How long does it take to make a milkshake?" Near the end of the day she came to me and said, "Take a break, kid. You earned it. Just do what you did today and we'll get along like lovers."

Lulu also introduced me to the art of soda fountain showmanship – those special movements that transform the simplest soda into a three reel Hollywood production. I became a whiz and called myself the 'Fizzician.'

One summer day, my artistry backfired. It was mid-afternoon on a Saturday. I was showing off in front of some girls, twirling and flipping a milkshake container from hand to hand, when I missed. Like a silver missile, the chrome container filled with milk, ice cream and chocolate syrup flew and landed in the lap of a lady sitting at the end of the counter. Stunned silence! I grabbed a towel and ran to her, staring at the oozing mess right in the crease of her lap. I gently lifted the container, and handed her the towel.

Doc Martin hurried over to the woman, who was making a noble effort to clean her dress. Before he could say a word, the woman said, "Please don't be angry with the boy. For the past fifteen minutes I've been enjoying a show I thought only existed in the movies." Doc

47

glared at me, then walked away without saying a word. He never mentioned it again. I had learned the hard way.

"I'm very sorry, lady." I said. I grabbed a napkin and wrote down an address. "If you take your dress here to be cleaned, it'll be like new and it won't cost a cent."

"Is it a good cleaner?"

"Yes ma'am. It's my Dad's place."

She took the slip of paper and walked out of the store not caring what anyone thought about that big, dark stain on her dress.

I don't have to tell you what my father thought of this Pushmondon.

The dentist's office was above the drugstore. One day Lulu handed me a tray of sandwiches and sodas to take upstairs. I never saw so many beautiful women in all my life. They looked like the classy pictures in Esquire. I just stood there, struck dumb. The dentist came out of his office. "That's fast service. What's your name?"

"Fred," I said. He handed me fifty cents.

"I'll return the tray when we're finished," he said.

Those beautiful ladies looked at me as if I'd entered a forbidden harem. I left there fast.

"Does the dentist always have beautiful girls up there?" I asked Lulu.

"Forget it, sonny. You're outa their league." Lulu always had a gentle way of putting a guy in his place. I never forgot those beautiful women, or my first fifty-cent tip.

One evening a Navy Lieutenant walked in and asked for a Bromo with aromatics. I mixed the antacid powder with water, and handed it to him. He drank it quickly. "I'll be here every evening at twenty-hundred sharp. I expect to see a Bromo on the counter." He handed me a dime and walked out. Doc explained what twenty hundred hours was.

Every evening at eight o'clock sharp, the Lieutenant walked in, drank the Bromo, put a dime on the counter and walked out without a word being said.

I had just turned 18 and received the personal greeting from the President. I was to report for my physical the next day. The Lieutenant walked in and picked up his Bromo.

"Sir, may I ask you a question?"

"Is it important?"

"Yes sir. Tomorrow I'm taking my physical and I want to get into the Navy." He looked at my thick glasses.

"How good are your eyes?"

"They're rotten."

"Tonight when you go to bed, block out every particle of light coming into your room. Keep your eyes open until they get so used to the dark, you can see everything in the room. The next morning, your eyes will be so dilated, you'll be able to read the chart with no trouble at all." I did as he instructed and passed the physical.

I left the willow tree, the sheep and the stream, and headed towards home, still thinking of Doc, and remembering the first time I started smoking.

"Doctor, I want to learn to smoke."

He looked at me thoughtfully. "Are you sure? There's nothing good about it."

"All my friends smoke, and I'll be going into the service soon."

He sold me the best pipe and tobacco fifty cents could buy. "Do you know how to smoke a pipe?"

"It's easy," I said, and began puffing faster than the Broadway Limited.

"You've got a customer," Doc said.

I put the pipe on the sink behind the drug counter, and went to wait on the lady. She wanted an ice cream soda. To make those fancy ice cream soda bubbles, you pushed forward on the handle, and soda water shot out of the tap in a fine hissing jet stream. If you pulled it towards you, it came out in a regular flow to fill the glass.

I was holding the fizz-water handle when everything started spinning. The tap went hiss-flow, hiss-flow as I rocked. I saw Doc leaning on the end of the counter, grinning.

"Doc, will you wait on the lady?" I didn't wait for an answer. I ran to the back door and made the trash can just in time.

I was sitting on the back step when Doc appeared with a glass of milky liquid. "Here, drink this."

"I want to die."

"Drink it," he said. I did. It eased the sickly feeling pretty fast.

"You were drawing on that pipe worse than a kid with his first soda and a straw. All you did was swallow nicotine and smoke. If you insist on smoking, do it slowly and don't inhale. Like you said, it's easy."

One day Doc asked, "Do you have a girl?"

"Me? Sure, lots of them. But I don't want them hanging around when I'm working," I lied.

Doc knew I was lying. He never called me aside when I spent extra time waiting on the girls from Harcum, Baldwin and Bryn Mawr College. On Saturday nights, some of my high school classmates would come in with their dates. How I envied them.

The fountain was getting so busy, Lulu took on additional help. I taught the novice the ropes. One day while I was tending the grill, the fountain burst into laughter. I turned to see a customer holding a dripping lemon.

"What the heck is this?" he shouted.

The new boy said, "You asked for a Coke with fresh lemon."

I ran to the rescue. After apologies and a new soda, the customer was appeased. Another time the neophyte was asked to make a Bromo. The customer looked at the murky, bubbling brown liquid and shouted, "This isn't a Bromo!"

"Yes it is," said the novice. "I added chocolate syrup to make it taste better."

Each time these events occurred, Doc would have his quiet meeting behind the partition where he filled prescriptions, and explain to his employee what went wrong. Always gentle and kind, never vindictive, Doc was a man of infinite patience.

CHAPTER 12

SO THAT'S WHAT
THEY LOOK LIKE

Doc Martin said, "Take a pint of vanilla ice cream with this order to Bryn Mawr College. Collect two dollars and forty-three cents. Take the bike and hurry back."

The college was just a few minutes away. I knocked on the heavy wooden door of Pembroke Hall East. No answer. I banged harder. A girl's voice said, "Come in."

I opened the door and walked into a partially naked girl crossing the hall. Other girls, some half-dressed, saw me and started yelling for help.

"What are you doing here?" I turned and saw a gray-haired Amazon, who quickly had my arm in her vise-like grip. "I ought to have you thrown in jail!" By now the hall was filled with girls. I was embarrassed.

"Lady, I only came to..."

"No excuses! Exactly why are you here?"

"Look lady, I'm trying to tell you. I'm here to deliver this ice cream and medicine. When I knocked, some girl said to come in."

"Is this true?" Brunhilda asked the girls.

"I-I thought it was one of us," a pretty girl answered. She was scared. I would be too if I had to live with that lady.

"You can go now," said the Amazon. "Next time, wait until someone comes to the door. What are you waiting for? I said leave!"

"Not until I collect two dollars and forty three cents for this," I said, holding up the package.

A girl came forward, handed me three dollars, and took the package. When I reached in my pocket, she said, "Keep the change. Just go. Please!"

Riding back to the drugstore, I said to myself, "So that's what they look like." I had seen cartoons and some pictures of naked girls. But tonight I saw a real live, almost completely naked girl. I never told my buddies. They wouldn't have believed me.

I was never again called to deliver ice cream to Bryn Mawr College.

RATIONING MEANS A FAIR
SHARE FOR ALL OF US

WITHOUT RATIONING

WITH RATIONING

RATION BOOK

RATION BOOK

Office of Price Administration
Washington, D. C.

WWII poster promoting the benefits of rationing.
Stamps were issued for sugar, coffee, meats,
cheese, fats, canned milk and other goods based
on family size, children's ages, and income.

CHAPTER 13

LAMENT

Every seat at the counter is taken. The noonday crowd seems to grow daily. I wait patiently as the customer reads the menu, which hasn't changed in over a year. Finally, he raises his head and says, "I'll have the usual."

"Coming right up." This ritual has been going on since I began working at the drug store nearly two years ago.

I've become familiar with the habits of many of the regulars, and chat with them while working. Unknowingly, I am gaining self-confidence, and learning social etiquette and quiet restraint, as was needed on a Sunday morning early in 1942.

A lady entered the store wearing an expensive dress, jewelry and a fur coat, and approached the soda fountain. "May I have three quarts of vanilla ice cream?"

"I'm sorry ma'am, I can only sell you one quart."

"That's absurd. I DEMAND three quarts of vanilla ice cream!" "I'm sorry, everything is rationed."

Her face became contorted. "Where is your manager?!" Just then, Doc Martin appeared from behind the pharmacy. "Did you wish something?" he asked calmly.

"Yes, this, this BOY!" she shouted, pointing at me, "refuses to sell me three quarts of ice cream!"

In a quiet voice, Doc replied, "The young man is correct. Under wartime restrictions, the law allows only one quart of ice cream to a customer. I'm sorry we can't oblige you."

With that same wicked look at Doc, then at me, she shouted, "I hope we lose this war!"

Doc looked grim. Quietly, he walked to the door, opened it, and said with careful emphasis on each word, "Leave this store at once and never step foot in here again."

After she left, Doc and I stared at each other. Without a word being spoken, we knew how each other felt. I remembered his instructions to me when I was hired. "Don't be disrespectful to customers, although some may deserve it."

Little did I dream that one day, soda fountains across America-- crammed with noonday lunch customers, afternoon shoppers, students and couples enjoying a quiet moment after a movie – would give way to mega-marts, bubble-packed toys and beach chairs. For me and for thousands of young boys and girls, the soda fountain was one of the great places to meet people from all walks of life. There was always time for conversation, especially at night, when the counter wasn't busy. Regardless of the number of customers, it was truly a one-on-one experience.

To the endangered species list, along with the condor, eagle and whooping crane, should be added the mom & pop shop, where kids like me could work after school and during the summer. Service stations, where boys learned to repair cars, are being converted into gas stations where lone souls sit in glassed-walled cages collecting money. Jobs where students can meet and talk with people, learn social graces and acquire self-confidence are disappearing fast. When the last soda fountain closes, bells across America should toll, for a large part of our nation's heart, grace and pride will die with it.

CHAPTER 14

THE TYCOON

I retraced my steps through a pastoral setting. Sheep were grazing by a stream shaded by sleepy willow trees. Red, yellow and ochre leaves danced their farewells in the autumn breeze as white castles floated in a crystal blue sky. Lancaster Pike felt like a quiet country road, remote from the war. I walked past Woolworth's, the Wilson Laundry, the Fire House, Jake's Hardware, Brennan's and The American Store.

It was at The American Store, on the southeast corner of Warner Avenue and Lancaster Pike, where this eight-and-a-half year-old tycoon began his first business venture, carting groceries for little old ladies in a wooden wagon with makeshift wooden wheels.

Saturdays were the busiest days. My younger brother Warren would occasionally accompany me, and some generous lady would give us both a nickel. I liked it when chauffeurs did the shopping. They would give me a dime to carry groceries to their long black limousines. The insides of some of those cars seemed bigger and fancier than our parlor.

The hardest trips were for ladies who lived in third floor apartments miles away. They also had the biggest appetites. There were never less than three bags, which weighed a ton. After three long trips up three flights, I'd drag myself back to the store with the nickel clutched in my hand.

Mr. Jefferies, the store manager, gave me a job stacking shelves and breaking and folding corrugated cartons in the cellar for fifty cents a week. One afternoon, when I walked down to the cellar, there was a boy I often saw at school.

"You ain't workin' here no more," he said. He looked mean. "Who said so?"

"Ah says so." His fists looked like two ham hocks.

No one, not even a colored boy twice my size, was going to take my job. "You're the one who's not working here." I was scared when I said it.

He hit me in the stomach, and I doubled over. He swung again and missed. I hit him on the cheek, which felt like a brick. It was a lucky punch, because I couldn't see much through the pain. We were rolling on the floor over cartons and against soda cases when I felt myself being lifted in the air.

Mr. Jefferies was holding me. Les, the butcher, was holding my adversary. Mr. Jefferies said to him, "If I ever see you within a mile of this place, I'll have you thrown in jail. Les, get him out of here!" Mr. Jefferies made me go upstairs and wash up. I was scratched up and hurt all over. When Les came back, he looked at me and laughed.

"Whooee, you must be crazy to fight a kid that big. Are you hurt bad?" "I'm okay."

Mr. Jefferies watched as Les tried to make me look human again. "Want to go home?" "No."

"Feel like cleaning up the mess down there?"

I nodded and went down to the cellar. This was no way to get rich.

When I arrived home, Mother saw me first. "What happened to you!? Your clothes are filthy!" she hollered. She pulled me to the back of the store where Dad was sewing. " Dad, look at him!"

"What happened, son? Are you hurt?"

"I was running down the stairs and tripped over a broken step. I'm okay." "Just like a clumsy Pushmondon," he said, and went back to his sewing. That hurt more than the beating I took.

"Take a bath, scrub yourself good and change your clothes," Mother admonished. I don't think she could speak if they took the words 'soap, bath and scrub' from the English language.

The job I hated most was working in cellars. I loved the outdoors. Being an American Store tycoon at least got me out of doors, out of white clothes, and out from under my parents' feet. "If he's working, he's staying out of trouble." Or so they thought.

I made many detours. If there was a delivery on or near Bryn Mawr Avenue, I would head for the spring on Morris Avenue near Old Gulph Road. A pipe fed the spring water into an old cement trough. The cold water tasted sweet. I would lean against the trough, feel the cool water dripping over the side onto my back, listen to the birds and daydream.

When deliveries took me by the grammar school or playground, I would watch a game of Ins and Outs, Mumbley Peg or Marbles. Sometimes they'd let me play. Mother could never under- stand how anyone could get so dirty pulling groceries.

When I did arrive back at the store, there was always one irate customer who wanted to know where that 'Slowpoke' was. I'd spend the next hour rushing to make up for my folly. It was worth it!

Dave, the Assistant Manager, was short and loud-mouthed. His great pleasure was to insult everyone he met. If a lady wanted her packages carried, he'd come out to my brother or me and say, "Hey, you damn Greek" or "You rotten Jew, get in here!"

I was in the cellar when Mr. Johnson, the Produce Manager, came to tell me that Dave was hitting my brother. I raced to the front of the store where I saw my brother getting slapped.

"Stop that!" I shouted as I ran towards them. Dave looked at me with an evil grin. "What happened, Warren?"

"That lady," he said, pointing to a customer, "wanted me to deliver her packages. "He came out and said 'Come in here, you damn Jew.' I told him I wasn't a Jew. He said it again, so I kicked him. Then he started to hit me."

I don't know what possessed me, but I plowed into Dave, hitting him over and over. His glasses flew off and he fell to the floor. I kept punching him until Mr. Jefferies pulled me away, dragging me to his desk at the back of the store. "Stay there and don't move," he ordered. I stood rooted where Mr. Jefferies put me, near tears and shaking violently. Warren came back to join me.

After a long time, Mr. Jefferies came back. "The lady is still waiting for you to deliver her groceries," he said to Warren. "Fred, go up front and grind coffee."

Nothing was said of the fight. The Assistant Manager never spoke to either of us for the remaining time he was there. A month later he was transferred. To China, I hoped.

Some of my neighbors were in the store at the time of the great battle. No one told my parents.

I hoped that, if Dad did find out, he wouldn't think his number two son such a Pushmondon.

The first home I remember was above our tailor shop on the corner of Lancaster Pike and Roberts Road. Mother wrote each bill in elegant Spencerian script. One customer confessed, "Her handwriting is so exquisite, we've framed her receipts."

CHAPTER 15

1049 LANCASTER AVENUE

Though I have blurry visions of other places, the first home
I clearly remember was above our tailor shop on the corner of
Lancaster Pike and Roberts Road. The store was large, with wicker
furniture, potted plants and genuine tapestries on the walls. A small
dressing room, a tall oak framed three-way mirror and a wooden
counter took care of the business end. The neon sign in the window
read "Bryn Mawr Cleaners and Dyers." There were also easel cards
'Featuring the finest in lady's and men's fashions.'

Like most Main Line merchants in the early thirties, Dad's
business depended upon the owners of the large estates, their help,
and the well-to-do high school and college students. In the late
spring, Bryn Mawr, Rosemont, Villanova and Harcum Colleges, and
the Baldwin, Shipley and Agnes Irwin Schools closed for vacation.
The estate dwellers trekked north to Bay Head, Newport, Saratoga,
and Bar Harbor. Bryn Mawr became a sleepy village.

When not cleaning the house or taking a bath, we could be
found in the playground at the corner of Lancaster Pike and Bryn
Mawr Avenue, across from the Bryn Mawr Trust Company. It was
a combination park and playground, with sandboxes, seesaws,
swings, a tennis court and a ball field. I was there under threat of dire

punishment and eternal damnation if I left the playground without my brothers and sisters.

Once in a while I'd steal away to play with "those ruffians" who lived behind us in the row homes on Markee Terrace and Floyd Terrace. The kids were tough and had a great sense of freedom. How I envied them.

We also played ball on the sidewalk in front of our store. The aroma of fresh-baked goods preceded the little gray-haired man with the bow legs and baggy pants. His old felt hat, shapeless from years of weathering, was pulled down to shade his eyes. The paper sacks he carried were filled with fresh breads, rolls of all sorts, and wonderfully tasty bagels. The wide step leading into our store was about two inches high; the old man never failed to trip on it and say, "Oy, Oy, Oy," much to our amusement.

In the store, Mr. Levy would tip his hat to Mother and describe the contents in each bag. Dad would purchase bagels and a large round loaf of rye bread with caraway seeds and glazed crust. When finances permitted, Dad would also purchase a loaf of braided challah bread. After Mr. Levy had gone, the hunger-inducing aroma filled the store.

Summer also brought itinerant tradesmen to our town. Making his periodic visit to Bryn Mawr was the knife sharpening man. As he walked down the street, he would call out, "Knives sharpened, scissors sharpened." Ladies would call to him from their windows, and merchants would hail him from their stores.

From his back, he would lower a small folding chair and a heavy grinding wheel on a three-legged stand. I watched with awe at the sparks when blade and stone met. He worked the foot treadle like a machine, regulating the speed of the wheel according to the dullness or quality of the steel. When each knife was finished, he would check it carefully. If it met his approval, he would give a nod and place it carefully on the ground. When he was finished and had collected his few cents from each lady, he would lift wheel and chair to his back and continue on his way. His cries of "Knives sharpened, scissors sharpened" faded into the distance.

Another visitor to our town was the umbrella man. On his back, he carried a bag containing umbrella staves of all sizes, umbrella poles, and repaired umbrellas for sale. String-tied cloth bags hanging from his belt contained the parts and tools of his trade. When a broken umbrella was brought to him, he would sit on a stoop and work. We kids would watch as he replaced bent staves, sewed the umbrella cloth to the end pieces, or repaired a spring catch. When finished, he would open and close the umbrella many times, checking every part. Satisfied with his work, he'd knock on the door, collect his few cents and continue on his way, calling out as he went, "Umbrella man!"

The produce vendor would go up and down the side streets with his push cart, loudly proclaiming the quality and beauty of his fruits and vegetables. How colorful they looked! Ladies came from their homes carrying baskets or bags, and checked each piece thoroughly.

At as much as two cents a pound, there had better not be a mark on them.

When the Snow Cone Man came, we kids would gather to watch him shave the big block of ice, then fill a paper cone with a large, round scoop of shaved ice. From the row of bottled syrups on his pushcart – root beer, strawberry, cherry, grape, orange, lemon, lime, chocolate and vanilla – he would pick the flavor chosen by the lucky kid who could afford a five cent cone, and pour a generous amount over the ice. Once in awhile, I was allowed to buy one. I would sit on the step of our store and savor every lick, wanting the joy to last and last. I did not know when, or if, I could have one again.

Just about dawn, I would hear the clop-clop of a horse, followed by the clinking of glass bottles. Johnny Marmer was delivering milk. His horse needed no commands. As Mr. Marmer went door to door, his wire basket filled with bottles, the horse followed slowly. Sometimes, Mr. Marmer would make an afternoon stop at Espenshade's Market across the street. The horse would stand patiently and let us pet him.

Though Bryn Mawr was an affluent community, it had a rural quality, neighborly and genteel. Now the old baker, the itinerant knife sharpener and the umbrella man are all gone. I still remember the first morning I heard the clinking of the glass bottles – but not the clop-clop of the horse. Instead, painted with the words JOHN MARMER MILK, was one of those new electric delivery trucks.

CHAPTER 16

BRYN MAWR GRAMMAR SCHOOL

Our parents believed it was wrong to begin school earlier than age seven, because our brains were not ready to absorb the three R's. My turn came on September, 1932. I walked that dreadful mile with my mother to the Bryn Mawr Grammar School.

Sophie Keefer, the Principal, was a big, stern-looking lady. Her gray hair was pulled into a bun at the back of her head. It seemed all gray-haired teachers wore their hair in a bun. On Miss Keefer's desk was a large paddle, no doubt once used by cavemen.

"So this is number four," said Miss Keefer, looking down at me.

"Miss Keefer, this is my son Frederick. I will repeat to you what I said when I brought in Newert, John and Arminnie. If Frederick ever misbehaves, you are to use that paddle on him. And when he comes home, his father will do the same."

Mother said goodbye to Miss Keefer, then looked at me for a long time. She knelt down, kissed me, and left the office.

"Follow me, Frederick." It was an order quietly given. I stole another look at the paddle, then followed Miss Keefer down the corridor to the first grade classroom.

"Miss Shoemaker," said Miss Keefer, "this is Frederick Shamlian. He is starting school today." I was seated behind Valencia Hinchey who, in a few months, would become a neighbor and a playmate.

My brothers, sisters and I always started for school together, crossing the light at Roberts Road. We passed Cardimone's Drug Store, Travalini's Barber Shop, walked up the Pike and through the alley next to the Seville Theater (now the Bryn Mawr Film Institute), cut across vacant lots to Bryn Mawr Avenue, and finally arrived at school. Somewhere along the way, I would stop to watch the birds, or catch grasshoppers, letting the others get ahead. The vacant lots were always full of wildflowers, attracting all sorts of bugs, which I would catch and bring home, to the annoyance of my Mother and sisters.

Though the winters back then brought heavy snows, the schools never closed. Snow would be piled along the curbs high over our heads. The merchants, including Dad, would spread ashes from their coal stoves on the slippery sidewalks. I spent so much time playing mountain climber on the curbside snow peaks, the last few blocks were a race to beat the school bell. At the door, Miss Keefer watched and waited until the last of 'her children' arrived. The smell of wet wool permeated every crevice.

Some winters were extremely cold, bringing successive days of below freezing temperatures. To stay warm, we wrapped newspapers around our bodies under our shirts. On the days I was insulated with the Evening Ledger, fear of crinkling kept me from raising my hand.

I disliked school, especially on rainy days when the world looked bleak. One day, the sky turned black and the rain struck hard against the windows. Thunder shook the building, and lightning bolts frightened the girls. The storm was still raging when the school bell rang and Warren and I dashed out into the rain. There was Dad, waiting for us in our Model A Ford, which served as both the family limousine and delivery car. That was the first and only time I ever rode to school in our car.

"Growing bodies need lots of rest," said Mother. All through grammar school, we had to go to bed at seven o'clock, even in the summertime. As Mother turned down the covers, she would sing the great arias. She sang 'The Bell Song' from Lakme as beautifully as Lily Pons."Un Bel Di" was a favorite of hers, and the strains of Madame Butterfly would float from our open windows. Mrs. Kelley, who lived across the street behind Kelley's Beer Parlor, would sit on her porch, close her eyes and listen. One day Mrs. Kelley came to our store and said to me, "Your mother has the most beautiful voice in the world." Only years later did I fully appreciate her gift.

On Sunday mornings, Mother and Dad listened to live chamber music on our only radio. To me, it sounded worse than death. Our parents insisted that we each learn to play a musical instrument, preferably the violin, which Dad loved. It was now my turn.

"Who are you?" asked Mr. Geist, the music teacher.

"Fred Shamlian, sir."

"Another Shamlian is it? Over there on the table is a violin. Open the case and bring the violin and bow to me." The violin looked so fragile. Its once fine finish showed the wear and tear of countless novices like myself. I gingerly picked up the instrument and bow, and took it to Mr. Geist.

"Now put the violin under your chin. You've seen your brother do it." The violin was still in midair when he took the violin from me. "Sorry boy," he said. "Violins are not made for left-handed kids."

At dinner I waited for the inevitable question. "How was your first violin lesson?"

"I didn't have a lesson." "Why no lesson?" asked Dad.

"Mr. Geist said they don't make violins for left-handed kids."

Not one more word was said. My brothers and sisters stared at their plates. Had they looked up, they surely would have laughed. The Pushmondon did it again.

During recess and at lunchtime, Miss Keefer would sit on one of the stone walls that flanked the front steps of the school. She didn't miss a thing. As she watched us, she had a habit of taking a strand of hair and rolling it around her finger. When she reached the end of the strand, she would give a yank. We all thought she would go bald, but at the end of eight years, her gray hair flourished abundantly.

Whenever she rose, staring like an eagle at her victim as she zoomed in for the kill, we froze, eyes wide. Back she would come, marching her frightened prey into her office.

What a relief when she passed.

As a boy, my thirst for books was insatiable.
By the 7th grade, I'd devoured the Tom Swift,
Rover Boys and Hardy Boys adventures, as
well as countless stories of great explorers
and faraway places.

CHAPTER 17

MISS HAZZARD

"I pledge allegiance to the flag of the United States of America, and to the republic for which it stands..."

Miss Shoemaker stood erect, facing the flag with her hand over her heart, saying each line intently. We all stood at attention, right hands over our hearts, repeating each phrase: "...one nation, indivisible, with liberty and justice for all." (Some years later, the words "under God" were added.) Miss Shoemaker then read a passage from the Old Testament, and ceremoniously placed the Bible on the corner of her desk. When we get to the third grade, each of us will read from the Bible.

Why the Supreme Court banned Bible reading in public schools, I shall never understand. The argument is, Bible readings do not adhere to the separation of Church and State. But while The Bible is the basis of many religions, it is not the Church. It is the book of God. Immigrants who, like my father, came to America to build a future in a nation founded "under God" accepted reading the Bible in school. It was as natural as reciting the Pledge of Allegiance. The Supreme Court ruling does not separate Church and State; it separates God and country.

Learning to read opened the world – and the universe – for me. Once I passed Dick, Jane and Spot, stories from the Readers whetted my appetite for more. I developed an insatiable thirst for books. By the time I reached the seventh grade, I'd read most of the adventures of Tom Swift, The Rover Boys and The Hardy Boys. I read Mark Twain, Dickens, Frank Merriwell stories of great explorers, astronomers and faraway places; anything I could get my hands on.

I would spend many hours in the classroom fantasizing about heroic deeds in enchanted lands, much to the dismay of my teachers. Not having many friends, the Ludington Memorial Library became my oasis, and books were my great escape.

Unfortunately, school wasn't just reading. There were daily classes in composition, grammar, history, arithmetic, music and geography. We also had gym and woodworking shop. I still use the shoeshine box I made in the eighth grade.

Grammar, with its meticulous breakdown of sentences, was especially boring. Little did we know that with each lesson, we were learning to write correctly. Together with reading and writing assignments, and surprise spelling quizzes of words from our readings, we were going to write and speak properly... or else!

How I loved history, especially the American Revolution. By the time I left grammar school, I could name most of the major events of the Revolutionary War – and almost all of its heroes. I could draw from memory a map of the United States, with a reasonably accurate placement of the 48 states and their capitals.

Geography wasn't limited to the United States. It was worldwide. We could name the capitals of most countries, as well as their outstanding products.

My nemesis was arithmetic. Miss Hazzard was a small, thin lady with a stern bun of gray hair. Like all of our teachers, she demanded nothing less than excellence. One day in class, she announced, "Now that you've learned to add and multiply, you will learn subtraction."

She went to the chalkboard and said as she wrote, "Here are 379. From it, we will subtract 187. Seven from nine is two. Eight from seven cannot be done, so we take one from three and make the seven a seventeen. Eight from seventeen is nine. The three becomes two, since we took one from it to make seventeen. One from two is one. The answer is 192. Now, you subtract 432 from 519."

I put the figures down and tried and tried, but could not get the right answer. Neither could Bobby, who sat across from me. Miss Hazzard stood over us with the ruler poised. "You will try again and again until you get it right!" I looked at the paper, then stared out of the window wishing I was out there sledding. I don't know what happened, but when I looked back at the paper the answer was there. Quickly I subtracted 432 from 519, and blurted out, "I know the answer.

It's 87!"

"Very good, Frederick. Now do the remainder of the problems." I did them all correctly, turned to Bobby and said, "It's easy. Want me to teach you?" Arithmetic isn't so bad after all, I thought. Little did I know that next to come were division and fractions.

Each teacher must have thought she was the only one assigning homework, for we came home each day burdened with books, pads and pencils. We began our homework when we arrived home, and continued after dinner until bedtime. Sometimes we took it to bed. Yet somehow we managed to listen to the adventures of Jack Armstrong, The Lone Ranger and Little Orphan Annie. Our imaginations soared with each new peril faced by our radio heroes.

Come Spring, when the sky was blue with towering clouds, the world was turning green, and the breeze from the classroom windows smelled clean and fresh, I would gaze outside and day-dream of daring feats of bravery. It was always during those reveries the teacher would ask, "What is your answer, Frederick?"

Caught again!

CHAPTER 18

GRADUATION

"Pansies, lilies, roses, flowers of every hue.

Take each one that's coming straight from heaven to you."

There we were, the eighth grade graduating class, on stage singing for our parents. The girls wore fancy homemade dresses. Most of the boys, like myself, were wearing our first pair of long pants. Ever since I could remember, I either wore short pants or brown knickers of heavy- ribbed corduroy, which swished when I walked. Finally I could walk without waking the dead.

The girls fidgeted, giggled and waved from the stage. The boys (well, most of us) stood there annoyed with the whole thing. Miss Thomas waved her arms frantically, trying to keep us in time with the music. Her mouth kept moving as we sang. Some said she was singing.

I think she was praying.

Mother was just 18 when my sister was born in the Bronx. Armenian for "new rose," Newert was a happy, independent woman. She earned multiple degrees and shared a love of language, literature and learning across a lifetime of teaching.

Newert at Beach Haven, Long Beach Island, around 1940.

With son Louis, an IT specialist and musician.

Newert never lost her joyful spirit. Below, with Aunt Nevrig.

CHAPTER 19

NEWERT

During the Depression, our whole family pitched in to help pay the bills. Newert worked after school and on weekends. In her first job, shelving books at Bryn Mawr's Ludington Memorial Library, Newert earned the staggering sum of twenty-five cents an hour. For my sister, who loved books and learning, the serenity meant more than money. It was a joyous reprieve from our boisterous home.

Newert also landed a second job making sandwiches and mashed potatoes in a little restaurant on Montgomery Avenue. Her potatoes were so good, the customer asked for seconds.

Newert graduated from Lower Merion High in 1937. As she and her classmates stood patiently outside the auditorium in their caps and gowns, waiting for the school orchestra to play "Pomp and Circumstance," a friend ran towards her shouting, "Newert! Newert, you won, you won the scholarship!" She had submitted her application at the start of the school year, then completely forgot about it. But there was her name in the program!

Our Mother had great ambitions for her five children. Dad, however, could not easily abandon some old world views. Earlier that year, Dad had announced that Newert would marry a man from the old country. To our great surprise, my obedient, mild mannered sister saw red, and shouted belligerently: "If you dare try that, I'll run away." After that, Dad's All-American girl had no more fear of an arranged marriage. Newert began her studies in Romance Languages that Fall at the University of Pennsylvania.

As an 'A' student, Newert's scholarship could be renewed. Regrettably, she did not realize that! And knowing that Mother and Dad could not cover her tuition, she took a summer job as chambermaid at Happy Creek Farms on what is now Darby-Paoli Road in Radnor. Working for the Harrison family earned Newert enough to continue her studies that Fall. Newert returned to the estate after her sophomore year. At Summer's end, she was about to give notice and return to Penn when Mother and Dad visited.

"Newert," Dad said carefully, "John's teacher believes he could win a scholarship to The Curtis Institute of Music if he receives advanced bassoon lessons. But the lessons will cost $100, which I do not have. Will you lend John the money?"

One hundred dollars! She would have to wait another year to return to Penn. Nonetheless, my selfless sister gave Dad the money, and John went on to win the scholarship.

In 1939, both Newert and Minnie were hired by the Bryn Mawr College Library. Newert was able to continue taking courses in Spanish and Latin, tuition-free. Three years later, the college gave her a partial scholarship, and the Spanish House had a new House Mother. During my Mother's illness, my sisters had taken charge of the cooking, cleaning and laundry, and looked after Warren and me – the perfect training for Newert's latest post!

Occasionally, Newert would brings home friends from Spanish House. I heard them talking and laughing in the parlor as I climbed the stairs to my room on the third floor. Once, a pretty girl was dancing the Mexican hat dance as the other girls clapped in time to the music.

By 1944, the years of working and studying had taken their toll. Newert was ready to quit. But College President Margaret

McBride interceded, and convinced her to complete her final year. At commencement, Newert received her Bachelor's Degree in Languages – quite an achievement for the daughter of a poor tailor.

Post-graduate summer courses took Newert to Middlebury College in Vermont. A partial scholarship covered her studies, and she waited tables in the dining room to pay her room and board. Then in 1947, Newert was hired to teach Spanish at Juniata College in Huntington, PA. Despite meager pay and non-existent raises, she persevered for two years.

It took four summers, but in 1949, Newert earned her Master's from Middlebury – and received a scholarship to the University of Michigan School of Library Science in Ann Arbor. The first course, Cataloging, was her downfall. "So many spaces from the left for the Author's Name; so many spaces for the Title; a semi-colon here, a period there. It was deadly."

Then, joy! A substitute teaching position at Central Michigan University. Her students, mainly ex-G.I.s, volleyed questions and answers back and forth like a tennis match. I remember Newert describing the thrill of teaching these students. It was, she said, her most rewarding teaching experience.

Unfortunately, the best job of her life lasted only one year.

To complicate matters, many immigrants from the Spanish Civil War were given college teaching posts simply because Spanish was their native tongue. After a long and futile search, she took a job with the Free Library of Philadelphia. Newert operated the very first "Bookmobile," visiting hospitals, prisons, schools and neighborhoods across Philadelphia.

After completing her rounds, she and her friend Frances would meet at the Melody Record Shop at 52nd and Market, owned by Frances' friend Mort Kaplan. Then, they would head to Frannie's apartment to listen to classical music. Mort would drop by, and accompany Newert home on the trolley.

Mort was not in the best of health, and he wasn't a worldly man. But despite the parallels between Mort and Dad's shops . . . and in spite of Dad's painful experience courting Mother, he objected to their courtship. Mort was unsuitable for his daughter.

On January 4, 1955, Newert and Mort were married by a Justice of the Peace in Millbourne, PA. A second service followed on February 27, when Rabbi Theodore H. Gordon married the couple in Wynnewood, PA. Dad did not attend. Throughout the ceremony, I kept thinking about how my mother's father had refused to attend their wedding. Ringing in my ears were the words, "All we learn from history is that we do not learn from history."

My older brother John, top, was our family's Golden Boy,
a musical prodigy with movie-star looks and charm.

As a child, John taught himself the violin and the clarinet. In high school, he played the saxaphone and glockenspiel until his music teacher urged him to play the bassoon.

After serving in the Canadian Navy, John completed his studies at London's Royal Academy of Music. He played for nearly forty years with the London Symphony, the Royal Philharmonic and the Philadelphia Orchestra.

On leave in Scotland, John met Peggy Walden, who served in the Royal Navy signal corps. They were married in England, where their son Peter was born. Below: John and me.

CHAPTER 20

BROTHER JOHN

In my parent's eyes, John was the Golden Boy, a musical prodigy who ascended to the highest heights to perform with the London Symphony, the Royal Philharmonic and the Philadelphia Orchestra. Blessed with movie star looks and a quiet charm, John enjoyed friendships with great men like Leonard Bernstein, and his sons Peter, Mark and David all share his musical talents.

Later in life, John achieved true international fame – as a bassoon repairman. Musicians from the world's great orchestras would make the pilgrimage to his Haddonfield, NJ workshop to bring their bassoons, contrabassoons, oboes and clarinets, and John made them sound better than new. Though he charged his fellow musicians very little, and did much pro bono work for local school orchestras, musicians selling their instruments would advertise "repaired by John Shamlian" to command the highest price.

John Victor Shamlian was born December 16, 1920, shortly after Mother and Dad moved from New York to Philadelphia. As a young boy, he and Newert attended a one-room schoolhouse in Garrett Hill, and he taught himself to play the violin and the clarinet. At 12, John sold subscriptions to *Liberty, The Saturday Evening Post* and *Ladies Home Journal* magazines to help with the family finances. Then at 16, he was hired by Railway Express – a sought-after job which required background checks of our whole family. We passed the test.

At Lower Merion High, John played the saxophone and the glockenspiel until one day, Music Director Dr. Bruce Beach introduced him to the bassoon. "I had no idea how to play that thing," John said. I just pumped on it for hours every day." But he stuck with it, graduating in 1939 with a full scholarship to Philadelphia's Curtis Institute of Music.

One evening as I sat in the dining room behind the store doing homework, Dad came in, turned two chairs to face the radio, and said "Quiet now." Mother came in from the kitchen and sat down.

"Good evening, ladies and gentlemen," the announcer intoned. "Tonight we bring you the Woodwind Quartet from The Curtis Institute." When he announced "John Shamlian, bassoonist," both mother and dad turned in their chairs to see if I was listening. How proud they looked. During John's solo, they gazed at each other with tears in their eyes. I dared not move, lest I muffle a single note.

While still a student, John was selected to play with the Boston Symphony at Tanglewood, in the Berkshire Mountains of Massachusetts. In the Summer of 1941, he took mother with him. Sitting in the audience listening to her son play for celebrated conductor and composer Serge Koussevitzky was her proudest moment.

Although just four years younger than John, I felt a generation apart. When Warren and I had to go to bed at seven, John could stay up till nine. How I envied him for all of his friends, who spent so many happy evenings in our home. One night after a concert at Bryn Mawr College, John invited the Curtis Orchestra to our home. Still in their tuxedos, his friends filled the second floor parlor, lined the stairway, ringed the dining room, and just barely fit in the kitchen.

I had just returned home from my late night shift at Liggett's Drug Store and was relaxing in the kitchen when John walked in. "Feel like grabbing a milkshake?" he asked. We jumped in his 1934 Plymouth Coupe with rumble seat and drove to a late night restaurant in Villanova. We didn't say much as we downed our thick shakes, but that night was the closest I had ever felt to my big brother.

When America went to war, John tried diligently to enlist. But childhood polio had reduced the size of one lung, and no U.S. Armed Service would accept him. Refusing to be shut out, John enlisted in the Canadian Navy. The evening John left home for Canada, Mother and Dad, Newert and Minnie, and a small parade of John's friends from school, church and Curtis all waited with him at the Bryn Mawr station. As John boarded the train, his friends from Curtis gave him a rousing musical send-off. Mother cried all the way home.

About a month after John's departure, I was building a balsa wood model airplane, and needed a single-edge razor. Knowing John would have some, I broke all the rules and ventured into his room. Mother had preserved it exactly as he left it.

John served aboard the HMCS Niobe, saw combat in the Mediterranean and, throughout the war, played clarinet and saxophone with the Navy Band. While on leave in Scotland, John met Margaret (Peggy) Walden, who was serving in the British navy signal corps. They fell in love, and married on a future port visit, before John returned to Canada.

Mother and Dad couldn't understand why John chose to get married in England, and cause his parents to miss his wedding day. Perhaps seeing how Newert's choice of husband was judged, and knowing all too well Dad's strident instructions to marry an Armenian girl, was all the reason he needed. John never spoke of Peggy at home. But when we went for walks along Bryn Mawr Avenue, passing estate homes where sheep grazed in large pastures, John would open up. In a voice so low I had to strain to hear, he spoke longingly of his wife and their son Peter back in England.

When the War ended, John learned to his dismay that one could not be discharged from the Canadian Navy without proof of a job. John was given leave to travel from the Halifax Naval Base to New York City, where a former teacher arranged an audition with the Indianapolis Symphony. Maestro Sevitzky offered John the position of Second Chair – and his freedom!

John had completed only two years at Curtis before the war began. In 1947, he returned to England and his wife, and was awarded a grant to finish his degree at the Royal Academy of Music.

After graduation, John accepted a position as bassoonist with the London Symphony. At that time, only British citizens could join the Musicians Union. Remarkably, John was the catalyst for a national resolution extending membership to non-citizens who served in his Majesty's Armed Forces.

When John arrived at Royal Albert Hall to play his first concert with the London Symphony, his trunk with his concert clothes had not yet arrived. John had to wear a suit too small, and instead of black shoes, he wore moccasins. "Fortunately," John assured me, "we were performing *Pocahontas*."

During his five years with the London Symphony, John was permitted to tour with Sir Thomas Beecham and the Royal Philharmonic. When a tour took him to Philadelphia, John learned to his surprise that Eugene Ormandy was holding auditions for the Philadelphia Orchestra. What a dilemma for John! My brother yearned to return home. Peggy, however, was perfectly happy in England with her British culture and family ties, and thought she was creating the foundation for their idyllic life in England with their young son, Peter.

John did audition, receiving a lifetime contract from Ormandy, and joined the Philadelphia Orchestra as third assistant bassoonist in September, 1951. Peggy and Peter followed, after a considerable delay. I don't know if she ever forgave John for dragging her so far from home. I do know that John wanted to live close to his family, clustered around Philadelphia's Main Line, but Peggy insisted that they live in New Jersey, forty-five minutes away. To her children, she essentially denied the Shamlian side of the family, always promoting the "English" as superior, and sought to undermine anything having to do with John's relatives.

All those years, I was largely unaware of John's difficulties. Always the quiet one, John never spoke of the bruising cold war that beset his marriage, the dark encounters with Peggy's unpredictable angst, and her relentless propaganda to deny her sons the love of the grandparents, aunts, uncles and cousins who lived just across the river. Our visits were always welcomed with smiles and tea, and their home looked like how I imagined an English cottage would. The parlor was beautifully decorated in elegant traditional style, and Peggy's museum-worthy watercolors graced every room. Her soft pastel colors exuded warmth and quiet charm.

Haddonfield is a lovely town, but it succeeded in keeping John apart from the rest of us. As far as his sons were concerned, Drexel Hill, Bryn Mawr and King of Prussia were an ocean away. Peggy passed away in September, 2006.

When I was working downtown in my first job after college, I'd walk from my office at Barr's Jewelers to meet John for lunch. Then we'd head back to The Academy of Music for the 2pm concert, which I watched from backstage. The first time I returned late to the office – thirty minutes late! – I immediately apologized to my boss, Meyer Barr. But when I explained why, he gave me his blessing to attend future concerts and stay for the entire performance! I was privileged to meet many great musicians and to observe, up close, legendary conductors like Ormandy, Igor Stravinsky, and Otto Klemperer.

Bassoon reeds were costly, and many are required for rehearsals, practice and concerts. Ever resourceful, and a skilled maker of model airplanes and tin toy soldiers, John proceeded to produce his own. He converted the basement of his Haddonfield home into a series of paneled rooms. The largest was Peggy's art studio. The smallest became his workshop.

John ordered special cane in bulk from overseas, and with the help of a friend at RCA, even crafted his own tools. He became so proficient, he was soon selling his reeds, and orders flowed in from orchestras around the world.

One day as I watched John put the finishing touches on some reeds, I asked, "How do you know if the cane you bought is any good?"

"You don't," he said. "Not until you make your first reed with it. I just made this one from a fresh shipment. Terrible." Disgusted, John threw the burlap bag under the steps.

Five years later, when the Philadelphia Orchestra was about to tour the country, and John needed a large supply of reeds, his only option was the cane he'd thrown under the steps. To his amazement, "It produced the richest sound I have ever heard from my bassoon."

John retired from the orchestra after thirty-one years in 1982, devoting himself to making reeds, repairing bassoons, and teaching a select group of students. Word of John's uncanny abilities spread quickly, and his reputation grew.

When the Fox Instrument Company of Indianapolis sent John a prototype of their new bassoon for testing, John replied by letter detailing each flaw in design and manufacturing. Sometime later, a second bassoon arrived, along with a letter explaining that the company had corrected all of the problems John had identified. John found the instrument to be as good as any made in Germany or France, at a much lower price, and recommended it to his students. John and Peggy were invited to Indianapolis, first class and all-expenses paid, to see the instruments being made, and a banquet was held in his honor to thank John for his invaluable contributions.

According to my nephew David, his father "was like a bassoon whisperer. He had a Zen-like quality about him when he worked on a bassoon. To others who repaired wind instruments, many of dad's adjustments were counterintuitive. But, they worked."

Musicians from Europe, Asia and the Americas would arrive at all hours asking for his help. Late one night, John was awakened by a distraught young woman just arrived from Germany. Her bassoon was defective, and the manufacturer said they could not repair it.

While she slept in the guest room, John went to work. When she awoke, he had just completed his labors, and asked her to test it. As she played the bassoon, tears streamed down her face. "How could you do what the manufacturer could not? It sounds so beautiful, I fear the charge must be more than I can afford."

John kept the charge very small.

Though Minnie never married, she had many loves:
travel, cooking, opera, art, and above all, the Main Line,
the gracious heart of her carefully-crafted life.

When America entered WWII, Minnie joined the WAVES. Trained as a Radioman, she served at the US Naval Station in San Diego, handling highly classified communications.

ARMINNIE
SHAMLIAN
720-94-84
O   T.5/43
USNR   P

THE CUNARD STEAM-SHIP COMPANY LIMITED
NEW YORK
EMPLOYEE IDENTIFICATION CARD
No: 345

XX MISS A. SHAMLIAN

IS AUTHORIZED TO GO ABOARD COMPANY'S VESSELS
WHILE IN PORT IN PURSUANCE OF OFFICIAL DUTIES.

ISSUED FOR
1966

Minnie's years with Cunard,
the pinnacle of oceangoing luxury, were among her happiest.

CHAPTER 21

MINNIE

Arminnie Shamlian came into the world the same year as Jack Kerouac, Judy Garland and Ava Gardner. The year was 1922. The Twenties were just starting to Roar. President Warren G. Harding introduced radio to the White House; the first U.S. Aircraft Carrier was commissioned; and construction began on Yankee Stadium.

That September 4th, Sophia and Vahan, now 20 and 28, living in an apartment above the Tailor Shop, gave their 3 year-old daughter and almost 2 year-old son a new sister. Her Armenian name means "Energetic Helper." A more appropriate name would be hard to imagine, for our Minnie, or simply "Min," was a taut bundle of energy.

My father's perfectionism and creative streak were evident in each of his sons and daughters. When my brother Warren re-built an engine . . . when John carved a bassoon reed . . . when Newert taught languages, it was as if we were channeling Dad as he cut his own patterns, searched for the perfect warp and weft, and sewed every masterful stitch of every suit by hand.

The teacher, the musician, the marketer and the mechanic all inherited Dad's passion for excellence. And though her career spanned several industries, Minnie was no exception. I believe she may have been the most passionate of us all, and worked the hardest to build a life that fulfilled her.

For Minnie, there was simply no such thing as doing half a job. Whether playing tennis, roller skating, drawing, cooking, playing clarinet in the school band, or making travel arrangements, everything Minnie did was powered by her sharp critical mind, generous spirit and unflagging and exceptional service.

Given her passion for world travel, her love of the sea, and the way she felt so at home among high society, it's no surprise that Minnie excelled as a travel specialist with the Cunard Steam Ship Company, the pinnacle of oceangoing luxury. From her mid-town office at 1616 Walnut Street in Philadelphia, Minnie's passion for helping and delighting others bloomed. She crafted itineraries, satisfied special requests ("a portable playpen for my grandson aboard the S.S Scythia"), entertained Cunard passengers, and made everyone she touched feel cared for and special.

Transatlantic air travel, however, was gaining ground, and in her fifth year with Cunard, the firm closed their Philadelphia office around 1969. Offered a position in New York, Min chose to stay close to home, becoming a salesperson for the elegant Bonwit Teller Department Store. Her charm, refined taste and love of fine clothes continued to delight her customers. Many asked for Minnie by name.

Throughout her life, Minnie expressed her love for her friends and family with fine gifts from the best Main Line shops. My children, however, never looked forward to Aunt Minnie's steadfast birthday and Christmas presents because, invariably, she gave them clothes. But what clothes! Rick and John wore the finest corduroy and worsted wool slacks and Merino wool sweaters from Jacob Reed & Sons Clothiers, and our daughter received embroidered cashmere sweaters and dresses I only wished I could afford for Gerry.

Minnie had a keen business mind, and proved herself a skilled secretary and bookkeeper for Main Line scions Perry Gresch, Cummins Catherwood and The Catherwood Foundation. For nearly twenty years, she was entrusted with key financial and management responsibilities. In later years, Minnie moonlighted as a salesperson for Her Royal Highness, dressing her privileged clientele – and her nieces and nephews – in the finest European children's clothing.

After Minnie's passing on February 7, 2012, we discovered just how wisely Minnie had managed her own finances. Despite a modest income and a life of remarkable generosity, including regular contributions to the Philadelphia Orchestra and Art Museum and numerous other charities, she had amassed a healthy savings.

Minnie never married. Quite possibly, she never experienced an intimate relationship. I don't know. Later in life, Minnie shared with me that when she was young, our parents convinced her that men were not to be trusted and wanted only one thing, planting in her psyche such a fear of men that it stayed with her. For someone so bright and vivacious to go through life with such a crippling phobia feels terribly cruel and sad. At the same time, it speaks volumes about the courage it took for Minnie to go through life so independently, and to bring so much joy to others.

Minnie did have one true love. It was the Main Line. Aside from her years in the US Navy during WW II, she lived there all her life, drawn to the lifestyle like a moth to flame. Min was always sharing stories and photos of her Main Line friends, peppering her conversation with names like "Bunny" and "Dottie." She would talk about them as if I knew them intimately, as if by sheer force of will she could fuse her two families into one.

The Greshes, the Catherwoods and others welcomed Minnie into their families and lives. She was a devoted friend, a beloved babysitter, a ready helper – and a frequent house guest in summer homes from Saratoga to Bar Harbor, and from Newport, Rhode Island to Cuernavaca, Mexico. Dad used to tell Minnie "You dress better than the people who can afford it." In my entire family, only Minnie acquired that distinctive "upper crust" vernacular, a la Katharine Hepburn in "The Philadelphia Story." A vase was always a "vhas."

Minnie, however, was no snob. She lived simply, generally cooked at home, drove a Honda Civic, and for much of her adult life shared a modest two-bedroom apartment with our Mother in a house on Moore Avenue, close to Bryn Mawr Hospital. Minnie and Mother were extremely close, and shared much in common. They were both very private people who loved classical music and opera, and shared a strong sense of how a thing should be done. They did not, however, always agree on the "how," particularly in matters of cooking. Their not infrequent quarrels could be quite shrill. When mother passed away, Min continued to live there on her own, until failing health necessitated the move to assisted living.

Minnie remained very close to her big sister all her life, and after Mort passed away, Newert and Minnie traveled together to Canada, Mexico, Puerto Rico, and Disney's Epcot Center. Sometimes I imagined fellow travelers observing this odd couple: Minnie, tall and thin as a rail, and Newert, short and stout. Minnie, the ever energetic helper, had both a fabulous appetite and a turbocharged metabolism. She never gained an ounce.

Growing up, Minnie and Newert lived a life quite apart from me. Then came the War, military service, college, and busy lives. I really did not get to know Minnie until September, 1995, when she brought me home from Lankenau Hospital after my bypass surgery. Nothing was too much for her... the cooking, the cleaning, the laundry. A consummate nurse, Minnie made sure I walked a little more each day. It wasn't as if we suddenly had soul-searching conversations. But from that moment, our lives drew closer, and we experienced a bond that continued to grow.

Having shared a few highlights of my sister's life as I knew her, I invite you to see what she meant to others. Here, from Minnie's years at Cunard, are notes from passengers fortunate enough to know her:

105 East 72nd Street - Penthouse
New York, New York 10021

Sham Dear,
        I tried to say goodbye to you at Helen's sailing, but it was frightfully hectic. You looked so chic! Helen was thrilled with her cabin and you were wonderful to her in all ways. We must see each other again before too long! - *Lots of Love, Hester*

The United Clay Products Company
Washington DC
Office of the President

Dear Miss Shamlian,
        You are now a member of our family. How wonderful
to know what a grand character you are! Our stateroom was the
nicest we ever experienced, and our friends left feeling we must be
millionaires. We're counting on you to come see us soon, as we want
to show our appreciation by entertaining you in Washington. All of
our friends, including the girls in the office, join Mrs. Chewning and
me in sending our love.   - *Sincerely yours, E. Taylor Chewning*

Treetops
Thornton Hough
Wirral (UK)

Dear Sham,
        At long last I am writing to thank you for your card and
the tea towel. I shall always think of you and our wonderful day in
Philadelphia. It stands out in our memory as one of the best days of
our trip. With all good wishes and hoping to see you again someday.
                        - *Yours sincerely, Margaret Carrell*

I wish this tender moment at the shore with my brother Warren, just 2 years younger than me, truly expressed how close we were. It was not to be.

Grease and gasoline were like perfume to my brother. By age fifteen, he was a skilled mechanic. His passion grew into one of the most respected Jaguar repair centers in California.

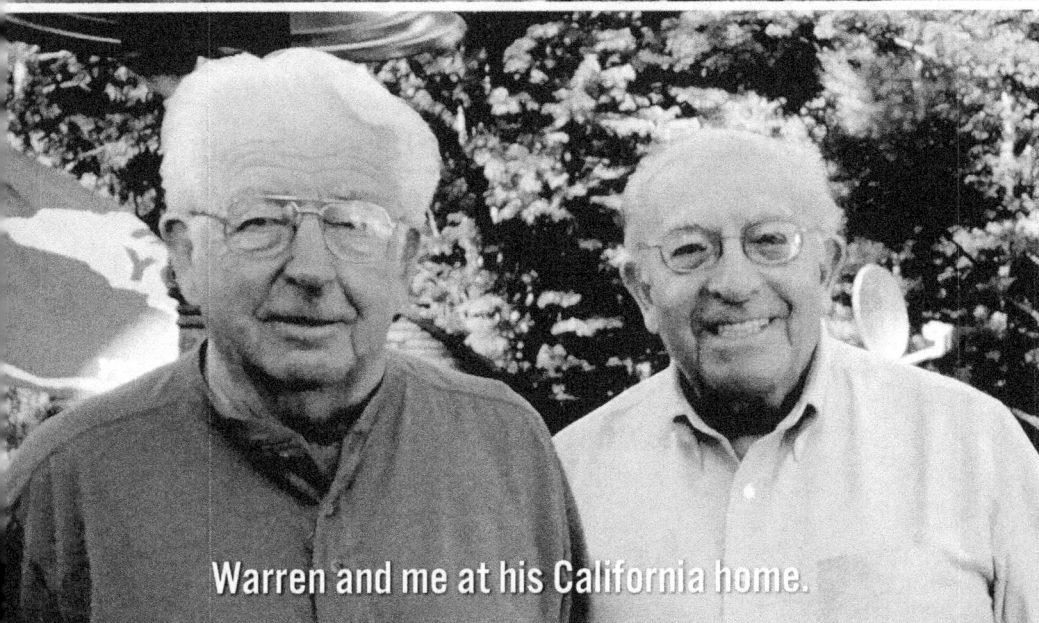
Warren and me at his California home.

When I arrived home from the Navy in the Summer of '46, Warren was going steady with Louise. A Becke tradition required that when someone married into the family, a home would be built for the couple – for not less than $75,000 – when the average home cost less than $5,000.

CHAPTER 22

WARREN

Grease and gasoline were like perfume to my brother Warren, born twenty-five months after me on August 16, 1927. His lifelong love of cars grew into one of the most respected Jaguar repair centers in southern California, serving over 600 faithful customers.

As a kid, Warren would watch the itinerant handyman, Olaf, repair our family car. Later, he accompanied Dad to Pat Schmader's Garage. And at Lower Merion High, to no one's surprise, Warren chose Vocational Studies, learning Automotive Repair from Mr. McGrath.

Sometimes Warren practiced his newly acquired knowledge on Dad's car. Between the back of our house and the Downey's home was a massive oak. Taking full advantage of a thick branch, Warren used a block and tackle to lift the motor from the car. I remember watching as each greasy part was carefully placed on one of mother's old oilcloth tablecloths, then cleaned in a bucket of gasoline, and inspected thoroughly. Later that day, I returned just as Warren was completing the job. When dad came out of the house, Warren replaced the hood, sat behind the wheel, and started the car. The motor hummed magnificently, and Dad beamed appreciatively.

By the time he turned fifteen, Warren had become a skilled mechanic, and began working at Tapper's Gulf Station. Dad always said that standing in the pit with oil dripping on his head explained why, of the three Shamlian brothers, only Warren retained a full head of hair all his life.

Once, a local banker offered Warren $100 if he could make his car go faster than 80 miles an hour. A few days later, with police permission, Warren took the car to a remote location and tested it. The speedometer needle flew past 80, and bumped impatiently against the 120 mile limit. The grateful man gave Warren $300, but Warren kept his secret to himself.

It's after one o'clock in the morning when I'm awakened by the wail of the Firehouse siren. In less than a minute, Warren is out of bed, dressed and dashing down the stairs. I hear the kitchen screen door slam, and the sound of his tires over the rutted dirt driveway. As the bells and sirens fade into the distance, I fall back to sleep – and wake up the next morning to the comforting smell of wood smoke from Warren's clothes. He made it home safely.

On Tuesday afternoons, the firemen assembled for training. The Firehouse had just received a new Hook and Ladder truck, with a ladder that reached many stories high. Each man had to climb the nearly vertical ladder to the top, then descend on the other side of the ladder. I marveled at Warren's agility.

Warren was also a skillful driver. One icy winter day as we were returning home after making deliveries for Dad, the car began to slide. Warren slowed the car to a crawl and stopped the skidding. Then, just blocks from the store, we hit a lump of frozen snow. The car veered and slid sideways down the usually busy Lancaster Avenue. My heart was thumping like crazy, but Warren stayed cool, manipulating the wheel until the car faced forward. We came to a halt at the curb just a few doors from the store.

When we entered the store, Dad asked, "How are the roads, son? Did you have any trouble?"

"They're pretty slick, Dad, but I just had to go slow," Warren replied casually. That's all he ever said about it.

Before becoming a mechanic at Tappers, Warren worked briefly behind the counter at Parvin's Pharmacy. One afternoon, girls from Harcum Junior College entered and sat at the soda fountain. As he waited to take their orders, Warren couldn't help hearing that they were upset. They had an errand to run, but no transportation.

"Show me a driver's license and I'll lend you my car," he said.

One girl handed him her license. "Louise Becke. Is that you?"

"They call me Sis," she said, smiling.

Warren dropped his keys on the counter. "Here you go. Don't keep it out too long."

When I arrived home from the Navy in June, 1946, Warren and Sis were going steady. A frequent visitor at our home, Louise came from a well-to-do family living in Bethesda, Maryland. Her mother was a major stockholder of the Safeway Stores, and her father worked for the Federal Reserve in Washington DC. A Becke family tradition required that anyone marrying into the family had to have a home built for them – for not less than $75,000. This was at a time when the average home in Washington cost less than $10,000. Their lovely new home was built in affluent Chevy Chase, MD, and the couple moved in soon after their were married.

To this day, I can't fully explain why Warren and I fought so much as kids. Even though school, work and friends meant that Minnie, Newert and John led very separate lives, the two of us never bonded. Was it sibling rivalry?

Though he was my little brother – or perhaps because of it – Warren would tease me until the taunts flared into an argument.

They usually took place at bedtime. When they became too loud or physical, Minnie or Newert would rush to tell Dad, who came and settled the argument . . . fast.

As we grew older, our physical confrontations ceased. Carrying fifty and hundred pound bags of potatoes, onions and flour up the basement stairs of The American Store had made me strong, and my success as a wrestler at Lower Merion High School had made me tough. So I ignored his taunts and would no longer fight Warren. I feared that, in my anger, I would really hurt him.

The passing years did little to bring us closer. While John was in the Canadian Navy, Warren sold his car without asking him. He also sold the fabulous Navy pea coat and Shetland wool blankets I sent home. I believe he needed the money to entertain Sis in the style she was accustomed to. Warren never apologized.

Even in our seventies, when Minnie and I visited Warren in California, he continued to belittle me, calling me the poet of the family. Why he felt the need, or never allowed himself to feel close to me, I simply don't know, but it always left me dejected.

Looking back, I often felt unappreciated. John was incredibly handsome and talented, and Warren was the youngest, doted upon for his beautiful boyhood curls, which mother preserved in a satin pouch. It seemed to me the world revolved around them. I tried to do everything right, but somehow, I never quite fit.

In the third grade, Miss Reese observed me squinting at the blackboard, and sent me to the school nurse – who sent me home with a letter saying I needed glasses. That's all Mom and Dad needed during the Depression – another bill to pay. The glasses did *not* improve my looks. At Lower Merion High, I tried the shot put, and almost broke my toe. Between my jobs and my shyness, I never saw a high school football or basketball game, and never attended a school dance, not even my own prom. Though Dad never said it, I believe he thought I was a genuine Pushmondon.

Warren and Sis had four kids together. Christopher, the youngest, was killed by a drunk driver at the age of 3. Vicki, now a beautiful and vivacious mother of two, is a Spa Director living in Gaithersburg, MD. Of Warren's two surviving sons, the apples fell remarkably close to the tree. Sandy founded QuickSilver RacEngines in Frederick, MD in 1973, specializing in custom engine development for race cars. And Brandon sells luxury cars in Florida.

One day in 1961, after fifteen years of marriage in which Sis vied with Warren's automotive passions and long hours in the shop, Warren came home to find Sis with another man. It was after their divorce that he moved to Cathedral City, California and opened *Jaguars Only*. Over the next two decades, Warren married four more times. Wife number four, Leanna Mortizavi, was by my account the most decent and caring of his wives. I'm not sure he ever found the right one.

Sophia among the Armenians

I was eight when we moved to 1008 Lancaster Avenue. Aunts Nevrig and Myrack (standing) and Uncle Kegham would frequently visit us in our clapboard house.

CHAPTER 23

DEPRESSION YEARS

I was about eight years old when we moved to the three-story clapboard house at 1008 Lancaster Avenue, just two blocks up the street. That's the home I described earlier that once housed a bakery, the one the health inspector nearly condemned - and the home I remember most and loved the best. At the back was a large corrugated steel section which once housed the big ovens. Now, moved a short distance to the top of our steep driveway, it served as a doorless two-car garage. Our Model A Ford was lost in it. A kitchen was built where the corrugated section once stood. Later, Dad put in a potbelly stove and the kitchen became the center of our social life.

We walked home from school for lunch along Old Lancaster Road, turning onto Warner Avenue and down our rutted dirt driveway to enter through the kitchen. The kitchen smelled of soap, bleach and starch mingled with the aroma of homemade soup. From the radio came "Aunt Jennie's Real Life Stories." Listening to the romances and heartbreaks of Helen Trent, "John's Other Wife" and other soap opera characters helped lighten our parents' heartaches.

Our new home had a backyard – a weed covered patch that Dad tried to make into a playground and garden. We all helped. Most of our time was spent digging up rocks, broken bottles, empty shotgun shells and other junk. I think the landfill came from the city dump.

Dad loved the outdoors. On Sundays we spent the afternoons at Valley Forge Park climbing the cannons and playing hide-and-seek in the military redoubts. How we managed to keep our white linen clothes clean was a miracle. Once in awhile, Aunt Nevrig and Uncle Kegham, and our cousins John and Pauline, would join us. While we played baseball, our parents played pinochle. We could hear their shouting throughout the ramparts. We kids would just look at each other, laugh, and keep playing. If Dad or Uncle didn't shout or bang on the table, it was a very poor game.

Next door to us, separated by an alley, was Scanlon's Saloon. The unpainted tongue-in-groove wood walls were decorated with pictures of sports greats like John L. Sullivan, Jack Dempsey, Connie Mack and the Philadelphia Athletics.

Across the street, behind Espenshade's Market, was Hammond's Mill. Early in the morning I would lie in bed just listening to the ring of the blacksmith's anvil. From somewhere, a rooster would crow, or the Paoli Local or a long freight train would rumble by. I often ran up the bank to watch the massive steam engines fly by, waving to the engineers. It was a thrill when one waved back.

At night, the wail of that train whistle set me dreaming of faraway places and the great exploits of Tom Swift and the Rover Boys. Sadly, that haunting sound, which had sparked such a wanderlust to see the world, would soon be replaced by the coarse, frightful blast of the diesel horn. I wonder if its demise contributed as much to the decline of rail travel as did the automobile and the airplane.

A worldly, principled man whose schooling ended in the 6th grade, Dad acquired his deep knowledge of the world and its people through his travels. Victor had no time "for liars, cheats and teeves."

CHAPTER 24

TEEVES

"Good morning, Reverend," said Dad to the minister who had entered the store carrying a black suit.

"Good morning, sir," answered the minister smiling. "Is it possible to have this suit cleaned and pressed for Saturday?"

"It will be ready then," said Dad.

I listened to this, thinking what a nice man the minister is. When he left, Dad handed me the suit to enter our store number on the inside of the jacket pocket, and on the underside of the right back trouser pocket.

None of the small merchant tailors could afford the costly cleaning equipment. They sent the clothes to a professional wholesale cleaner who only worked for tailors and dry cleaning shops. Each store marked its own identification number in indelible pencil on the clothes pockets.

There was just enough room on the inside of the jacket pocket for our number. I put a line through other numbers and wrote in ours.

When I lifted the trouser pocket I said, "Dad, there's no more room for any more marks on this pocket."

"Let me see," said Dad. "You're right. Put a big X on this pocket so the cleaner will know to look at the other pocket. This old suit has been cleaned many times."

I was sweeping the floor Saturday morning when the minister walked in. I took the suit off the rack and handed it to Dad, who handed it to the minister.

"How much do I owe you?" asked the minister.

"There is no charge," answered Dad, who looked concerned as the minister looked the suit over inside and out.

"Is there something wrong with the cleaning?" "This is not my suit. I brought in a brand new suit."

I stood there with my mouth open. Dad's stunned expression was mixed with disgust and disappointment. He spoke very slowly at first, so each word would be said correctly.

"When you brought the suit to be cleaned, I saw that it was very old. It had been cleaned so many times, there was little room to put my mark." He took the suit and pointed to the pockets as he spoke. "I felt pity on you, a man of God, and charged you nothing. Now you tell me it was a new suit. You are a disgrace to your church. Take the suit and leave. Never come back."

The minister calmly took the suit and left the shop.

Dad went back to his sewing. Before I left to go carry groceries, Dad said to me, "I have no time for liars, cheats and teeves."

At the American Store, I could make as much as a dollar in tips on a Friday afternoon and Saturday. One Saturday, I came home with more than I had ever earned before. I handed the money to Mother saying, "Here's two dollars and sixty cents." I had no sooner finished saying that when Dad walked into the kitchen, took the money from

Mother, grabbed me by the arm, and practically dragged me to the American Store. He pulled me through the store up to Mr. Jefferies, the Manager.

"Do you know how much is here? How did my son come by so much money?" He said it so loud, customers turned to listen.

"Mr. Shamlian, yes, I know how much is there. Exactly two dollars and sixty cents, which Fred earned by carrying groceries and breaking cartons for me. He earned every cent of it."

"Good. I want no teeves in my home. Tank you sir." Dad turned and walked out of the store with me following behind. I didn't dare look at the customers. As we approached our shop, Dad said, "Hurry son. Mother has dinner ready and I am now hungry."

CHAPTER 25

JAKE'S HARDWARE

When I grew too old to be a delivery boy at The American Store, I took a part-time job at Jake's Hardware, lugging bags of fertilizer and waiting on customers. Mr. Jake Finklestein was dead, and his wife ran the business. She was so deaf, one had to scream to be understood. One day a customer came in.

"May I help you, sir?" I said. "Yeh. I want a bastard file."

I had never heard of that file. I thought he was being smart. "What kind of file do you want?"

"Damn it kid, you hard of hearing too?"

"What does the man want, Frederick?"

I walked to Mrs. Finklestein and said, "He wants a file." "I want a bastard file," interrupted the man.

"Speak louder. I can't hear you," said Mrs. Jake.

"He wants a bastard file," I said a little louder, embarrassed. "A what?"

"THE MAN WANTS A BASTARD FILE," I shouted.

"Oh, that. They're on the top shelf over there."

I climbed the wooden ladder to the top shelf. There was a long box with a yellow and black label, NICHOLSON BASTARD FILE. I'll be darned, I thought.

"What are you doing up there, sleeping?"

"No sir," I said, climbing down the ladder. "I've got the BASTARD right here."

Working in the hardware store was a learning adventure. There were no plastic bubble- wrapped packages. Every nail, screw, nut, and bolt had to be weighed or counted. I loved learning the language of craftsmen and their tools--though it took a while to understand why they called them male and female fittings.

CHAPTER 26

COAL THIEF

I stood at a distance, watching as the boys from Markee Terrace placed old horseshoe nails on the railroad tracks. How daring they were! The coal cars shook as they passed over the nails, causing some coal to fall to the ground, where the boys gathered it and took it home.

One morning when no one was around, I gathered a small pile of old nails from behind Hammond's Mill, and ran to the railroad bank. I stood a few feet from the tracks, watching the slow approach of the gondola cars filled with coal. On the track, I placed a few nails. I waived to the engineer who, unaware of the heinous crime about to be committed, greeted me with a wave of his cap. To my dismay, the huge engine flattened the nails without the slightest bump. After the front wheels of the first car had passed, I crept back to the bank, and with great fear and excitement, quickly laid more nails on the track. Though the trains moved slowly, it was dangerous work, and timing was critical. This time, the gondola cars passing over the nails rocked and some coal fell to the ground. The line of coal cars seemed to go on forever. I continued to place more nails on the track. Finally, the last car passed, and I ran along the bank filling my burlap bag with coal.

Below the front window of our store was the cellar window, where the driver would pour coal with a chute from the truck. I pushed opened the window and emptied the contraband coal into the bin below. I hid the empty bag in the space between our shop and the shoemaker shop next door.

Our hot water was heated by a small coal stove called a bucket-a-day stove. Each of us had to take turns keeping the stove going. The coal in my little bag kept the stove going for almost half a day. After the bag was safely hidden, I entered the store with clenched fists, lest my parents see my blackened hands. I raced upstairs to the bathroom and washed until all evidence was removed. If my parents knew, I would have been whipped, not just for endangering my life, but for stealing. I would have been the lowest of all Pushmondons. But today, I was proud and happy. I had proved myself the bravest of the brave.

Many years later, while describing my exploits during the Great Depression to my children, I told them about the coal-collecting incident. Weeks later, seated around the dinner table, our sons Fred and John were discussing their day at school when our daughter Germaine piped up.

"Know what we talked about today?"

"What did you talk about?" her mother asked.

"The Nun asked what our parents did during the Depression." "What did you tell her, dear?"

"I told her my Daddy stole coal."

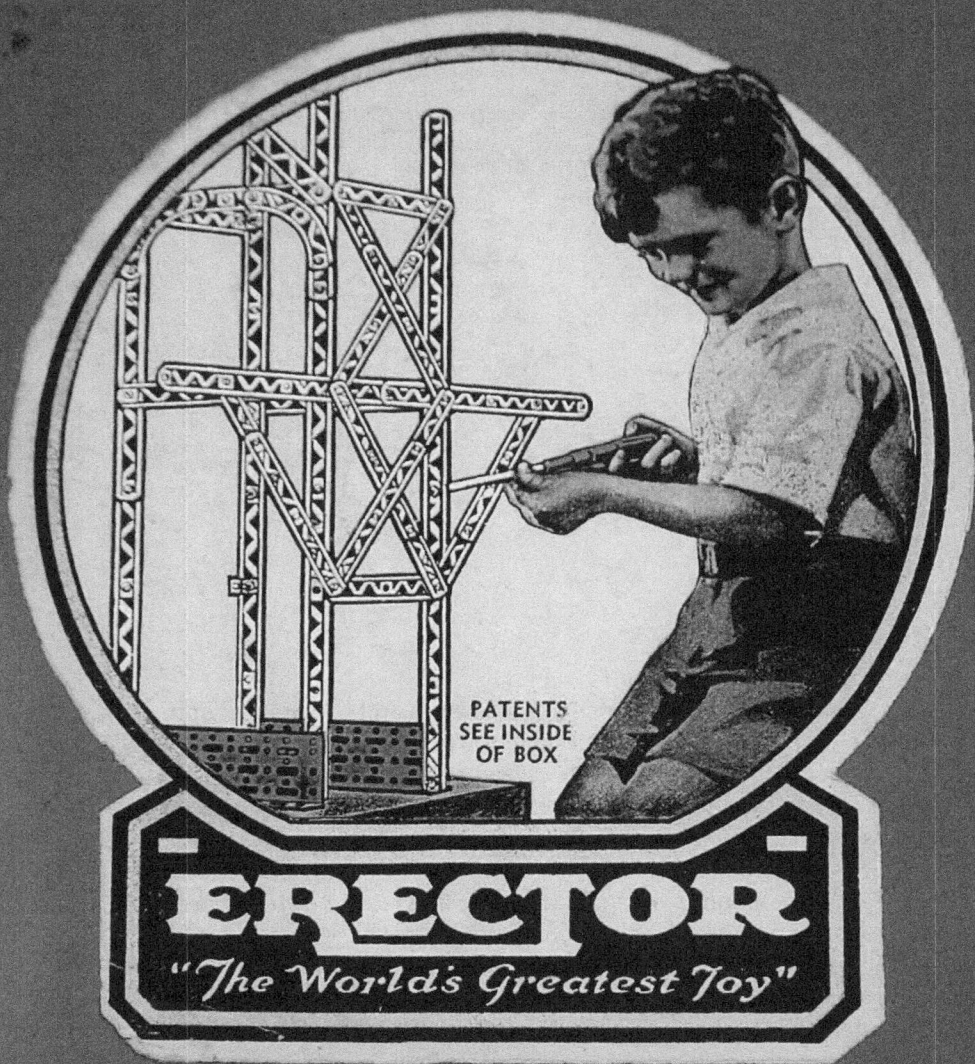

PATENTS
SEE INSIDE
OF BOX

ERECTOR

"The World's Greatest Joy"

Santa always brought each of us one special gift.
John's Erector Set boasted chromed metal strips,
plates, wheels, and screws to build skyscrapers,
bridges, trucks…whatever you could imagine.

CHAPTER 27

TOYS

A boy had to be the richest kid in the world to own a scooter. So we made our own. I had spent the morning foraging through the back of Hammond's Mill, our cellar and garage, and assorted trashcans until I found everything needed to make my super-speed scooter.

Three wooden orange crates were lined up in the back yard. They were about three feet long and fourteen inches wide and deep. I was sitting on the back stoop looking them over when Dad came to the door of the pressing shop for some fresh air. It was hot, and the steam made the room unbearable.

"What are you doing, son?"

"I'm trying to find the best looking one." "Is it for your room?"

"No, I'm making a scooter."

"A scooter. What is a scooter?" "I'll show you when I'm done."

I selected my crate, then nailed a three foot length of two-by-four to the center of the upright end, making sure the opening faced inward, and that the long bar was flush with the front. Next, I took an old roller skate, separated it, and nailed the two-wheeled sections to each end of the bar. In the garage, I found a long spout oilcan with a tiny bit of oil to lubricate the wheel bearings.

To test my handiwork, I turned the crate upright and stood on the bar, rolling backwards and forward to make sure the rusted wheels rolled. I then jumped on the bar to make sure nothing would come loose.

For handles, I broke apart a crate, and nailed two of the one-by-two pieces reinforcing the ends at slight outward angles on the top right and left. Almost done. Now, all I needed were headlights. I took two empty vegetable cans, minus their labels, and nailed them to the top with the openings facing front. I had a candle stub for each can. I went to Dad.

"Dad, can I borrow your matches?"

"What do you need matches for?"

"I'm making headlights. Come, take a look!" Dad followed me to the back step.

"This is my scooter. These are my lights," I said, pointing to the shiny cans. "I want to put a candle in each one." Dad didn't say anything. He handed me a book of matches and watched as I melted the candles on the bottom and fastened them to the inside of each can.

"There, it's done!"

"Will this work?" Dad asked, looking over my magnificent craftsmanship.

"Sure it will. Let me show you." I rode it up and down the alley between our store and Scanlon's Saloon. The scooter worked great.

"That's good, son. Please break up the other crates and put the wood in the cellar." I was hoping for more enthusiastic words of praise. Well, at least for now I wasn't a Pushmondon.

Newert and Minnie had another use for orange crates. Putting two side-by-side, with the openings facing front, they would wrap colorful chintz cloth around them, with the ends of the cloth meeting at the front center. On top, they would add more chintz or some other colorful material, and then adorn the edges with frilly ribbons. Voila! A set of bookshelves or a vanity table which no one would ever suspect of being orange crates.

My brother John had a Daisy Air Rifle. I loved shooting the BB gun with my brother. John also had a mold to make lead soldiers, which he would let me play with only when he was using it.

John was meticulous about his possessions. I dare not mark or scratch anything.

To make more soldiers, I would scour the neighborhood for empty cigarette packs. I dug through the trashcans behind Scanlon's Saloon, picked them up from the streets, and saved Dad's empty packs. The liners were covered with lead foil, which we peeled off and made into a ball. When the ball grew to approximately three inches in diameter, John placed it in a wood- handled crucible and set it over a fire. We would watch and wait until the ball melted, then pour the molten lead into the mold. Once cooled, we took the soldiers from the mold and trimmed off the excess lead over the crucible.

We took turns shooting at the soldiers. First, we lined the back wall of our garage with folded corrugated cartons. In front of them, on a board set on wooden crates, we placed our army. We were both pretty good shots. When the rifle chamber was empty, we picked up the spent BBs, removed the ones embedded in the cartons, cleaned them off and started all over again. Before John put his rifle away, it was cleaned, polished, and filled with clean BBs.

Dad had lots of empty wooden spools that once held sewing thread. With one spool, two large buttons, a rubber band and two wooden matchsticks, I made an army tank. With my trusty Buster Brown penknife, I cut V-notches around the entire circumference of each end of the spool. My invincible tank now had treads. Next, I inserted the rubber band through a buttonhole until it protruded just enough to insert half of a matchstick. I dropped the rest of the rubber band through the hole in the spool, and used the unbroken matchstick to grab the other end of the rubber band. Then I pulled it through a hole in the second button, and inserted the long match through the protruding loop. The match and button snapped tightly against the spool. I wound the rubber band until the tension was just so, set my tank on the back stoop, and watched it roll down the steps and along the walk until the band completely unwound. I took it into the kitchen to show Mother this mighty wonder. I rewound the rubber band, put the tank down on the kitchen table, and we watched it knock over the salt and pepper shakers.

"This is the great army tank I made."

"That's very nice, dear," said Mother as she straightened up the kitchen table.

Making balsa wood airplanes required patience and skill acquired with practice. Each part, outlined on thin balsa sheets, had to be carefully cut out with a razor blade. John kept a small supply of Gem or Treet single-edge blades, which I preferred. Dad's old double-edge blades were hard to manipulate; I always ended up with bandaged fingers. No matter how hard I tried, my planes never looked as finished or sleek as John's. His favorite models were hung from the ceiling in his room.

When one of us finished a plane, we would climb out of the second floor hall window onto the kitchen roof for a test flight. I slowly wound the propeller to tighten the long rubber band motor, held the plane aloft, let go of the propeller, and with a gentle push, watched the plane soar through the air and land in the small field behind our house. They weren't just model planes. They were the daring male pilots, Captain Eddie Rickenbacker or the Flying Tigers.

To make slingshots, we sawed out the forked sections from fallen branches, then cut up old automobile inner tubes. We practiced our marksmanship skills by lining tin cans on the fence and shooting at them with pebbles.

Each Christmas, Mother and Dad made sure that Santa Claus brought one toy or special gift to each of us. How they did it is still a miracle. One year, John received a Gilbert Erector Set.

With its chromed and perforated metal strips and hundreds of nuts, screws, metal discs, plates and wheels, one could build derricks, skyscrapers, bridges, trucks...whatever you could imagine. The possibilities were endless.

Warren's gift was a metal truck with large rubber tires and a brand new feature, battery operated headlights. I received a large round box of Lincoln Logs. The truck would carry the logs to the imaginary construction site where we would build a log cabin or our version of a colonial fort.

Store bought toys were treasured possessions. John still owns the Lionel train set he received when he was about eleven years old. The metal passenger cars and engine were painted pale green and had solid brass fittings and handrails. On rare occasions, he would let me work the transformer. For a few minutes, I was the engineer on the first overland express.

Bryn Mawr's Seville Theater was as romantic
as its namesake. A grand hand-painted mural.
Crystal chandelier. Oak-panelled Walls. Velvet
drapes. An organist! Newsreels! Westerns!
And Lana Turner and Gary Cooper!

CHAPTER 28

THE SEVILLE THEATER

There was something magical about the movies. For three and a half hours, I shared jungle adventures with Tarzan, sailed the seven seas with swashbuckling heroes, invented the telephone with Alexander Bell, and helped William S. Hart, Buck Jones and Tim McCoy rid the West of desperadoes. On Fridays, I was constantly looking at the classroom clock, hoping the day would end, and that Dad would let us go to the movies tomorrow.

On Saturdays, if all the household chores were completed, and the store was cleaned to our parents' satisfaction, if finances permitted, Dad would give us each a dime for the movies. Many Saturdays, we were not so fortunate.

I was always in a hurry to get to the theater, but if Newert, John or Minnie had extra pennies, they had to stop at the Bryn Mawr News Agency, where Mr. Stevens would sell them a grab bag of candy for a penny. The small brown bag was filled with broken or leftover candy. Some of the pieces were hard from age. Who cared? It was candy.

The Seville Theater, at the upper end of Bryn Mawr, had an arcade of shops, including Mr. Nitti's barber shop. We called him the Barber of Seville. The dark green ticket booth with the brass-framed windows was centered up front, near the sidewalk. One walked through the arcade to the theater entrance.

The minute I was inside, I would run down the carpeted aisle, only to be stopped by an usher. "If I catch you running again, you'll be told to leave. Now walk to your seat." The flashlight was pointed right in my face, and it took a few seconds to focus. Did somebody take my favorite seat? No, there it was: on the aisle, on the right side of the center section, about one-third of the way down. Once seated, I kept looking at the clock, or up at the large, circular, hand-painted mural and huge crystal chandelier. Velvet drapes and ornate gold lights adorned the oak-paneled walls, and floor-to-ceiling curtains covered the movie screen. At the foot of the stage was an organ. In the evenings, the organist performed before the movies began. Hurry up, one o'clock!

Exactly at one, the lights would dim, the din of hundreds of kids would hush, the curtains were slowly drawn, and for the next fifteen minutes I would watch the Paramount, Movietone or Pathé News. There were films of people in the Midwest made homeless by dust storms, of the Japanese invading China, Amelia Earhart embarking on another flight, sports greats Dizzy Dean and Babe Ruth, and the latest women's fashions. Though interesting to watch, I couldn't wait for the cowboy movie and the serial. Little did I know that I was watching history and the making of legendary heroes.

I yelled and shouted with the rest of the boys when Tim McCoy appeared on screen, and for the next half hour, I rode along with my Western heroes. When the movies introduced singing cowboys, I felt let down. Gone was that ramrod-straight, steely-eyed, raw-bone look of the old- time cowboys. Even their cohorts sang. As far as I was concerned, they didn't need their six- shooters to capture the villains. They could sing them to death.

After Tim McCoy rides into the sunset, I laugh at the "Pete Smith Specialty" about the bumbling husband creating chaos as he tries to repair his home. John always sat on the aisle seat on the right section of the theater, and I could hear his laughter above the others.

Many of the exotic places and famous American patriots, explorers and inventors I read about were brought to life when a Burton Holmes

Travelogue or John Nesbitt Passing Parade graced the screen-sepia-colored tales of great moments in science.

Next, the coming attractions filled the screen with words like SPELLBINDING, BREATHTAKING, BOLD, DARING, CAST OF THOUSANDS, FOR THE FIRST TIME ON THE SILVER SCREEN, UPROARIOUS COMEDY, and DON'T MISS THIS GREAT EPIC. How they whetted my desire to see the pictures!

Sometimes during an intermission, the Manager would come on stage to announce a paddle ball, yo-yo or talent contest. Kids my age would sing, dance, do acrobatics or show off their prowess with a baton or musical instrument. It took courage to perform before five hundred kids. Most of us weren't that brave. Even if we felt sure we could do better, nobody ever said it, because our friends would've said, "Yeah, if you're so good, why weren't you up there?" Respects for the contestants' courage (and fear of reprimand) are probably why there were so few boos and catcalls. To choose a winner, the performers lined up on stage and the Manager passed be- hind them, holding his hand over each kid. The one who received the most applause won either a small trophy or coveted tickets to next Saturday's matinée.

After the lights dimmed, it was time for the cartoon. There had to be a car- toon! Then came what I was truly waiting for: the new chapter of the hair-raising serial. I sat spellbound as Buck Rogers, Zorro, Rin-Tin-Tin or Flash Gordon faced one peril after another. Each of the twelve to fifteen chapters ended at the very moment our hero faced imminent death. I was still reliving their exploits when the feature film began. I liked the adventure and mystery movies best. Coming out of the theater, I had to squint to accustom my eyes to sunlight.

On Monday before school, my classmates were usually prepping each other for an upcoming geography or history test.

"What is the longest river in Brazil?" "What is the main crop grown in Kansas?"

"Who was the first to sign the Declaration of Independence?"

I, too, was concerned about Brazil, Kansas and the Declaration of Indepen- dence. But if I had missed the movies, my first question was, "Did Flash Gordon escape the exploding spaceship?"

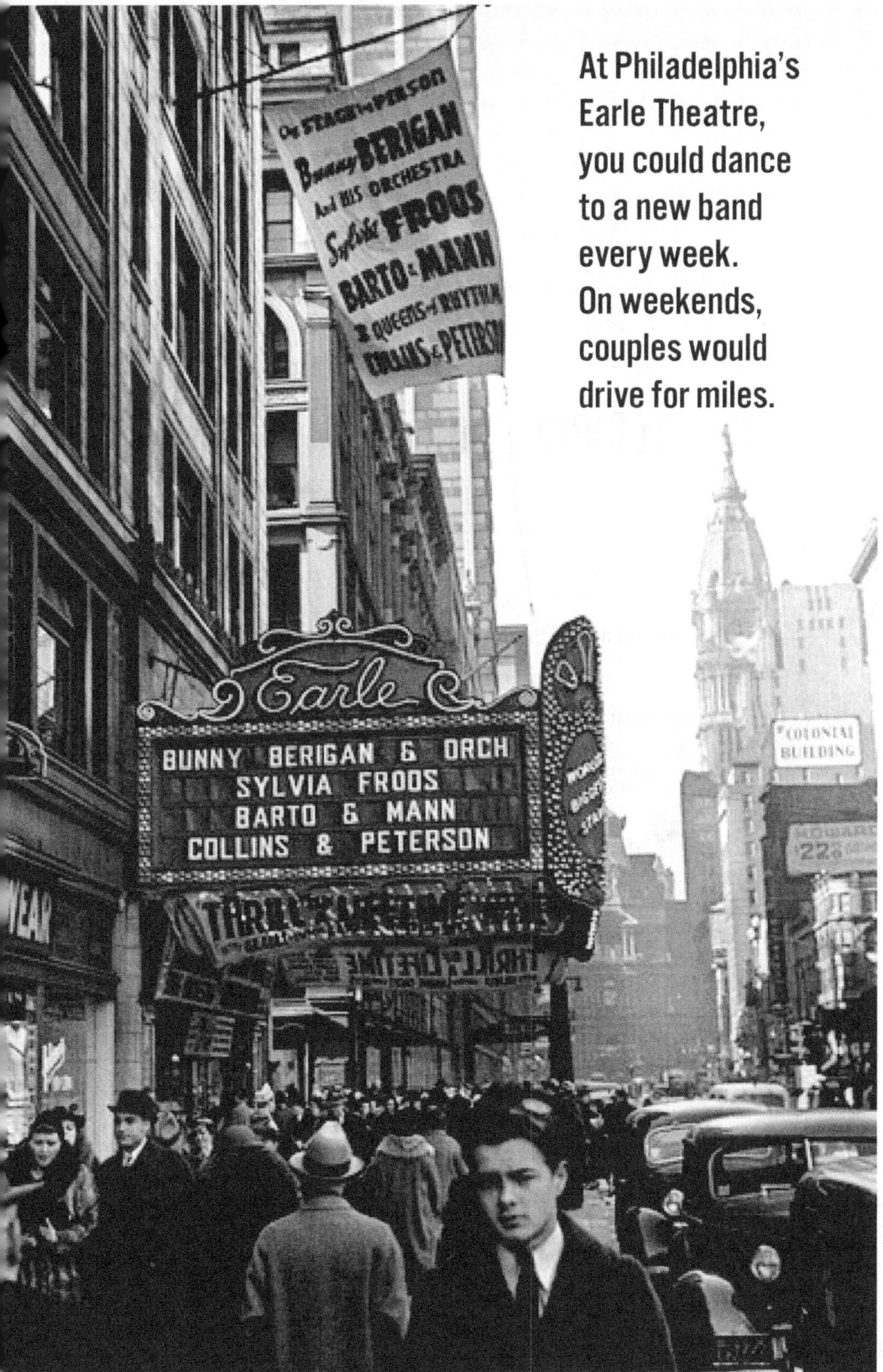

At Philadelphia's Earle Theatre, you could dance to a new band every week. On weekends, couples would drive for miles.

CHAPTER 29

THE RECORD SHOP

"Did we get another radio?" I asked Mother. " No. Why do you ask?"

"I hear music upstairs."

"Newert bought a record player. She and Minnie are in the parlor listening to it."

In the parlor? The most sacred room in the house! What is so magical about this record player? I had to see for myself.

Newert and Minnie were seated on the sofa listening to Tchaikovsky from a large floor model phonograph and radio console of polished cherry mahogany. It couldn't fit in any room but the parlor. Newert had saved the money working as a parlor maid at a local estate. It was the first automatic record player I'd ever seen. I walked over to examine this new wonder.

"Don't touch it!" said Newert.

"I'm not going to touch it. I just want to look at it."

132

I watched this marvel of automation in awe. Newert had put multiple records on the spindle, which held them above the turntable. When the first record completed its cycle, the tone arm raised and swung back, while a pin recessed into the spindle just long enough to let the next record drop. Then the tone arm slowly swung back in position above the record and gently lowered itself until the needle touched the rotating disc. After the last record played, the arm rose, slowly swung back onto its rest, and the phonograph shut off – automatically.

The sound coming from the built-in speakers was full and rich. Beethoven, Tchaikovsky and Mozart never sounded so good. I wondered how Benny Goodman, Tommy Dorsey and Artie Shaw would sound, but I was forbidden to touch the instrument.

Newert and Minnie purchased their classical records at the Bryn Mawr Record Shop. It was owned by Mr. Hammond, who also owned the mill behind Espenshade's Market. My sisters were such frequent visitors; they were on a first name basis with co-managers Bill and Jim. Single records were displayed in special pockets, or wells, in the counter. Albums were arranged on shelves lining the walls. Each single was in a paper sleeve with a circular cutout on each side so you could read the record label.

Most classical recordings were on twelve-inch discs. Popular music was on ten-inch discs, which were used in all jukeboxes. Most saloons and diners had a beautiful illuminated Wurlitzer jukebox. Drug stores and restaurants had compact, chromed music selection boxes on the counters and in each booth. For five cents, one could hear a favorite song.

All records were 78 rpm and made of shellac. An album of four or five records was quite heavy. When America entered World War II, shellac became a priority in the manufacture of war material. Records were now made of a new plastic, which warped quite easily. Gradually, the plastic was improved to reduce warping.

I seldom visited the record shop. When I did, it was usually on my way to work at Liggett's. I would select a record and take it to one of the two soundproof listening booths. Slightly larger than a double telephone booth, each room had a large window, a built-in bench and a phonograph on a table-high shelf. A small cardboard box contained a few steel needles. The weight of the needle and tone arm hastened the wear of the record. When the war began, steel needles were replaced by wooden ones. Though they quickly wore out, they were much easier on the records.

How I envied my classmates who came with their girlfriends. It isn't much fun listening alone. Once in a while, a boy and his girl would start jitterbugging, causing both booths to vibrate and the tonearms to slip and scratch the records. The Manager quickly put a stop to it.

The Earl Theater in Philadelphia, at Eleventh and Market Streets, featured a different band each week. The shows would start right after the feature movie. There were as many as six shows, each filled to standing room only. On weekends, couples would drive for miles to dance to their favorite band.

Walk down any street in the early evening and you'd hear music coming from a phonograph in an upstairs bedroom, where someone was studying. There were always record parties, where everyone would bring their newly purchased records to dance to.

The Record Shop was more than a store to buy records. It became a place for friends to share a common bond of music.

When Sophia married a recent immigrant who was neither wealthy nor Jewish, her father disowned her. In the apartment over the shop, with only a pot-bellied stove for warmth, Sophia and Victor weathered the Depression with unshakable devotion to their family.

CHAPTER 30

A VERY SPECIAL PERSON

I was sweeping the changing room of dad's tailor shop when the store bell clanged. I looked out from behind the partition at a gray-haired man. There wasn't anything special about him. You'd pass him on the street without noticing. Dad was standing at the counter.

As he approached, he asked, "Are you Mr. Shamlian? Mr. Victor Shamlian?"

"Yes."

"This is your store? You are the tailor?"

"Yes."

"You have five children?"

"Why all these questions? Is something wrong?"

"No, Mr. Shamlian, there's nothing wrong. I'm from the Department of Welfare," he said, reaching into his jacket pocket for his wallet. He removed his government ID and showed Dad.

"Mr. Shamlian, we know that your business, like many, many others, is very slow. You have expenses to meet and a family to support. We can offer you welfare assistance to help you through these trying times."

I couldn't see Dad's face. I could only imagine the hurt expression as he answered. "Since I was a boy, I have learned the tailoring trade. All these years I have supported my family without help from anyone." As he spoke, Mother came up beside me and listened.

"Mr. Shamlian, there is no doubting your craftsmanship, but in these trying times even the best of us need help. I am here to offer you financial aid until business conditions improve."

"Tank you very much. I cannot take your money."

"Mr. Shamlian, we only want to help, hopefully for a short time."

"Sir, you don't understand. I do not want welfare! I WANT WORK!"

The man lowered his head and said softly, "Mr. Shamlian, I did not mean to offend you. I'm sorry." He left the store. When Dad returned to his sewing machine, there were tears in his eyes. Mother walked back into the kitchen, wiping her eyes with her apron.

About mid-morning the next day, the store bell clanged. Dad rose from the kitchen table and walked into the shop. At the counter was the man from the Welfare Department.

Before Dad could speak, he said, "Mr. Shamlian, this suit is soiled. I would like it cleaned and pressed with rolled lapels."

"It will be like new. Tank you very much." Nothing else was said. Dad stood at the counter and watched the man until he disappeared from sight.

That afternoon, the driver for the company that cleaned clothes for tailors came by. While he was checking the few items, Dad handed him the suit belonging to the government man. "Henry," Dad said, "Be extra careful with this suit. It is for a very special person."

CHAPTER 31

THE HORSE FARM

When I first saw him, I imagined King Arthur and The Lone Ranger astride him. He was the tallest, most magnificent white Arabian stallion I had ever seen. In fact, he was the first. Old Eohippus would have been proud. Mr. Thomas led him to a stall and gently backed him in. As he maneuvered the steed, he spoke to him in a soft, low voice.

The horses boarded on the Thomas farm were all thoroughbreds owned by the local gentry. Mr. Thomas cared for each as if it was his own. He spoke with the same low voice to each horse as he opened the gate, then watched as the handler led it to the entrance. Some of the horses nudged Mr. Thomas in an expression of friendship. After they were watered, they were taken to the corral, which opened into the pasture.

I was fifteen when Mr. Thomas hired me to work on his farm in Newtown Square. My job was to spread the hay after it was lifted to the loft from the hay wagon. I would pull the huge forkfuls of hay inside the loft door and unclamp the hay, which dropped to the loft floor in a shower of dust. Then I spread each load evenly over the entire loft.

It was steamy under the barn roof. As the hay grew deeper, the heat became more intense.

When there was a lull between hay loads, I would sit by the door and watch the barn swallows. If a load of hay contained a tiny field mouse, it would quickly flee to a sheltered nook. With all of the cats and owls on the farm, the mouse had a poor chance of survival.

Each morning before the workers came to reap the hay, I would enter the barn and emulate Mr. Thomas, talking soft and low to each horse, including the great stallion. After a week, I managed to pet some on the nose. When I first approached the stallion, he snorted and rolled his eyes in fear. But after a week of trying, he stood calmly and stared at me as I spoke to him. I was determined to become his friend.

Watching Mr. Thomas, I learned how to offer a horse a piece of sugar or an apple slice in the palm of my hand. The first time I offered the stallion a lump of sugar, he reared back. "It's okay. I'm not going to hurt you." I said. Slowly he came forward, stretched his head until his nose was near my hand, then backed up without taking the sugar.

I repeated the offer each day until one morning, to my delight, he took it from my hand – and did so each day after. It took a few more days to muster the courage to rub his nose. When I succeeded, I knew I had won a friend.

Mr. Thomas had warned me not to go near the stallion. I don't know if he knew what I was doing in the barn. If he had found me talking to the stallion, would he have fired me?

The handler was a surly, rough looking man. His job was to tend to the stalls, take the horses to the water trough, and brush them down. Up in the loft, I would hear him swearing at them. One day I heard a commotion, followed by a yell of pain. I rushed down the ladder to see the handler holding his bloody shoulder. Just then, Mr. and Mrs. Thomas rushed in.

"That goddamn horse bit me," said the handler, pointing to the stallion. Mrs. Thomas ran into the house and came out with a towel, which Mr. Thomas wrapped around the wound. It was bleeding badly. Mr. Thomas looked at the heavy rope in the handler's hand.

"Did you use that on him?" he asked.

"He wouldn't do what I said," answered the handler.

It was some hours later when Mr. Thomas returned from the hospital with the handler. His shoulder was bandaged and his arm was in a sling. Mrs. Thomas took him to a room in his home. When she returned to the barn, Mr. Thomas said, "Once his shoulder heals, I'm firing him. No one puts a strap to my horses."

One evening before taking me home, Mr. Thomas said, "I have to bring the horses from the pasture." As he opened the corral gate, he said, "All you do is whistle and they'll come running. Want to try it?" I whistled. Nothing. I tried again. No luck.

"Stand away from the gate," said Mr. Thomas.

He let out a sharp whistle. Without hesitation, each horse lifted his head. Their hooves thundered as they raced to the corral. Even the great stallion, kept in a separate pasture, reacted to the whistle. He raced to the fence and whinnied to be let into the corral.

After each ten-hour day, I took a hot bath to rid myself of the straw, sweaty dirt and ticks. My first week's pay was eight dollars – the largest amount I had ever earned. When the haying came to an end, so did my job. I wished it could have lasted longer.

Dad and I drove through the Main Line countryside in a 1936 Ford sedan with yellow hubcaps. The finely stitched, cleaned and pressed clothes were hung on a wooden rod across the backseat.

Sometimes, when Dad made his deliveries, he was invited in to sit and discuss world affairs with captains of industry, such as Richard Bond, CEO of Wanamaker's and John Zinszur, the Chairman of Sharp and Dome.

CHAPTER 32

THE OLD COUNTRY

The little bell above the screen door clanged as I entered our store. "It's only me," I shouted.

At the back of the store, Mother was making a list of the clothes Dad had to deliver. "Want me to come along and help, Dad?"

"I would like that," he replied. We can be home early for dinner."

Before I carried the clothes through the dining room and kitchen and out to our car, Mother inspected each bundle to confirm the billing details. Sophia wrote every one of the shop's monthly bills in Spencerian script so exquisite, one customer told Dad that he framed Mother's invoices.

Our 1936 black Ford sedan with the yellow hubcaps was both the family and business car. We hung the clothes on a wooden rod in the backseat, wired to the hand straps on each side. Invariably, whoever sat in the back hit their head on the bar.

Our delivery route took us through the scenic Main Line countryside, of which I never tired. Cruising up the mile-long driveways of the great Main Line estates, flanked by towering oaks or finger pines, I felt like we were entering magical, miniature kingdoms. The lawns were tailored as meticulously as my father's suits, and the gardens and fountains turned my imagination towards Camelot.

Usually, I carried the clothes to the kitchen door, where a maid or butler would take them. Those kitchens looked larger than our house. I remember one bitterly cold winter day, making a delivery to the Tyson estate. Mr. Tyson was a very successful businessman, and Mrs. Tyson was a member of the patrician Scattergood family. Entering through the kitchen, I was met by a maid, who took the clothes, and a moment later, by Mr. Tyson himself.

"Hello. Who are you?" he asked with a smile.

"I'm the son of Vahan Shamlian, the Tailor."

"I know John and Warren, but I don't recognize you."

"I'm the middle son, Fred."

"The middle son! So, where's your father?" When I told him dad was waiting for me in the car, his smile was displaced by a look of concern.

"On such a frigid day? Go at once and ask your father to please come inside."

When dad entered, he was warmly greeted by Mr. Tyson. "Good to see you, Victor. Will you sit a moment by the fire and get warm?

The two men walked into the parlor, and sat across from each other in those grand leather chairs. A butler brought a cut glass decanter, and poured the two men a drink. They sat and talked for quite a while, while I was brought hot chocolate and home-baked cookies in the kitchen.

Although born on a farm in Turkey, with no schooling after the sixth grade, and little to show for a lifetime of work raising five sons and daughters, in every way that mattered, Dad was an aristocrat too. A worldly, principled man who spoke softly, listened intently and thought deeply, Dad acquired his acute understanding of world affairs, politics, business and people through his extensive travels.

On many occasions such as this, Dad would be invited into these great estates to sit and discuss world affairs with Philadelphia's captains of industry. Among his customers were Richard Bond, the Director of Wanamaker's; John Zinszur, Chairman of Sharp and Dome; and Mr. McNeely, attorney for the Atlantic Refining Company.

Despite much that has been said and written describing the rich as aloof and greedy, my travels with Dad showed me a very different face of these old world Main Line families, who showed my my father kindness, appreciation and respect.

I remember pointing to one of those mansions and saying to Dad, "When I get rich, I'm gonna buy us a home just like that." I wonder what he thought about my claim, because the Shamlian family had never lived in a real house. We lived in a land of Mom and Pop shops like ours, making our home in the apartment above the store.

Once in awhile, Dad would tell me about the old country as he drove. From his narratives, I've tried to piece together his life story.

Born to Armenians on a small and prosperous farm in a village in central Turkey, Vahan's large family possessed that humble dignity that comes from living off the land, and from their deep faith in God and the Bible, which stated that Sunday was a day of rest.

One hot Sunday afternoon, Dad and I were sitting out in front of the shop when a long black limousine pulled up. The chauffeur opened the door, and out stepped a distinguished-looking gentleman, who approached my father.

"Sir, I have a problem and need your assistance. I must attend a meeting shortly, but a button has come loose from my jacket. Would you be so kind and sew it on?"

Dad invited him into the store and in a few minutes, had the button sewn on. When the man offered to pay, my father said, "Sir, I do not work on Sunday, so I cannot accept money for helping you."

The very next day, that gentleman came back and asked my father to make him a suit. He became a steady customer.

Another time while we were driving, Dad told me of an incident when he was a young boy. "One day, my father and I were taking the coach to the city (probably Ankara), when we were held up by highwaymen. They made us leave the coach and, one-by-one, searched the passengers for money and jewels. When the bandits came to my father and me, their leader called them back. They rode away without taking a thing from us."

"Our farm," he continued, "was near the highway. If people stopped and asked for food or a place to rest, my father asked no questions. He made sure that they had food to eat, a place to sleep and more food for their journey. He would not take money."

Late one night, men on horseback came to the farm and asked if they could rest. They were put in the barn to sleep on fresh hay. We took them bowls of beans, and fed and watered their horses. The next morning, before leaving, one of the men rode up to my father with some money. Though we needed it, my father said he could not take money for helping someone. Each man thanked my father, and rode away. Those riders were the men who robbed the coach."

CHAPTER 33

NOSTROTON HOJA

The greatest heroes of the war are the parents who sit at home, waiting for those letters that begin "Dear Mom and Dad," and listening intently to the radio for news.

On the way home, we passed the cornfield near Airdale and Montgomery Avenues, where it had become a tradition for neighborhood kids to help themselves to a few ears of horse corn at Halloween. The countryside was splashed with the brilliant colors of autumn. But dad's gray hat was pulled down low. He looked tired. Tired, I thought, of the struggle to keep a family together during the Depression and now, a World War. Three of his five children were in the service. In another year, his youngest son would probably have to go to war, too.

"Dad," I said, "Let's stop at the drugstore. I'll get some ice cream for dessert."

As I was getting out of the car, Dad said, "Your Mother likes chocolate, I like strombelly." Strombelly was Dad's way of poking fun at his English. At home, we never said strawberry.

There were six of us at the dinner table. John was somewhere in British Columbia with the Canadian Navy. Minnie was home on leave from the Naval Training School at Hunter College, New York. We joked, laughed and listened to Dad tell Armenian folk tales of Nostroton Hoja. Each story had a moral.

My first Nostroton Hoja lesson came when I attended Bryn Mawr Grammar School. We had to wear clean clothes from the skin out, everyday. Some of our clothes were handed down from one brother to the next. One night at the dinner table, I remarked about the patches on a classmate's clothes.

"Did I ever tell you about Nostroton Hoja and his best friend's wedding?" Dad didn't wait for an answer. "One day Hoja was working in the fields. He had been working since dawn. When he looked up and saw the sun directly overhead, he thought, "What a fool I am." At this very moment, my best friend is taking a wife, and I am not there to wish them good health and many fine children. Hoja dropped the hoe and ran from the fields to the house of his friend. The wedding feast was in progress. Hoja quietly sat down at the end of one of the long tables. He hoped his best friend would look his way. Large trays of food were brought to the table and passed from one person to the next. Hoja realized he had not eaten since daybreak, and watched with great hunger as the trays came closer. After the person beside him took his food, he passed the tray to the person across the table. He did not look at Hoja."

"This happened to every tray of food that came his way. Hoja looked about him. Everyone was wearing their finest robes, their finest silks. It was going to be a long celebration. Hoja went home, bathed in the river, trimmed his hair, and put on his finest silks, and returned to the feast.

As he sat down at the same seat, his best friend shouted, "Hoja, welcome! I am glad you came. Pass the food to my friend Hoja."

When the food was set before him, Hoja looked at it, deep in thought. Then slowly, he began taking the food and--to the amazement of the other guests--began putting the food in the pockets of his best clothes.

"Have you gone mad?" cried his best friend. "Surely he is mad," shouted others.

Hoja looked at them with such sadness that everyone fell silent. "I was working in the fields," he said, "when I looked up and saw the sun overhead. I remembered that it was the time of my best friend's wedding, and I ran here to wish him happiness and good health. When I arrived, soiled from working in the fields, no one even acknowledged me. I went home, bathed and dressed in my best clothes. Now, everyone knows me and you present me with food. But since I am the same person who was here before, you are not pleased to see me. You are pleased to see my fine clothes. So, let my clothes eat!"

I never made fun of patches again. We all learned from Dad and Hoja.

On my first weekend liberty in Maine, I was offered a ride by a couple straight out of Grant Wood's *American Gothic*. During the long drive, the '31 Ford rolled through the countryside at 20 miles an hour.

"Here we ah, sailah. Glad to do ah paht."

To my amazement, the happy couple turned and headed back in the direction we came from.

CHAPTER 34

BRUNSWICK, MAINE

The ten days passed quickly. My orders read "U.S. Naval Air Station, Brunswick, Maine." I enjoyed the train, the soot, the crowds of servicemen and their families. It was all new and exciting. Before the war, the furthest I'd ever traveled was Long Beach Island, New Jersey.

The Naval Air Base on the outskirts of Brunswick, a small college town, was no Pensacola, but it served one major function: to train English airmen to fly the F4U Corsair, the most graceful of all Navy fighter planes.

Did I go to special schools for carrier personnel? No. Did I work in the hanger on the planes? No. I ran the mimeograph machine.

One day I was running the mimeograph when an officer stopped and asked, "How are you doing, sailor?"

"Lousy," I said, without looking up. "I joined this man's Navy to fight the war, not print it." The officer went off without a word. Another sailor who worked in the Headquarters Building rushed up to me. "Sham, you shouldn't have talked to the Old Man like that."

151

"Who?"

"The Old Man. The Skipper," he said.

I could have kicked myself. All I saw was a sleeve with gold stripes. Not only did I open my mouth to the Commanding Officer, I never looked him straight in the eye. I was to have that pleasure soon.

Maine was unspoiled and picturesque. The grays and browns of fall were brightened by the rich greens of the fir trees and a brilliant blue sky. The few people I had met possessed that simple, quiet Yankee dignity I'd read about. One afternoon, while hitchhiking on my first weekend liberty, a 1931 Model A Ford, just like the one we used to own, stopped.

"Going somewherah, sailah?"

"Are you heading towards Lewistown?"

"Ayah. Hop in sailah."

The couple looked like they stepped out of Grant Wood's American Gothic. "I hope I'm not taking you out of your way."

"That's all right, sailah."

We rode without saying anything. I watched the countryside glide by at twenty miles an hour.

"Here we ah, sailah."

"Thanks for the ride. I really appreciate it."

"That's all right sailah. Just doing ah paht." "Ayah," said his wife.

"Ayah. Good luck, sailah."

"Thanks again," I yelled as the Model A pulled away. I couldn't believe it. They were heading back in the direction from which we came.

It was my first visit to Lewiston. I was walking towards what I thought was the center of town when I felt a tug at my sleeve.

"Will you take me dancing, sailor?"

She was about five feet, six inches tall – and about as wide. Her motley red hair looked like a steel-wool version of Orphan Annie. Her hips were extraordinarily wide, and her legs looked as if they could support a concert grand. Her face was all brown freckles and gooey eye makeup. She wasn't my version of a sailor's dream.

"I can't dance," I said.

"Please take me dancing. I have no one to go with."

I was so naive; I didn't know how to turn her down.

"Okay. But only for one dance."

"Take me home first so I can change," she said.

All the changing in the world won't help this girl, I thought.

"My name is Carmen."

"They call me Sham."

"What's a Sham?"

"It's short for Shamlian, Fred Shamlian."

"Are you stationed at the airfield?"

"Yep."

"What do you do there?"

"I'm relieving a Wave."

"Here we are," she said. As we walked up the porch steps, I heard someone say, "So, you snagged one."

"Yes, Daddy, and he's taking me dancing. Keep him company while I change."

"Sit down sailor. This may be a long wait. I'll get us both a beer." While I waited, and waited, her "Daddy" told me of his adventures as a sailor in World War I.

About ten years later, I heard the screen door open, and turned to see the most beautiful girl in the world.

"Ready to go dancing?"

"I'm waiting for Carmen."

"I'm Carmen."

I literally fell off my chair. I couldn't take my eyes off her, and kept tripping over the rocker each time I tried to pick it up. Her Dad just sat there, laughing. I finally managed to stand up.

"You're Carmen?"

"That was my Halloween costume. I was coming from a party for the kids at the school. See what six pairs of heavy wool socks, six skirts, a closetful of towels, tons of makeup and a wig will do?"

Her jet-black hair was long and wavy against her flawless skin. Her eyes were the greenest I had ever seen. And her figure would have shamed Lana Turner. She was every young man's dream and every old man's fantasy.

I saw her every liberty, and prayed I would never leave Maine. It was not to be.

It was my turn to be Master at Arms in the Beer Hall, complete with MAA armband, billy club, leggings and web belt. My duty was to tell sailors to put their empties in the rack, and return the empty pitchers to the bar. I was also charged with preventing any physical "discussions" resulting from excessive hops.

My station was a table about twenty-four inches in diameter. On it was a card that read MAA STATION. At seventeen hundred hours, the doors opened and I think all 250 English cousins came rushing in.

Three of them approached my table.

"Hey Yank, how about getting up and letting us sit there." "Sorry, for the next four hours, this is my station."

"But there are no more tables."

"There's nothing in the rule book says you can't sit here. But there is about me giving it up."

"Damn Yanks."

"Think you own every bloody thing," said another.

The third slammed his beer on the table saying, "Bloody Damn Yank." I was brushing suds from my uniform when one said, "Serves you right, Yank." I slammed him hard with the billy stick, and all hell broke loose.

"Fight! Fight!" These words rang out loud and clear. I think all ninety American sailors joined in. It was a masterpiece of a donnybrook.

The Shore Patrol came and broke up the fight, and the entire base was confined to barracks. The next morning at muster, I was ordered to report to the Commanding Officer, ON THE DOUBLE. He looked at me and said, "Shamlian, you're the worse excuse for a sailor I've ever met. Of all the stupid tricks! I don't want to hear any excuses. I know how it started and ended."

I stood at attention, thinking, I've been in the Navy just a few months. Now I'm about to be kicked out before I even have a chance to fight.

"Come over to this the window," he ordered.

Pointing to the few Englishmen at muster, many with black eyes, bandages and arms in slings, he said, "I guess you're proud of that." I didn't answer. "Shamlian, I'm transferring you as of this moment."

"I'll go pack my sea bag, Sir."

"It's already packed and in my car."

As I turned to leave, he said in a friendly manner, "Shamlian, this is off the record. It took a green boot to show them their comeuppance. I only wish you would have completed the job." He smiled reassuringly. "You're going to a good duty. You've earned it. And you won't have to print the war. Now don't disappoint me."

"I won't, Sir. Thank you." We shook hands goodbye.

I walked down the steps between two rows of Marines carrying M1 rifles and entered the Skipper's station wagon.

I never saw Carmen again.

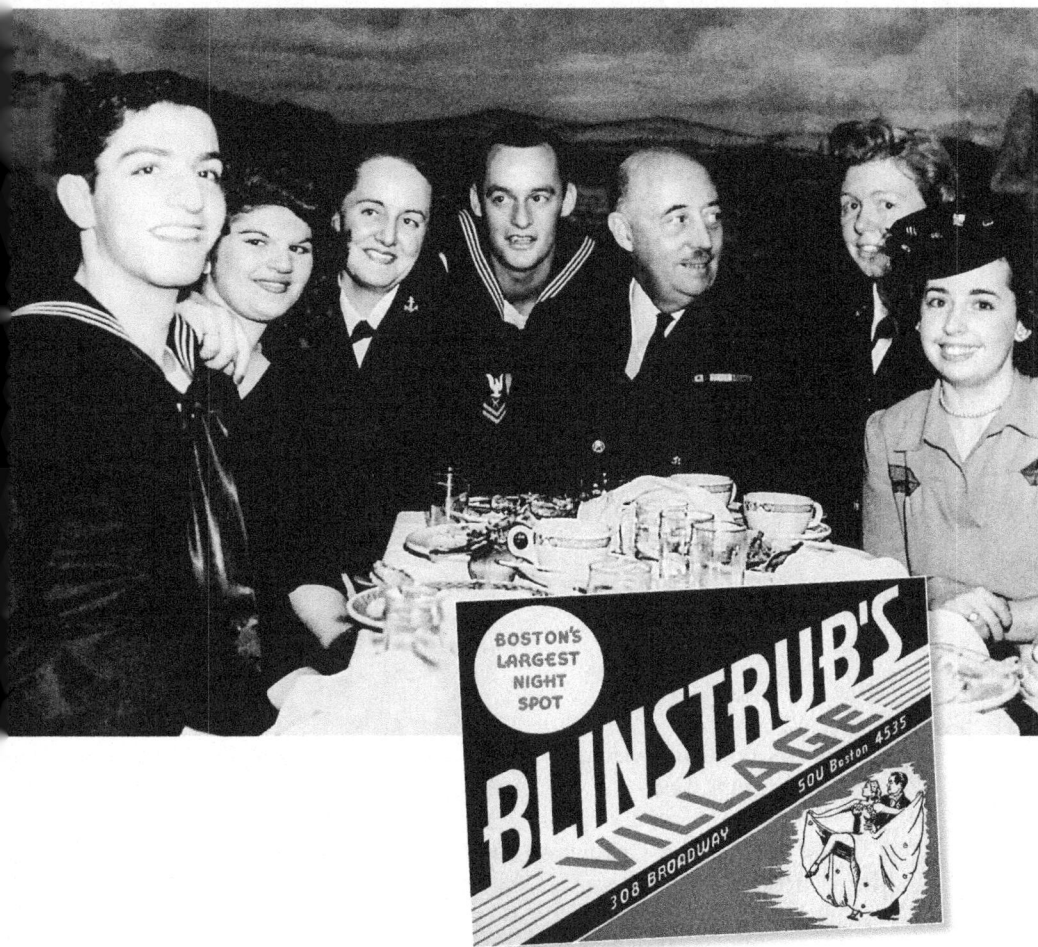

BOSTON'S LARGEST NIGHT SPOT

BLINSTRUB'S VILLAGE

308 BROADWAY

SOU Boston 4535

While stationed in Boston, the city became my world, from the Silver Dollar Saloon to the Boston Commons, designed by the Yankee ancestors of my friend and crush Ensign Sue (2nd from right). Some nights, against regulations, we would meet after work for a drink.

CHAPTER 35

BOSTON

I rode out of Brunswick with the Skipper's driver, Frank, who was also being transferred.

A few miles south, we opened and read our orders: Report to First Naval District Headquarters for assignment to duty.

"Frank, why are they transferring *you*?"

"They don't want the Brits to know where you're going."

"Why?"

"So they can't get even for last night."

At District Headquarters, we were informed that we were on subsistence, and must find our own accommodations. I had very little money. The only place I could stay until payday was the YMCA. Frank went home to Dorchester. The next morning, we reported for duty.

"What you do and say here will determine your future in the Navy. At no time will you discuss your work with anyone, and that includes Admirals. Understood?"

Lt. Henry Lewellyn Bixbee looked at me with the most penetrating blue eyes. He was a big man, a man of few words, with a thin layer of white hair. He began his naval career as cabin boy on the last of the Navy sailing ships. At the outbreak of the war, he was recalled from retirement.

A Wave officer escorted me to a cubbyhole containing a desk, chair, lamp and wastebasket.

It was about the same size as the listening booth in the Bryn Mawr Record Shop. "Wait here," she said and abruptly left.

Nothing in the room indicated what type of place I was in. It was another cellar, only with neon lights and many small offices. What kind of mess did I get myself into? Even the initials on my orders told me nothing. I was thinking of Carmen when a junior lieutenant approached, handed me a portfolio stamped CONFIDENTIAL, and said "Read this. I'll wait."

When I finished reading the contents, I handed him the report.

"Did you read it all?"

"Yes sir."

"Do you know what you read?"

"No sir."

"Good. From now on, whatever you see and whatever you do, you don't know a thing. It that understood?"

He left. Twice I was warned to keep quiet. If I had any sense, I would have given my table to the English, and I'd still be seeing Carmen.

For two weeks, I was given menial clerical work that any five year old could do. Was there something in my IQ tests that I didn't know? I thought no one spoke to Frank or to me because we were new. We were so kept busy , we saw little of each other. Day after day, it was the same treatment. When anyone did speak, it was strictly business, terse and aloof. I went to chow alone and worked alone in my broom closet. I took longer showers, used more deodorant and mouthwash, and took care to check all thirteen buttons. The freeze continued, while outside my office, enlisted men, women and officers talked and worked together.

Then one morning, Lieutenant Bixbee roared, "SHAMLIAN!"

I rushed to his office.

"Come in, Shamlian. Sit down. These gentlemen have something to say to you." The three were dressed in conservative business suits and identified themselves as FBI and Naval Intelligence. My insides began to leapfrog. They began...

"Frederick Shamlian, you live with your parents, brothers and sisters at 1008 Lancaster Avenue, Bryn Mawr, Pennsylvania..."

They told me about the schools I attended. How and when my parents came to America. Where my brother John was stationed in Scotland, and that Minnie was stationed at the San Diego Naval Base. They took turns telling me what I did since I arrived in Boston; every movement I made, every word I spoke, even the few girls I'd met. The narrative ended with, "You've been quite selective of those you've met." My mind flashed back to an incident on the Boston Commons.

I had a date with Elizabeth who lived in Watertown. We were to meet at the Duck Pond. I arrived early, and was sitting on the grass watching kids in a Swan Boat when a man sat down next to me.

"Nice day," he said.

"Yes it is."

"Come here often?"

"Nope."

"Where are you stationed?"

"The Navy Yard."

"What do you do there?" "Nothing. I'm a pencil pusher."

"I like sailor uniforms," he said, and put his hand on my leg. "You look great in yours."

"Take your hand off me or you'll carry it home in a sack!" He left, fast.

The agent continued. "Your work here is classified Top Secret and shall not be mentioned at anytime. You will be stationed here for not less and not more than one year. Any questions?"

One year. I'll never get to sea, I thought.

"Just one. Do you have my brother's address?" They laughed. I was serious. It had been months since his last letter. I was excused by Lt. Bixbee and was halfway to my desk when he shouted from his office, "Shamlian, when you come back from lunch, bring me a bottle of milk." From that moment, the atmosphere totally changed. Officers and enlisted men came to my cubbyhole and introduced themselves. The leper had been healed.

The classified nature of the work became more apparent as my responsibilities increased. Codebooks and coding apparatus had to be constantly updated and distributed with extreme secrecy.

My favorite duty was going aboard the ships to deliver "the merchandise." For a few minutes I was part of the real Navy. How I envied them.

Each week, we had to take time for target practice with a 45-caliber sidearm. But instead of live ammo, a spring-powered needle was inserted into the barrel. A paper target about seven inches in diameter was placed just a few inches away. When you pulled the trigger, the needle shot out. Even without real bullets, the recoil had a kick. Hitting the bullseye was harder than it looked.

About fifteen feet from the office was "the vault," a large, windowless room with an iron door where all top secret literature and equipment was kept. When ordered to go in, we were given the keys and a loaded 45. Immediately after entering the room, we locked ourselves in.

One day, Lt. Bixbee handed me a slip of paper. "I want a count of the books with these serial numbers. Leave the door open, I'll be right there."

"Sir, the orders are to secure the doors after entering." "I said leave the door open! I'll be right there."

I had just entered the vault when a man dressed in overalls rushed past me, picked up a wrapped codebook and started to walk away.

"Put that back," I shouted.

He stopped, turned and said, "I need some nails."

"There are no nails in here. Put it back."

"I'm taking these nails," he said.

"You do and I'll shoot you," I said, reaching for the gun. I had never pointed a weapon at a human being. It was a frightening experience. He started to walk away with the book. I lifted the gun from the holster, released the safety, cocked the firing pin and aimed at his chest. "One more step and I'll kill you." The gun shook in my hands. He dropped the book and fled. I shouted for Lt. Bixbee. All at once, the area was filled with Marines with M1's.

In the Exec's office, I had to relate every action and every word. He asked question after question. "What color was his hair? What color eyes? Describe his clothes. Where were you standing when you pointed the gun?" Then Lt. Bixbee asked, "You were told to always fire a warning shot. Why didn't you?"

"Because he was too near the steps and might have gotten away with the book."

"Would you have shot him?"

"I don't know, sir. I think I would have fired a warning shot if he started moving again. But he wasn't going to take that book."

Back in my cubbyhole, I kept repeating, "goddamn war, goddamn war" as I shook all over.

The next day, Lt. Bixbee came to the cubbyhole, dropped an official-looking paper on my desk and said; "Shamlian, sign it." I started to read it.

"I didn't say read it. I SAID SIGN IT!" he roared. I signed it at once. He picked up the document and replaced it with a Third Class Petty Officer's stripe, "Here, you've earned this." I just stared at it.

"What's wrong with it?" he asked. "Does it have to be a Yeoman?"

I think he understood "Shamlian, I wish it could be different, but we can't let anyone know what we do here. This is the only type of rating I'm authorized to give."

"Thank you sir," I picked up the rating and looked at the crossed quills. As he was leaving he turned and asked, "What rating would you have wanted?"

"Quartermaster."

"Quartermaster?"

"Yes sir. I intend to go to sea. And when I do, I want to be at the helm." He just stared at me, shook his head and left.

Ensign Sue came from a long line of Yankees who colonized America. It was either her grandfather or great-grandfather who designed the Boston Commons and the famous houses on Marlborough Street. She had bright red hair, a pug nose, skinny legs and a twinkle in her blue eyes.

Sue didn't have that officiousness that some Wave officers carried like chips on their shoulders. When she worked, she hummed quietly. Her smile was infectious.

We met shortly after I passed the government investigation. She stood in the doorway of my cubbyhole, her dark Navy uniform in sharp contrast to her red hair.

"Hi. I'm Ensign Sue."

"I'm Fred Shamlian. Most folks call me Sham. Won't you step into my parlor? Don't be afraid, I'll keep the door open."

She laughed. There was no door.

"Some other time. If you need any help, just ask. Good luck, Sham." I liked her at once.

As the weeks passed, we became friends. On a few occasions, against Navy Regulations, we met after work for a drink in some hideaway restaurant.

When it was my turn for night duty, the officer in charge was Sue. Around midnight, Sue was at her desk, rubbing the back of her neck.

"Anything wrong, Sue?"

"My shoulders ache."

I offered a massage, and Sue happily accepted. She purred like a kitten.

"Sham, that feels so good, it's making me sleepy." I don't know how long I stood behind her, but I remember kissing her on the neck.

Despite the years which have passed since that Summer of '44, I still treasure that friendship.

Frank lived in Dorchester with his wife, Alice, who was expecting their first child. One day Frank said, "Sham, I'm going out and getting drunk tonight." Knowing Frank, I knew he meant it. We were told to drink only with our fellow workers in the interest of national security.

"I'm with you," I said. "I haven't had more than one drink since I got here."

We started at four-thirty. Frank ordered rum and coke. I ordered the weakest beer I could think of.

"You'll never get drunk on that stuff," he said.

"You know me Frank, I do everything slow."

We stopped at bar after bar. I marveled how one man could drink so much and still keep going.

"I'm hungry for Chinese," Frank said. We made our way to Number 9 Tyler Street and climbed two flights of stairs. The restaurant was elegant, with white linen tablecloths, fine china and crystal.

Frank ordered Subgum Chop Suey. I ordered the same. I didn't even know what it was.

The instant the waiter walked away, Frank's head hit the table with a loud bang. He was out cold. I couldn't wake him. Everyone in the restaurant watched with amusement or dismay as I poured a pitcher of water over his head. I didn't give a hoot what they thought.

I called the waiter, who watched the drama with an expressionless face, gave him a five dollar bill and said, "Cancel the order."

I finally managed to get Frank to his feet, take off his glasses and put them in my jumper pocket. With one arm around his waist and one of his arms around my neck, we reached the head of the stairs, where he began to mumble incoherently. Frank broke loose from me, slid face down the two flights of stairs, and became wedged between the two front doors. I ran down, picked him up and half carried him to a cab.

"543 Boyleston Street."

We were inside the front door of the apartment building when Mrs. Gorman, the landlady, saw us. "I'll have no drunks in my house!"

"He's not drunk, ma'am. He's sick."

"I should know a drunk when I see one. Get him out of here and if you come back with him, I'll throw you out, too!"

I left him sitting on the sidewalk against the building, went to a corner telephone booth and called Sue. Within minutes, her coupe pulled up and she stepped out wearing a coat over pajamas. I told her what happened.

"I wish I could help you Sham, but my landlady will do the same."

The cabbie came to me and said, "I've been watching this circus. If you trust me, I know a place we can take him and keep you both out of trouble."

"Let's go!" The cabbie helped me carry Frank to the cab.

Sue waved goodbye. I didn't know where the cabbie was taking us. Finally he stopped and pointed to a large gray stone building. "Go in there and tell them the story. They'll help you." The sign on the wall read PRECINCT 21.

"It's a police station!"

"Don't let that worry you. They're good people."

Inside was a high wooden desk. Rising from each end of the desk was a black pipe with a round globe light. Framed between the lights was a ruddy, white-haired police sergeant.

"Can I help you, sailor?" he asked in a heavy Irish brogue.

"Yes sir. I have a buddy outside in a cab. He's too drunk to go back to base. May I bring him in so he won't get into trouble? I'll stay too."

"Aye, bring him in."

Frank was still out cold. The driver helped carry him to the door. When I couldn't carry him anymore, I dragged Frank across the floor. The sergeant stood up, leaned over his desk and peered down at him.

"Holy mackerel, HE IS OUT!" He called two policemen to help me carry Frank to a cell. "I'll be taking his ID card and neckerchief, and notifying the Shore Patrol."

"You can't," I said. "The cab driver said if I brought him here everything would be alright. I'm staying here with him."

"A cabbie, you say?"

"Yes sir. He's outside waiting for his money."

He ordered a policeman to go talk to our driver. The officer returned and whispered something to the sergeant, who was reading Frank's ID card. "We will not notify the Shore Patrol. How did your friend get this way?"

"His wife is expecting their first child in a couple of weeks. I guess he needed to get something out of his system."

"Aye, I see what you mean. A nice Irish boy trying to live the good life has to go out and loosen up."

Frank was put in a locked cell. After I paid the cabbie, I was given the cell next to his, unlocked. About dawn I was awakened by loud yelling.

"Let me out of here!" Frank was shaking the cell door as if trying to pull it from its hinges. Seeing him in his skivvies, scratched face and angry expression, I wanted to laugh, but put on a sober face.

"Sham, what did I do??"

"Frank, if I tell you, you'll never live it down," I said with a concerned expression. "You may have to stay in there for keeps. I begged the Sergeant to ask the Shore Patrol and FBI to drop all charges."

"Oh Jesus, Mary and Joseph. Is it that bad?"

"It's that bad, Frank."

"I'll never drink again!"

The policemen standing out of Frank's view were laughing and nudging each other. After a while, they brought us our personal belongings and uniforms, which looked as if they had been pressed. After washing up and a hot cup of coffee, we were told we could leave, but that the next offense could mean life imprisonment. Frank fled the station.

Ensign Sue gave us a sheepish grin as we reported for work. Near the end of the day, she came over and I had to relate every detail. Imagine the two of us in that proper, top-secret office laughing like kids.

Refusing to let the effects of childhood polio
keep him from serving in WWII, my brother John
enlisted in the Canadian Navy, went to sea
and played in the band.

CHAPTER 36

BOSTON POPS

Along Tremont Street, Boston's theater center, the big movie of the day was "The Song of Bernadette" with Jennifer Jones and Vincent Price. The Hotel Touraine, on the northeast corner of Tremont and Boyleston Streets, across from the Boston Commons, was a great place for sailors to meet girls. Heading north on Tremont, I soon came to Park Square and the famous Parker House, then into Scully Square, Boston's Barbary Coast, with burlesque houses and the infamous Village Barn, a haven for thirsty sailors. It was every sailor's duty to pay his respects to the Square, to the innkeepers, and to those wonderful artists such as Lily St. Cyr.

Boston was a city of contrasts...from the quiet parks and stately homes on Beacon and Marlborough Streets, to Symphony Hall, where Serge Koussevitsky conducted the Boston Symphony; from historic Christ Church to bustling Washington Street, home to Filene's Department Store and the Silver Dollar Bar.

In the summer, you can sit on the grass by the Charles River and listen to the Boston Pops. There was always a parade. On Sunday mornings, I'd awake to the din of bagpipes, fifes, drums and trumpets. From my window, I could watch Scotsmen in their bright plaid kilts...the Daughters of the American Republic...or other historical groups. Boston had much of that English respect for tradition. The city became the center of my universe. On off-duty weekends, I would hitchhike wherever my thumb pointed.

I first saw the town of Concord on one of those Technicolor days when the world was a hundred shades of green trees, fields and bushes, and the sky was deep blue with enormous white clouds skyscraping into the heavens. By the bridge, the bronze Minuteman stood at readiness. Birds were everywhere – and unusually quiet, considering their numbers. The silence was broken by the crunch of my shoes on the gravel path. I didn't know a pastoral peace like that existed. I felt I was trespassing on hallowed ground.

Early one Sunday morning, while strolling down Main Street in Lawrence, Massachusetts, searching for a cafe and enjoying the church bells, I came upon a radio station nestled between a row of stores. The stairs led to the second floor. I went up.

"Can I help you, sailor?" asked a man behind a control panel.

"Is it okay to come in?"

"Come in. What brings you here?"

"I have a date for lunch. I was just looking for a place to get a cup of coffee when I saw your sign and wondered what a radio station in Lawrence looked like."

It was a small place with a large glass wall separating the studio. I watched a lady playing church music on an organ.

"Ever been in a radio station before?"

"Yes, when I sang with the school choir in Philadelphia."

"Did you like it?"

"I guess so. I liked watching the blonde soprano in front of me."

The coffee he gave me tasted good. We talked about Philadelphia and Boston. It was surprising how little I knew of Philly and how much I knew about Boston. As we were talking, a farmer came in with two bushel baskets overflowing with apples. "Thank you for mentioning my ripe apples," he said as he left.

"Is that how you get paid for doing commercials?"

"No, not really. We don't ask for money when a local farmer or group needs help. It's that Yankee pride that won't accept something for nothing."

I don't remember much of Lawrence, but I learned a lot about New England that day.

I've always been drawn to the sea. I've walked barefoot on the sands of Nantucket, Scituate and Hampton Beaches. From Massachusetts to Maine, I've watched the surf smash against the huge rocks, as if trying to free itself. Sometimes the sea would turn black and wild, telegraphing an impending storm; or it would be a calm blue-gray, building strength to attack the rocks once more.

The New England coast is an endless series of coves, which protect the seafarer from the tempestuous sea. From the rocks in the coves, I would watch the aerial ballet of the seagulls above the sailboats. In winter, the small villages looked like scenes from Currier & Ives prints. When the stars were bright and the cold air was crisp, the church bells and chimes playing Christmas carols could be heard for miles around. From somewhere would come the sound of sleigh bells, which made New England winters a time forever remembered.

One day I received a call from my brother John. His ship was in port for a few hours. When I saw him in his Canadian Navy uniform, he looked a foot taller and much older. In my apartment overlooking Boyleston Street, we talked of his ship, my duty and of home.

The Toby House Restaurant was just below my apartment. Over our dinner of lamb with mint sauce, John asked "Do you get to Symphony Hall to hear the concerts?"

172

"I haven't been at all."

"Will you do me a favor?"

"I'll try, John. What is it?"

"In the summer of '41, when I was playing at Tanglewood, Leonard Bernstein and I bought Maestro Koussevitsky a bottle of his favorite cognac –a gesture of thanks for allowing us to play with the Boston Symphony. Immediately after the last performance, we rushed to his dressing room with our gift, but he had left for the airport just moments before – to conduct in Europe. We sat on a high curb under a street lamp in Lenox, talking and taking turns sipping the cognac until the bottle was empty. If you get a chance, could you take him a bottle for me? I'll pay you after the war."

As we shook hands goodbye, I realized how much I looked up to John, and how much closer we had become.

A few weeks later, I had a chance to purchase the cognac. I went to Symphony Hall with the package neatly wrapped. When the concert ended, I approached the stage entrance.

"What do you want, sailor?"

"I must see Serge Koussevitzky."

"He doesn't see anyone after the concert."

"It's very important. Could you take him a message?"

"I'm sorry. He refuses to take messages, too."

"It's very important. It's from one of his musicians."

"It can't be done. He refuses to be interrupted."

I carried the bottle to my apartment. It was many weeks before I drank it.

Whoever laid out the city of Boston must have wanted to avenge the Gods. Streets change course without reason. Street names change as you ride around the Square. Nonetheless, I thought I knew Boston like a book.

One day Commander William Davis Miller, our new Commanding Officer, asked if anyone knew how to get to the First Naval District Headquarters on Causeway Street.

"I do, sir," I shouted smartly.

"Good. Come with me and direct my driver."

Approaching the car, I saw that Frank was the driver. I started to say something, but he winked as if to say, "Shut up, you're getting out of work."

"How do you get there, Sham?" Frank asked. I gave him the directions and we rode and rode and rode. We passed Beacon Hill, MIT and were headed for parts unknown. We were lost. Finally, the Commander had Frank stop and ask directions from a policeman. What should have been a fifteen-minute trip took two hours. Finally, we reached headquarters.

I didn't speak all the way back to the base. Back in my cubbyhole, I was feeling pretty sorry for myself when the Commander came in. I was prepared for the worst.

"Shamlian, I want to thank you."

"I can't imagine what for, sir."

He suppressed a smile and said, "During our morning spin, we passed Beacon Hill. For the first time in forty years, I saw the home where I grew up. It brought back many fond memories." He left, leaving me speechless.

"What did the skipper want?" asked Frank.

"He said you were a lousy driver. Couldn't even follow directions. Why didn't you say you knew the way? Why didn't you stop me when you knew I was giving you the wrong directions?"

"I just wanted to pay you back for scaring the hell out of me that morning in jail."

CHAPTER 37

SPECIAL ASSIGNMENT

I awoke and looked at the calendar. Today is the day! I was now a Second Class Petty Officer, grown up and confident. Nothing was going to stop me.

I knocked on Lt. Bixbee's door.

"Come in, Shamlian. What can I do for you?" "It's a year today, sir. My time is up."

"Yes, what about it?" "I want to go to sea."

"All the compliments are full."

After passing my Navy physical at the Philadelphia Armory and being sworn in by the Admiral, a Petty Officer said, "Shamlian, Kowalski, step forward. You men are classified Special Assignment and are on active duty as of this moment. You have one week leave. Report here at 0800 hours, Friday, 17 September 1943."

When I told my parents I'd been accepted and was classified Special Assignment, Mother was frightened. She though I was to start fighting the enemy at once. I thought I was something special. All through Boot Camp and the short tour of duty in Brunswick, Maine, I waited to find out when I would be called to perform some great heroic feat.

"Sir," I said to Lt. Bixbee, "when I was sworn in, I was told that I was Special Assignment." "Shamlian, Special Assignment means limited service because of your eyes. You are ineligible for sea duty."

My world collapsed. I just stared at the Lieutenant for a long time. "I'd like to find that out for myself, sir."

"How?"

"May I have your permission to go to District Headquarters and speak to the Admiral?" "The Admiral?" He sat straight up and stared at me. From the expression on my face, he knew I meant it.

"The Admiral may not see you," he said. "I'd like your permission to try."

"You have it."

"May I leave now? I'll return as soon as I see him." I took the trolley to the First Naval District Headquarters.

"Who do you want to see, sailor?" asked the Lieutenant as he checked my I.D. card. "Admiral Danforth."

"Admiral Danforth?"

"Yes. My commanding officer told me to report to him," I lied. I got through. Outside the Admiral's office sat a formidable looking gray-haired woman. The desk plaque read M. Delaney.

"May I help you, sailor?"

"Yes ma'am. I wish to see the Admiral."

"About what?" she asked with raised eyebrows. "I want to go to sea."

"Please let me have your I.D. card." She wrote my name and serial number on a pad and handed back the card.

"Does your commanding officer know you are here?" "I have the Exec's permission to see the Admiral." "What is his name?"

"Lt. Henry Bixbee, ma'am."

"So, Hank said you could come." My God, she knew him! "Yes ma'am. May I see the Admiral now?"

"I'm sorry, he's too busy to see anyone."

"But I want to go to sea. I've waited a year for this day!" "How good are your eyes?"

"They're great! I don't need glasses to fight Japs and Germans."

"Go back to your base." "But..."

"Go back sailor. The Admiral can't see you."

Disappointed and angry, I walked away. I would be a desk jockey for the entire war. Back at the base, Lt. Bixbee asked, "Did you get to see the Admiral, Shamlian?"

"No, sir. Some old lady standing guard outside of his office said he was too busy. I'll try again in a few days. By the way, sir, she knew you. Her name is Delaney."

He laughed aloud. "Nobody gets past Marge."

The next morning, Lt. Bixbee handed me a large brown envelope. "Shamlian, this is for you." I opened it. After fifteen days leave, starting immediately, I was to report to Shoemaker, California via troop train for assignment to the U.S.S. Lavalette, DD448.

I was going to sea!

CHAPTER 38

CURTAINS

In bed, I watch the curtains gently wave as they catch the breeze. They mute the sun's rays, adding a soft yellow hue to the room, and soften the harsh gray bleakness of the winter sky. At night, I fall asleep watching a gossamer moon.

On my trips across America's southwest, I saw the tiny houses of the railroad workers and their families. The houses were almost the size of a large room. The yellow paint on the wooden boards was badly peeling or had faded to a dull brown from the constant sun, heat and winds.

Without curtains, those houses looked cold and forlorn. Many had broken windows or no panes at all. They were covered with oil-coated paper to repel the rain and dust. How dark and dismal those houses must have been. The curtain-less windows made the houses and all inside vulnerable to the world.

When Mother would take the curtains down to wash, my room became vulnerable to the world, too. When they were replaced, softness and tranquility returned. How comfortable and at peace I felt behind my sheer cotton wall.

CAMP DWIGHT MORNING SALUTE

With Easter approaching, choir boys from the Church of the Good Shepherd shifted into high gear selling Mrs. Minter's Coconut Cream Eggs. If you sold a dozen boxes, you won a week at Camp Dwight. At night, around the campfire, we listened to stories and sang songs.

CHAPTER 39

ON LEAVE

In my bed, I watch the curtains dancing in the chilly winter breeze. I snuggle deeper beneath the blankets, too warm and too lazy to get out of bed and lower the sash.

The church chimes are playing "The Church's One Foundation." How many Sundays have come and gone since I sang that hymn with the choir? When my brother John played the chimes, he had a way of blending each note with the next, allowing the music to flow gently over the village. Now he's at sea, and the chimes sound so different. I wonder if he will play them again. Will things return as they were?

I look over to see if Warren is awake. His bed is empty. I forgot that he went to work at Tapper's Service Station. There is no one to talk to. Listening to the chimes, I remembered my choir days and how much of a role the church played in our lives.

The Church of the Good Shepherd in Rosemont is a gray Gothic structure with old world stained glass windows and bright red doors. Inside the stone walls, carved wooden arches stretch towards the ceiling like hands in prayer, creating a feeling of hushed reverence.

Although he belonged to the Armenian Church, Dad wanted us to grow up American, so we were sent to the Episcopal Church. I was about eight when John escorted me to church to meet Dr. Willoughby, the choirmaster. Of slight build, with thin wisps of gray hair, gray-blue eyes and rimless glasses, he looked like a scholarly English professor. He sat at the piano and played the scales, which I had to sing, followed by a hymn. After the ordeal, he said, "You will sing in the soprano section."

Whether I wanted to or not, I now had to attend church every Sunday. In fact, I liked singing in the choir, and even going to choir practice. Every month, each choirboy received a small brown envelope with a dollar and a half inside. The older boys received a little more.

We gave the envelopes to our parents. In 1933, a dollar could buy food for almost a week.

Later, Warren joined the choir. During Father Lander's sermons we would sit upright and angelic, under the scrutiny of the "old men" in the bass section, while surreptitiously playing tic-tac-toe on the Church Sunday Bulletin.

With Easter approaching, the choirboys sold Mrs. Minter's Coconut Cream Eggs. Whoever sold twelve boxes went to camp for a week. If you sold two dozen, you went for two weeks. Each box contained one hundred and twenty coconut eggs with a thick, rich dark chocolate coating. They sold for a penny a piece. If a person wanted, they could purchase a box for one dollar.

We went from door to door selling our eggs, greeting the unfortunate person who opened the door with, "Easter time is the time for eggs and the time for eggs is Easter time." I think they bought them just to get rid of us. We sold our dozen boxes each. I couldn't wait to go to camp.

Camp Dwight, a YMCA camp, overlooks Downingtown, PA. We were met by Mr. Yost, who gave a short welcoming address as our parents looked on. The counselors showed us to our tents, which were on platforms. The sides were rolled up, revealing two sets of two-tiered bunks, one on each side of the platform. Warren and I shared a tent with two other boys. Brother John, an experienced camper and Boy Scout, avoided us like the plague. Wherever we were meant trouble.

Living in the hills opened a world I never knew existed. Wildlife was prolific. There were all sorts of grasshoppers, beetles and toads never seen at home. I had to investigate every creature that moved. At night, we sat around the campfire listening to stories and singing songs.

The last song each night was the camp alma mater, "There's a camp along the Brandywine, Camp Dwight is its name…" We went to our tents by the glow of the fire. The sides were down and secured for the night. The protective flaps over the screen windows were rolled up to let in the evening breeze. I fell asleep immediately, not having stopped since six a.m. reveille.

Breakfast consisted of tons of flapjacks with lots of old-fashioned tub butter and syrup, sausages, cold cereal, all the bread and jam a guy could eat, and pitchers of milk by the gallons.

We went swimming in a large pool. I didn't know how to swim. One afternoon in my zeal, I ran to the pool and leaped in. There seemed to be no bottom. When I popped to the surface, I kicked my feet and paddled, trying to reach the side rope just a few feet away. The more I paddled, the further I was from the rope. The lifeguard leaped in, pulled me to the side, lifted me out of the water and threw me on the concrete.

"Why did you do that?" I yelled, trying to hide my shame.

"I thought you were drowning."

"Me? No, I was just trying something new."

"Next time, try it at the other end of the pool."

Each day I practiced swimming until I could manage an unorthodox paddle across the pool, resembling a crippled bullfrog.

Near the end of the week, our counselor led us on an evening hike with blankets and warm clothes. It was near dark when we arrived at the mountaintop. "Tonight we sleep under the stars," he said. The campfire was just glowing embers when we wrapped ourselves in our blankets. We used our rolled-up clothes as pillows. One by one, the whispers and murmurs faded into sleep. I laid on my back, hands under my head, looking up at the heavens.

There was no moon, but millions of stars, each one brighter than the next. I saw the Milky Way with its mysterious curtain and the Big and Little Dippers. My reverie was broken by the first falling star I'd ever seen. Its fiery trail traced an arc across the sky. Was it just a star or some great planet? I wondered if we would get to Mars and Saturn like Flash Gordon and Buck Rogers. I don't remember falling asleep, because I kept seeing the heavens all through the night.

When our parents came to pick us up on Sunday, I vowed that next year I would sell a million boxes of eggs.

John, Min and Newert belonged to the Young People's Fellowship sponsored by the Church. They had their own special Young Adult Sunday School, and went to concerts and roller skating rinks, and on picnics and special trips. After these events, their friends Margie and Bill Warren, Stan Cavanaugh, George Armour, Jim Snyder, Miller Seidel and Alice Coogan would usually end up at our house, sitting around the kitchen table in front of the potbelly stove.

We had a magic icebox; it was never empty. There was always lots of milk and homemade cake Mother "just happened to have." To refuse food meant you were either sick or shy. Our folks cured everyone of both.

In wintertime, when the potbelly was hot, Dad would clean the top of the stove and cook hamburgers. He would mix ground meat with fresh parsley, chopped onions, black pepper, an egg or two, and sliced white bread dipped in milk. The aroma filled the house, stoking ravenous appetites.

On Friday or Saturday nights, some of their friends would drop by. Before long, a pinochle game was in full swing. Others would sit in the kitchen chatting, or listen to Dad tell stories from the old country. Dad would interrupt his stories to hear the news on the radio, then say to the group, "I don't like this Hitler. He will have us in a war soon." No one took Dad seriously. Hitler, or whatever his name was, couldn't hurt us three thousand miles away.

The Church fostered togetherness and respect among the young people, and gave them an outlet for their energies. In 1939, the Fellowship went to the New York World's Fair, with its great Trylon and Perisphere. Shortly after their visit, on September 1, the lights in the Polish Pavilion went out. It was the start of World War II, and the beginning of the end of innocence in America.

The chimes have stopped. I smell bacon and fresh coffee. I brave the cold to shut the window.

All of a sudden, I'm very hungry.

Cod Liver Oil was good for the heart, brain and kidneys. Once a week, we each had to down a whole tablespoon! And just when I thought the wretched taste had faded...

CHAPTER 40

HOME REMEDIES

I had been home from Camp Dwight just a few days when a lump began to form under my right arm. I said nothing. Each day, it grew larger and hurt more. I couldn't lower my arm without pain. Mother saw me favoring the arm.

"What is wrong with your arm? Let me see it." "It's nothing, Mom."

"I want to see it now."

Off came the shirt. When Mother saw the lump, which by now had grown to the size of a baseball, I could tell by the tone of her voice that she was frightened.

"Victor, come here and look at this."

Dad came from behind the sewing machine, looked at the lump and asked, "How long have you had this?"

"It started after I came home from camp." "I will take you to see the doctor," said Dad.

Since our family doctor lived at the edge of Philadelphia, Dad took me to the doctor we saw in cases of emergency. He looked at the swelling, probing and hurting the lump more. Finally he said to Dad, "Frankly I don't know what it is. I have to take him to the hospital and practice on him."

"What kind of doctor are you!?" shouted Dad. "No one practices on my son. Get dressed, son. We will go now."

At home and still very angry, Dad said to Mother, "What kind of doctor is he? He wants to practice on Fred. I will take him to Dr. Christensen."

After looking at the lump, Dr. Christensen said to Dad, "Mr. Shamlian, you have seen this kind of thing before. You know what to do to draw it to a head. When it's ready, bring Frederick back here."

There was no discussion about treatment, just a nod of understanding between two men. Lump or no, we were not going to miss dinner at Aunt Nevrig and Uncle Kegham's home.

When we arrived at the Kash's house, there was a discussion among the grown-ups. All four of them approached me. "Remove your shirt," Dad said. There were all sorts of exclamations and whispers, half in English, half in Armenian. They went to the kitchen and, after a short search, found the great secret medicine: flaxseed.

They filled a pot with water. When it began to boil, Aunt Nevrig poured in the flaxseed. All four of them had to look, and Aunt Nevrig had to keep pouring until all agreed there was enough. As it boiled, they took turns stirring until it reached the magic consistency. They spread what looked like Wheatena on a cheesecloth, which they rolled into a long tube and tied around the lump. The hot flaxseed hurt terribly. In a little while, I began to feel a drawing sensation and the pain increased. Every so often, they would untie the bag and look at the lump. Like great doctors in consultation, they would shake their heads and say in unison, "Not ready yet."

It was after dark when they agreed that I was ready for the doctor. I rode in the car with the bag still tied around my arm. The lump had grown larger. Each bump was excruciating. I just sat there with tears in my eyes and gritted my teeth.

Dr. Christensen looked at the lump and said to Dad, "You did a fine job." He took a white kidney shaped bowl and placed it under my arm.

"Will you hold the tray while I lance this?" he asked Dad. A sickly, thick yellowish stream came forth, almost filling the bowl. The pain subsided at once. Dad turned such colors, Dr. Christensen said to him, "Thank you for your help, Victor. Please sit down." I doubt if Dad could have stood a minute more.

"There's still a lot of infection in there. I'm going to insert a drainage tube. You need to change the dressings often."

That night I slept peacefully for the first time in days. Two weeks later, Dr. Christensen said that the infection was gone and pulled out the tube.

There were other home remedies and preventatives. Once a week we had to take a tablespoon of cod liver oil. The taste never seemed to leave. Just when I thought it had gone, I had to repeat the torture.

I cannot remember a Sunday without homemade chicken noodle soup, roast chicken, pilaf and fresh vegetables. Frozen foods were not around then. The only instant food I recall was "G. Washington Instant Coffee," a silver tube about two inches long, crimped at each end. Beans, oatmeal and fresh vegetables were all part of our daily diet. "Healthy food is the best medicine," Mother would say.

We had more uses for ground beef than anyone. We used it to stuff cabbage, stuff peppers, stuff tomatoes, stuff squash and stuff ourselves. We cooked it with eggplant and string beans, which Dad called String Bean Stew. Ground beef also made hamburgers, meatballs, meatloaf and goulash.

The Armenians call yogurt Mazoon. When I was a child, Mazoon was as foreign to most people as Mars. Armenians, then and now, make their own Mazoon. When our parents and aunt and uncle made it, it was thick and creamy. It cleansed the blood and kept our stomachs in fine order. We drank it to keep cool in the summer and dabbed it on our faces at night to clear the skin.

Sore throats were dreaded because of the swabbing with Argyrol, the brown liquid with the horrible taste. Another feared remedy involved cutting raw onions in slices and rolling them in a linen handkerchief, which was tied around our necks. The same thing was done with hot salt.

After the onion treatment, on hot days anyone could tell of our approach ten miles downwind.

We bathed and bathed again. Every Saturday, beds were stripped and the springs were wiped down with soapy water liberally laced with smelly Creolin or Lysol. Newert and Minnie had to wipe down the woodwork. Hospitals were never so clean. "Cleanliness prevents disease," said Mother.

During the great polio epidemic, we had to wear a block of camphor on a string around our necks to ward off bugs, germs and friends. We also had powered mustard for mustard plasters, which were put on our chests when we had severe colds. It was hot and burned. We smelled like hot dogs. There wasn't a remedy that did not smell.

One summer day, I came down with a severe case of bronchitis. It kept me in bed with a high fever for many days. I was given Spirits of Niter in sugared water to reduce the fever.

Every morning, Dad would climb the two flights of stairs with a glass of orange juice. "How do you feel?"

"Pretty good."

"Drink this. Stay in bed."

When he handed me the juice, his fingers were yellow from tobacco. The glass smelled of tobacco. I remember lying there, looking at the sky. The street sounds from the open window sounded distant and muffled. I didn't know I had fallen asleep because the sounds and the sky were still there. When I opened my eyes, Mother was sitting by my bed holding my hand. When I looked at her, she just smiled at me. I smiled back. I felt good.

The greatest home remedy is love.

CHAPTER 41

CHARLIE MACK

I awoke early and had just finished brewing a pot of coffee when Dad came into the kitchen. The radio was tuned to his favorite news station. Dad never said much until he had his first cup of coffee and had listened to the news. I took the old brush broom, a dustpan and a paper sack and went to sweep the sidewalk in front of the store. "No respectable merchant has a dirty sidewalk," Dad repeated time and time again. God help us if we were caught sweeping the dust into the gutter.

Charlie Mack arrived to open his laundry. I leaned the broom against the store and walked over to Charlie. "Good morning, Mr. Mack."

"Good to see middle boy," he said, smiling. "How many days you home?" "Fifteen days."

"You come to see Charlie. I have many newspapers. You read picture, I read you Chinee."

To the right of our store was the shoemaker's shop. Squeezed between it and Harrison's Clothing Shop on the corner was a narrow green clapboard shed. A sign above the door read CHARLIE MACK LAUNDRY.

Though I always saw Charlie opening or closing his shop, I didn't meet him until I was about eleven, when a lady brought to our store a white linen skirt stained with ice cream. Dad showed the skirt to Mother saying, "Sophia, I can't send this to the cleaners. They will ruin it."

"Leave it with me, I know what to do." "No, I will send it to the Laundry Man."

I didn't know it then, but Dad was concerned for Mother. She didn't feel well and was under doctor's care. "Son, take this skirt to the Laundry Man. Tell him the stains are ice cream. He will know what to do."

The tiny shed smelled of soapy water, starch and hot coals. Through the counter window, I saw Charlie bent over a long narrow board, ironing. In front of the counter was a bench, just big enough for two, and some Chinese newspapers. Behind Charlie, towards the back, were washtubs and the coal stove which heated his irons – and his shop in winter.

"Yes?" His dark eyes studied me. His graying hair was cut short. His face was smooth. I never saw him with even the slightest hint of a beard. Were there Chinese men who didn't have to shave?

"Mr. Mack, my Father asked me to bring you this skirt. He said to tell you the stains are ice cream."

"You tailor boy?" "Yes, sir."

"Which one you?"

"I'm Fred, the middle boy." "Come back two days."

Two days later, I went back for the skirt. Charlie was at the washtubs. I sat down to wait and picked up a Chinese newspaper. On the front page was a photo of a naked infant, sitting alone in the midst of bombed wreckage, crying. I glanced up to see Charlie watching me.

"You read Chinee?"

"No sir, but I understand the picture."

"You no like?"

"No. Why hurt babies? Why must people kill each other?"

"Man cheap. Land mean more. Man get cheaper alla time."

I turned the page and asked Charlie, "What's happening here?" He bent over the paper and translated. He explained many of the pictures. As I got up to go, Charlie said, "You come again, Middle Boy. You read picture, I read Chinee."

I liked Charlie. When I would head to the grocery or hardware store, I would stop at the laundry, open the screen door and say, "Hi, Mr. Mack. Any new papers today?" He would wave me in and explain the headlines, which were mainly about Japan's invasion of China and the scourging of the land.

My short visits continued all through high school. When it came time for me to go to war, I went to say goodbye.

"When you come home, Middle Boy, you come see Charlie?"

"Yes I will."

"I visit tailor father and ask how is Middle Boy." As I left that steamy shed, Charlie waved goodbye with a hot iron.

I remember that iron well. One day as Charlie was reading the news to me, kids opened the door and shouted, "Chinky, Chinky Chinaman, sitting on a fence. Trying to make a dollar out of twenty-five cents!" Charlie picked up a hot iron and went as far as the front door shouting in Chinese. I never saw kids move so fast.

"In China, one does not disgrace another," he said. "Man must have dignity inside to have dignity on outside."

When I went into the Navy, I had a good picture of the Japanese. Besides Pearl Harbor, Wake Island, Guam and Guadalcanal, I remembered the stories Charlie read to me. Of babies bayoneted and waved in the air while their mothers were raped. Of old people, especially scholars, publicly beheaded. To deprive the invading Japanese of food and shelter, the Chinese burnt their own homes and fields, which were family owned for centuries. I was going to fight a short, crafty killer trained in "all of the tricks of the trade."

In her letters, Mother wrote that Mr. Mack sent his greetings. I never did write to Mr. Mack. I think it would have meant a lot to him. Mr. Mack seemed to accept his life as a matter of destiny. The hours of toil over the tubs and ironing board were as it should be. I never heard him speak ill of anyone, but he spoke of hope for those who did not have dignity.

About nine months after the war ended, I was discharged. I was home for just two days when I developed a high fever, which turned out to be Scarlet Fever. I was quarantined for twenty-one days. My brothers and sisters had to find another place to live. Dad slept in the store. Only Mother was allowed to see me.

My plans to get a job on a newspaper were shot down. Near the end of the quarantine period, Dad came up one morning with juice. "The Laundryman says hello."

When Dad referred to other merchants, he called them by their trade: Mr. Laundryman, Mr. Shoemaker, Mr. Druggist. I remember some years earlier, Dad and I were in the store when the mailman came in.

"Good morning, Letter Carrier." said Dad. "Good morning, Letter Carrier," I echoed.

Dad slapped me so hard, I bounced off the wall. When I picked myself up, Dad said, "You will say good morning to Mr. Britton and apologize to him." I did both.

Recalling the incident years later, I realized that only a merchant has the right to call another person by his trade. It was the old world respect. Besides, a boy should address older men as "Mr." or "Sir."

At the end of twenty-one days, my brothers and sisters came home. We were a family again. When my feet stopped shaking and I could make it on my own, I walked to the laundry, opened the door and said, "Hello, Mr. Mack. Any new papers today?" He grinned, waved to me saying, "Welcome Middle Boy. I have many papers. You read picture, I read Chinee."

I sat down on the bench and picked up a paper. Mr. Mack sat down beside me and pointed to a photograph, saying "Middle Boy, land destroyed by war now..."

I was really home.

There were 7 Shamlians in our attic apartment.
A clothes line and blanket separated boys & girls.

We all pooled our savings for our week at the shore.
Bare feet, the crisp salt air, the sound of waves.
I loved it. Mr Middleton (right), the owner, taught
Warren and me how to crab with a piece of suet.

CHAPTER 42

BEACH HAVEN

The bureau in our bedroom had two drawers where Warren and I stored our memorabilia; old broken watches, torn movie tickets, Dixie cup lids with pictures of our favorite movie stars, Landon-Knox sunflower campaign buttons, etc. I was browsing through the drawer when I found a picture of Warren and I at Beach Haven.

During those Depression years of the thirties, we all worked. The money we earned, we gave to Mother. If we needed something, a few cents were set aside from our earnings.

I had always wanted a pair of Buster Brown high-top genuine leather boots with rawhide laces. On the right boot was a leather pocket with a Buster Brown penknife. From the tips I earned carting groceries, a few pennies were set aside each week. Impatiently, I watched the savings grow to the staggering sum of four dollars and fifty cents.

Dad drove Mother and me to the Father & Son store in Ardmore. Her critical eye watched as my feet were measured. She knelt, probed and poked, making sure the boots were healthy and fit like a glove. When she nodded to the sales clerk, I wanted to shout with joy. Now I could walk to school unafraid of the snowdrifts, and with my own penknife to play mumbley-peg.

Though we all worked, went to school, did homework and worked some more, we managed to have fun. There were always friends of Newert, Minnie and John at the house. On summer afternoons, we went to the playground. Sundays we went to Valley Forge, and later, to Lenape Park with its great Merry-Go-Round, where John and Minnie would catch the brass ring. We listened to the radio together. John and Min were our family's musicians, and Mother and Dad would try to attend their school productions.

As we grew older, one of Minnie's friends, Margie Warren, who we called Matzie, knew a man who owned a house in Beach Haven, New Jersey. We could rent his attic apartment for twelve dollars a week – a fortune! Twelve dollars could feed the seven of us for a month. We all saved for the shore from our earnings. Shore resorts were known to be expensive. We figured an extra ten dollars would take care of our needs. If there was money left after rent and food, maybe we could go to a movie.

Newert and Min held the fortune, since they were the oldest. Soon enough, we were on our way. Dad sat behind the wheel, his old felt hat straight on his head, and Mother sat beside him, wearing their Sunday best. The four of us were jammed in the back seat. John couldn't be with us. He was playing with the Boston Symphony at Tanglewood – his summer job while attending the Curtis Institute of Music.

I remember when the five of us could sit in the back of the old Model A. When the occasional tussle did occur, Dad would stop the car, turn around in his seat and with a great sweep of his hand, slap all five faces with a sound of a great arpeggio.

We filled the trunk of our 1936 Ford with our clothes and bags of food. The drive to Beach Haven took three hours. We prayed we wouldn't get a flat tire. The old Model A could only make the trip with numerous flats. In its trunk were spare tires, patched inner tubes, tube repair kits, a jack, lug wrench and hand pump. Minnie said she would write a song about our drives in the Model A, to be titled "A Trip In Five Flats."

We arrived at Manahawkin, crossed the dimly lit wooden causeway to Long Beach Island, entered Ship Bottom, and turned south towards Beach Haven, passing scattered groups of houses. Today, the causeway is a steel and concrete span, and I don't think there's an inch of space on the island for any more houses.

Mr. Middleton took us up the outside steps to the attic apartment, a long room with a small bathroom and kitchen at one end. At the other end were the beds. We strung a clothesline across the room, over which we hung a blanket to separate the girls' and boys' rooms.

The place looked great to Warren and me. All we wanted to do was unload the car and get to the beach, but first we had to help sweep the floor, put the food and clothes away and wash the dishes, despite how cleaned they looked. Then, after a meal that could have sustained us for a week, we went to the beach.

Mother and Dad, still in their Sunday best, sat on a blanket watching us run and leap into the water. The undertow was always strong and we had to be careful. I liked standing knee-deep in the ocean as the water receded, feeling myself descending into the sand until I had to dislodge my feet. The water was exhilarating, and the afternoon flew by. After we showered and had dinner, Mother and Dad left for the long ride home, but not before we received instructions on manners and helping each other.

Early the next morning, I ran to the beach ahead of the rest. Seagulls flew away in raucous anger, and the sandpipers fled a safe distance to continue searching for breakfast. I enjoyed watching them dash across the wet sands, always one step ahead of the surf. As the water receded, they would follow it down, seeking food washed up by the surf. They did this over and over, and never seemed to tire.

There were no such things as portable radios and television sets. Only the affluent could afford a portable wind-up phonograph. We devised our own game in the sand, a cross between golf and skeeball. In the evenings we joked, acted like clowns, read books or, if the mosquitoes were not too active, went for a walk.

A trip to the movie, at a lavish quarter each, was an experience. The aisle entrances were covered with large mosquito net curtains. Before we parted the curtains to go to our seats, an usher sprayed our clothes with citronella. You can imagine how the theatre smelled. Yet the mosquitoes still attacked! The aura of citronella lingered with us for days.

Mr. Middleton took Warren and me fishing in the bay and we caught our first fish, which Minnie photographed as we held it high. He also taught us how to crab with a piece of suet or meat tied to a string. Large blue shell crabs were plentiful; it was easy to catch a bushel-full. After a few lessons, Warren and I went crabbing alone, only to discover that our prowess with the oars was nil. Besides trying to keep from going in circles, we had to worry about the crabs escaping from the basket. We laughed so hard, we couldn't row.

In the summer of 1943, we rented the first floor of the Paxton house, near the end of Long Beach Island. The road ended just a few hundred feet past the house. Across the street were the dunes and the ocean. The bay was a few blocks behind us. We were met by the landlord's daughter. I remember her eyes, a pale gray-blue. She had a quiet, mystical quality. I felt as if I could see through her into infinity.

One night, I decided to take a walk. There was no moon, no streetlights, and during the war, windows were covered after dark. The island was lit by brilliant constellations. How bright the sky seemed. I wanted to sit on the beach, but a sawhorse barricade blocked passage. The beaches were patrolled by mounted Coast Guardsmen watching for attempted landings from German submarines. Some nights, we'd lie awake listening to the thunder of distant explosions. Were they depth charges? Torpedoes? Naval guns? In the morning, the beaches would be coated with a slick of oil. Was it from an enemy sub, or one of our own ships? How close the war was.

I had turned eighteen and registered for the draft before coming to the shore. No one knew how badly I wanted to join the Navy. I loved the sea. I was drawn to its majestic, mystical and frightening force – like a primal urge to return to where life began. I read books by Dana and London, along with epic tales of Magellan, Hudson, Commodore Barry and the great clipper ships sailing the seven seas.

I prayed that my poor eyesight would not keep me out of the Navy.

CHAPTER 43

THE WRESTLING MATCH

Decades of sports trophies were displayed for all to see in our high school hallway. One plaque read "Fred Shamlian, Light Heavyweight Wrestling Champion, 1943."

"That doesn't belong there," I said aloud. As I walked the three miles home, I recalled my wrestling match with Ed Malloy.

Every boy had to take part in a contact sport before he could graduate. Being practically blind without my glasses and totally uncoordinated, I was unfit for football and basketball. I had tried nearly every sport, and failed.

One day during gym class, Mr. Unger said, "Shamlian, today you wrestle." I was such a horse, it was easy to pin my opponent. After the match, the other boys and I reported to Mr. Unger for fresh lessons in the classic art. We sweated and groaned for forty-five minutes. Any Greek watching us would have denied his heritage. After just three sessions, Mr. Unger gave up.

The following week, I had to wrestle again. I won the match mainly because God made someone more uncoordinated than me.

A few days later, in Miss Hovey's English class, Frank James glared at me and said, "Sham, you better win or I'll break you in two. I bet fifty cents and a pack of Luckies on you."

"Win what?"

"The wrestling match." "What wrestling match?"

"Jesus, Sham, don't you know? You're wrestling Ed Malloy at lunch in the gym – for the championship! You better win, you hear?"

Stocky, about six-two and as strong as an ox, Frank was both a weightlifter and a fighter. He could hold his own against the world. His dream was to become a Marine. In a few months, Frank would realize his goal, and serve with distinction.

I didn't know whether Frank was joking or not. After class I raced to the music room and took my seat next to Ed. Ed didn't talk much. When he did, it was about his treks through the hills. "Ed, Frank said we're wrestling today. Did you hear about it?"

"I just heard it from Carl." There was a long silence.

"Ed, do you want to win?"

"Why?"

"I feel funny trying to beat a friend."

"I feel the same, Sham. Let's just give them their two bits worth."

Just then, the music teacher came in and told us to report to the gym after class. "One thing though, Sham."

"What's that, Ed?"

"I hope they let us eat afterwards. I'm hungry as a bear."

We sat in the locker room, waiting for our turn to enter the gym. I never saw so many kids in my life. The entire overhead track was packed, and kids lined the walls. Frank gave me a thumbs up. Approaching the large mat, I saw Mr. Unger wearing his official referee suit. Seated at a table were the teachers who agreed to mark points, time the match and give us fresh orange quarters to suck on at each break. When our names were called, we stepped to the center of the mat and shook hands.

"Good luck, Sham."

"Same to you, Ed."

The bell rang and we approached each other, bending low, our arms hanging ape loose, circling as we sized each other up. Suddenly Ed leapt forward so fast, I was flat on my back before I had a moment to react. I quickly twisted around and grabbed his leg. We were a jumble of limbs as we were told to relax and given orange slices.

When the match resumed, it was a seesaw battle, with each of us making points. All of a sudden, I wanted to win. I had never won anything before. I couldn't play a musical instrument like my brother John, or get all A's like my sisters, or take a car apart and put it together like Warren.

All I could do was flip sodas.

I was on my hands and knees. Bent over me, Ed had the advantage. His right hand gripped my right wrist, while his left locked onto my left arm. What was it that Mr. Unger tried to drum into our skulls during practice? When your opponent has the advantage, don't twist backwards. Drop on your right side and let your opponent roll over you. As soon as Mr. Unger slapped the mat, I dropped on my side and Ed rolled right over me. I lunged for his chest, held his shoulders, and kept pushing. I felt a tap on my shoulders.

"Get up, Shamlian, you pinned him."

Ed lay there for a minute, and then got up slowly. "You okay, Ed?" I was on my knees looking at him. "I'm okay. Some match."

"Sure was," I said, helping him up.

During the match, I was so intent on winning, I didn't hear a sound. Now, I couldn't believe the noise. Everyone was shouting! I did not notice Ed's slight limp on the way to the showers.

The next morning, I was in the music room when Ed came limping in. "What's wrong with your leg, Ed?"

"My trick knee. Every once in a while it goes out on me." "Did it go out during the match?"

"You remember when you dropped and I rolled over you? I landed on my knee and knocked it out."

"Is that why you couldn't move when I pinned you? Ed, why didn't you tell me about your knee?"

"No reason to. You won fair and square."

"You really won that match. You had more points than me." What a lousy way to win. I was still a Pushmondon.

A few weeks later, during Assembly, I received my letter and certificate, and quickly stuffed them in my pocket. When I arrived home, Dad was at the sewing machine.

"How was school today?" "Fine."

"Anything important happen?" "Just school stuff."

"Where are the letter and the certificate?" "How did you know??"

"Warren told me. He's proud of you. Better let me have them. You know how your Mother feels about sports. We don't want her to see them."

Mother was fervently opposed to any of her sons playing football – or any sport which could cause bodily harm: "You attend school to do great things with your brain, not your brawn. Learning develops character. Football develops broken necks."

At least she did not object when we played baseball at the playground. Reluctantly I reached in my pocket and handed the letter and certificate to Dad. He read every word. "I will keep them safe so your Mother does not find out."

I felt rotten. I wanted to say, "Dad, I didn't earn them. I won the match because of a trick knee." The look in his eyes prevented me.

All that week, local merchants or one of Dad's customers would stop and congratulate me on winning the wrestling championship. "Your father showed me the letter."

I made up my mind to find the letter and throw it away.

Mother and Dad were in the dining room listening to the radio. I looked under the counter shelf and opened the sewing machine drawer. Not there. But I got lucky. I lifted the cover of a thick book and there they were. I started to reach for them, but just as quickly changed my mind, closed the drawer and walked away.

The book was the Holy Bible.

Thursdays were pinochle nights. It was Uncle Kegham (left) and Aunt Nevrig against mother and dad (right). The games started calmly, but soon, the pounding of fists on the table reached all the way to the third floor. We fell asleep to the happy din.

CHAPTER 44

TROOP TRAIN

I went to say goodbye to Charlie Mack. As I was leaving, he said, "You come home, Middle Boy. You come see Charlie. I have many papers to read." Then I walked to Liggetts to say goodbye to Lulu and the rest. Tommy, the novice, had become a first class soda jerk. In between customers, we talked about the Navy. When he saw the half dollar tip I left him, the look on his face reminded me of a story Dad told us about Nostroton Hoja.

One day, Hoja, who worked hard in the fields, decided to go to town for a steam bath and massage. He wore his grimy work clothes, carrying the clean clothes he'd wear after the bath.

Hoja was received like a lowly dog. The attendants paid him cursory attention. With the old worn towels handed him, he entered the steam bath. There was very little steam. The fields were hotter than the bath, and the massage was nothing but a light rubdown. It is the custom to lie down in bed after the massage and, upon awakening, receive a hot bowl of soup. The bed Hoja was given was soiled, and the soup tasted like warm water.

As he was leaving, the attendants lined up for their tip. With a great flourish, Hoja presented them – to their utter amazement – a five dollar gold piece.

The following week, Hoja returned. As he entered the bath, the attendants rushed to help him. He was handed large, thick-pile towels. The massage was worthy of a Sultan. When he stepped into the bath, attendants shouted, "More steam for Hoja! More salt for Hoja!" Hoja was in heaven. Truly, this was the finest bath any man could have. The bed upon which Hoja slept had thick mattresses and clean sheets. When he awoke, he was given a rich broth fit for a king.

Dressed in his fine clothes and ready to leave, Hoja stood before the attendants, who were all smiles. With a great flourish, Hoja presented the head attendant with a five-cent piece.

"Hoja," asked the head attendant, "how come when you came in the first time and we treated you like a dog, you gave us five dollars in gold? Now, when we treat you like a king, you give us five cents?"

"You see," said Hoja, "the five dollar gold piece was in appreciation of today."

The next day, I left for Boston, unaware that in a few years, Liggetts would be closed, and soda fountains in pharmacies across the country would give way to shrink-wrapped sundries and toys.

The Fargo Building, located near the South Boston Dry docks, is a Naval receiving and debarkation center. I'd been standing with my gear since dawn, waiting for my orders. Late that afternoon, about two hundred of us were herded into a large room where our sea bags and rolled hammocks were searched for contraband liquor.

The search netted scores of bottles of every type of alcohol imaginable. Once smiling faces now wore expressions of gloom and anger. It's a safe bet that most of our ship's company never spent another dime on liquor during their tour of duty.

The troop train consisted of old coaches and freight cars brought out of retirement to serve the war effort. I was fortunate to be assigned a window seat in a coach. Others were assigned to freight cars converted into sleeping quarters, with bunks three-tiers high. Shore Patrol were stationed at every exit.

We were headed to California via the northern route. Gradually, the weather grew colder, and the snow deeper. I didn't know which was worse, the frigid air or the soot coming through the old wooden window frames. During the night, the train stopped. All I could see was snow. At dawn, we began moving backwards and continued until the train stopped at a small rail yard.

With no heat, our coach felt like a freezer. Late in the morning, we began heading southwest. Hot coffee eased our chattering teeth.

It was my first trip across the United States and I did not want to miss a thing. I spent the time looking out the window. At home, the Broadway Limited sped past our Bryn Mawr station. This old train lumbered along with a tired clickety-clack. Frequently, we would pull into a siding to wait until a high-speed freight or passenger train passed by.

During the nights, when I couldn't sleep, I watched the lights of the cities and towns. The light from a solitary farmhouse caused me to wonder what the people were like, and what were they doing at that moment.

At the beginning of the trip, the young sailors like me were full of high spirits. I wanted to see everything. Old timers with three or more hash marks on their sleeves would look at us like old dogs watching young pups though half-closed eyes, and fall asleep.

By day four, our spirits had waned. We were turning gray from the soot. It permeated our clothes, skin and duffel bags. Despite washing, soot was winning the battle. To pass the time, we read, wrote letters or played cards. If you could play hearts, rummy, cribbage or pinochle, you could always find a game. I thought back to the pinochle games at home.

Every Thursday, weather permitting, our parents would go to Aunt Nevrig and Uncle Kegham's house to play pinochle.

Occasionally Aunt and Uncle would come to our house. The games always started calmly, but soon, even way up on the third floor, we could hear the banging of fists on the table and the angry shuffling of cards. "Here we go again," said Warren. We fell asleep to the din.

Dad tried to teach us to play pinochle. The rules were never the same ones he followed when playing with Aunt and Uncle. One night Dad said to me, "You be my partner until your Mother is ready to play." All was going well until Uncle was dealt a hand that put he and Aunt ahead of us. The cards were dealt. Dad was first to bid. He looked at me and asked, "Do you have any aces?" I thought he was using strategy to make Uncle overbid. I laughed.

"Do you have any aces?" he shouted angrily. There was fire in his eyes. "Yes."

"I bid thirty," he said.

Aunt Nevrig passed. I had a run and bid thirty-two. Uncle looked at me with a twinkle in his eye and said, "I bid thirty-five."

"Do you have a run?" asked Dad. "Yes." I didn't laugh this time.

"I bid forty on his run," said Dad. We all passed. "Put down your run," said Dad.

As I laid down my cards, Dad shouted, "IT'S THE WRONG SUIT!" I practically jumped out of my skin. From that moment, I played the hand as if every wrong move meant the firing squad. We made our points. As Dad wrote down the score, Uncle said to me with a wink, "You played the hand well. I don't believe Vahan taught you."

Happily, the games were halted, and the gauntlets and battle-axes set aside for food and drink. The conversation turned to the family, school, health and business, and the closeness and concern for each other became apparent. Afterwards, the battle re-commenced. Years have passed since that first game, but I can still see and hear it clearly.

On the fifth day, we ran out of food. Sometime after dark, we pulled into a siding and, coach by coach, were marched into a Harvey House Restaurant for noodle goulash, rolls, butter and coffee. The Shore Patrol guarded the exits. I felt like a prisoner. Where could a bunch of gray sailors go in the middle of nowhere?

The next morning we pulled into a siding and were delivered a box breakfast of an orange, coffee, sugar, milk and a small box of cereal. You poured the milk into the wax-lined cereal box. Lunch was another siding stop, and another boxed meal. Dinner was more Harvey House goulash. This continued for the rest of the trip.

In Dodge City, Kansas, the famous cow town with the Long Branch Saloon, the tallest building was three stories with a high facade. We stopped again in Albuquerque, New Mexico, where I saw my first Indians. They were sitting in front of the depot, selling silver and turquoise jewelry. The station looked like one of Father Serra's adobe missions. Did the Alamo look like that?

In Odgen, Utah, the Rockies surrounded the city like a towering, impregnable fortress. I had to look straight up to see the sky.

I was to cross the United States three more times. Each voyage introduced me to a new world, and the enormity and beauty of this country became more apparent with each trip. I was mesmerized by the "amber waves of grain." Miles of wheat swayed gently in the breeze, undulating like the sea.

Late afternoon on the ninth day, the train stopped. From the window, I could see brown mountains, brown earth, very little vegetation, and a high fence topped with barbed wire. "Everybody out!"

"What for this time?"

"You're here. This is Shoemaker, California."

Comin' in
on a Wing and a
Prayer

Words by—
HAROLD ADAMSON.

★

Music by—
JIMMY McHUGH.

Revised words by
FREDERICK DAY.

"Can you sing *Comin' in on a Wing and a Prayer?*,"
the bartender asked. When Denny and I finished,
there were tears in his eyes, and fresh shots
of whiskey for us both. We must of sang that
tune half a dozen times that evening. Later,
we learned he had three sons in the Air Force.

CHAPTER 45

SHARPS PARK

The saloon was a small wooden building with unpainted walls. The window curtains were freshly washed, and the bar was hand-made. It was rustic, clean and free from that aroma of tobacco smoke and stale beer. There were a few tables and chairs and a jukebox. The barkeeper was tall and lean. His face was long and rawboned, and the crow's feet around his eyes spoke of years working outdoors.

Denny and I were finishing our second beer. I put a nickel in the jukebox and played "Sioux City Sue." I started singing quietly with the music and Denny joined in. His harmony was fantastic. We sang a little louder, not the type of loudness you'd expect from one under the influence, but softly, as if we were talking to one another. When we finished, the bartender asked, "Can you sing 'Coming in on a Wing and a Prayer?'"

"Know the words, Sham?" "Yep."

When we finished, there were tears in his eyes. He poured each of us a shot of whiskey and a beer, leaned on the counter and stared into space. What did that song remind him of? After a while he asked, "Where's your home?"

215

"I'm from Pennsylvania. Denny's from Minnesota. Have you lived here all your life?"

"My family moved here from Oklahoma a few years ago. Everyone here is from Oklahoma and Arkansas, mostly Oklahoma."

He said no more. Later, Denny told me that the people of Sharps Park were part of that great migration from the Dust Bowl of the MidWest.

Sharps Park is a little settlement outside of San Francisco, on the cliffs overlooking the Pacific Ocean. I was introduced to it as a result of a horse race. We were stationed at the U.S. Naval Advance Base Depot in San Bruno, California. Before the war, the base was the famous Tanforan racetrack. One afternoon, Denny came to the Master-at-arms room in the barracks and asked, "Sham, have you ever seen a horse race?"

"Nope, never." "Want to see one?" "Where?"

"Bay Meadows. Not far from here."

We hitchhiked to the track. Servicemen were allowed in free, which was good since I had little money. As I rubbernecked at the stands, the colorful pennants and the crowds, a formidable-looking man wearing a banker's gray suit, a homburg and a five-dollar cigar approached us.

"First time at the track, sailors?"

"Yes," I answered, looking both at him and at the sights.

"Bet on Blue Boy in the fourth to win. Good luck." The cigar never left his mouth as he talked.

I was amazed at how everyone yelled, and how quickly the race was over. What a fascinating mix of people! At the end of the third race, Denny said we should go down to the paddock. I didn't let on that I did not know what a paddock was. "Look the horses over carefully," he said. I didn't know what to look for. I figured a farm boy from Minnesota knew more about horses than I'll ever care to know.

"Which one do you like?"

"Den, I don't know a thing about horses, but number four looks like he can't wait to run."

"I've been watching him, too. Let's bet on him. How much money do you have?"

"About two bucks."

"Me too. Let's put two dollars on number four to win."

This time I watched the race in earnest and shouted like the hundreds of others. Number four won! We collected twenty-four dollars in winnings and left the track. My twelve dollars felt like Astor's millions. We were going to celebrate in style with a good meal and someplace to drink, hopefully meet a girl and dance.

Denny said, "I know a little place where the food and drinks are great. You'll meet some nice people. Let's go there and celebrate."

"Are you sure this is the right place?" I asked Denny. All I saw was a little village of small wooden houses, a barn and a restaurant, which served as the local saloon. "Don't worry, you'll like it here."

So I'm drinking ten-cent beers and wondering what I'm doing here when the bartender asks, "Will you sing "Coming in on a Wing and a Prayer?" And again, with the misty blue eyes, he poured us each a shot and a beer. Nothing was said between us. We just nodded thank you. It was beginning to be a joke.

The shots and beers were having their effect. Denny and I started to sing along with the songs from the jukebox. The barkeep kept requesting "On a Wing and a Prayer" and kept dispensing shots and beer. After I don't know how long, he came from behind the bar and pulled down the shades. "It's closin time," he said.

I wasn't feeling too steady on my feet. I said, "We better be going." I hoped it wasn't too late to find a girl and go dancing.

"Don't go. The party's just beginning," said the bartender. In the middle of his sentence, the side door opened and in came what might have been the entire population of Sharps Park.

"Folks, say hello to Pennsylvania and Minnesota. They sing real good." One-by-one, the men shook our hands and the ladies smiled and said, "Welcome."

Once more, the barkeep requested "Coming in on a Wing and a Prayer." When we finished, there was no applause, just a nodding of heads.

I asked the bartender if there was something to eat. "That's being taken care of," he said.

As Denny and I talked with the men at the bar, the side door opened and in walked a beautiful blonde, blue-eyed, barefoot lass carrying two plates covered with napkins. The townsfolk made room for us at the table. She placed the dishes in front of us, smiled shyly, and quickly left. On each plate was a big steak and home fries. The food was delicious and had a great sobering effect.

As we ate, they asked about hometowns, our parents, and what they did for a living. I liked these folks. Most were ex-farmers, now working as carpenters or skilled laborers. The conversation turned to our singing.

"The bartender really likes "Coming in on a Wing and a Prayer," I said.

"He has three sons in the Air Force," answered one of the villagers. Denny and I looked at each other. It was no longer a joke.

After dinner, the barkeep asked, "How about singing some songs we all can sing?" I don't know how many we sang, but sometime during the festivities, I looked at my watch. I could hardly speak.

"Den, it's almost seven a.m. We have to be at the base in one hour. How are we going to get there?"

"Don't worry, sailor, we'll get you back in time," said one of the men. The three of us sat in the front of his pickup truck, and in no time we were racing down the mountain. I looked down nervously. There was no guardrail, just a mile drop. I felt sure we would go over the edge. We pulled up to the gate with five minutes to spare. "You come back again," he said, and drove away. I didn't get to dance with a beautiful girl, but I did meet some wonderful people. Beneath their overalls, gingham dresses and calloused hands, there was something honest and rich in dignity.

And I owe it all to the number four horse named Blue Boy.

CHAPTER 46

THE DIPLOMA

"May I have a deferment until January?" I asked the Draft Board Registrar. If I complete at least three months of my senior year, I can receive my diploma."

"I see no problem with your request. I think a deferment can be arranged."

Two weeks later, I received a letter to report for a blood test and physical for Draft Classification. At the Draft Board, I was assured… "that the test and exam were just standard procedure." A few days later, I received my Draft Card. I was classified 1A and ordered to report to the Armory at 32nd and Market Streets in Philadelphia on September 10, 1943 for induction into the military.

I showed the letter to the official at the Draft Board. "I thought you were going to give me a deferment so I could receive my high school diploma?"

"Young man, we cannot make promises like that. You must realize we are fighting a war. EVERYONE must do their part."

"I want to serve my country. But I was told that a three month deferment could be arranged!"

"There's nothing we can do, and that's final."

I had been in the Navy over two years when I requested a meeting with the base's designated Education Officer.

"Sir, I would like to get my high school diploma."

"How much schooling have you had?"

"Eleven years."

"Why didn't you complete your education?"

"I turned eighteen in July and was drafted before I could begin my senior year."

"Shamlian, give me a day or two to check your records."

A few days later, he called me back. "Shamlian, I have your records. Your tours of duty, advancements in ratings, time aboard ship and length of time in the Navy should give you the required points to earn you your diploma. Give me the name and address of your school and the Principal's name. I will have a letter sent today.

Two weeks later I was called to the office. "No luck. Your Principal is a tough old bird. To earn your diploma, you have to take the Armed Forces Institute courses specified in his letter. I have to tell you, these courses are hard. It will require practically all of your off duty time."

"Sir, I want that diploma."

It had been a long time since I had opened a book. My studies in English, history, science and mathematics were extremely hard. The days passed slowly. Week after week, I handed in my assignments to the Education Officer for review before mailing to the USAFI office.

When finals day arrived, I took each timed test in the presence of a Monitor.

A few weeks later, the Education Officer read me the results. "Shamlian, on three subjects, you scored over one-hundred percent above the other test takers from the Mid-Atlantic states. In mathematics, you came out ninety percent above the average. I'm sending these scores to your Principal. I suggest that you leave this base and celebrate. You've earned it."

Two weeks later, I opened the letter from Dr. George Gilbert, Principal of Lower Merion High School. It read:

Dear Mr. Shamlian,

Your examination grades received from the Armed Forces Institute have been reviewed and prove satisfactory. Upon your discharge from the Navy, your diploma will be presented to you at the June graduation exercises.

I had no desire to receive my diploma with a lot of kids, and was thinking of ways to avoid the ordeal. Mother Nature came to the rescue. Three days after I arrived home, on June 2, 1946, I was quarantined for twenty-one days with scarlet fever.

The diploma arrived by mail.

CHAPTER 47

COMING HOME

I had never driven cross-country in a bus. In fact, it was the first time I'd traveled further than an hour by bus. After receiving my Honorable Discharge in Shoemaker, California, I took the ferry from Oakland to San Francisco to book passage home. The trains weren't running due to a railroad strike. Flying was reserved for the wounded and VIPs. The Greyhound Bus Lines were booked solid. I finally found bus passage on the Burlington Route to Philadelphia.

Seated next to me was the only other ex-serviceman, a sailor on his way home to Omaha, Nebraska. When the bus pulled away from the depot, I settled back in my seat for the long ride.

The ride was a totally new experience. Trains approached the cities by way of rail yards on the outskirts of the towns. But the bus traveled through the main streets of the cities and small towns. There was no rest room on the bus, so the driver made frequent stops in the small towns along the way for bathroom breaks and for meals.

As we headed eastward, I noticed the changes – in the architecture of the stores and homes, in the dress of the people, and in the food served at the bus stops. I enjoyed talking with the passengers, who were from all parts of the country.

We stopped for lunch outside of Cheyenne, Wyoming. I spent so much time putting things in my duffel bag; I was the last one off the bus. Where had they all gone? I saw no one, only a long one-story building. I opened the solid wood door and entered a room filled with poker tables, a roulette wheel, dice cages, slot machines and a long mahogany bar. The bartender and I were the only occupants.

"Where do you eat around here?"

"We don't eat our meals, sailor. We drink 'em." "I'm not thirsty. But thanks anyway."

"How bout tryin' your luck?"

"Why not?" I gave the barkeep a five-dollar bill and was handed five silver dollars. I put one coin in the slot machine and pulled the lever. Down dropped three silver dollars.

"I sure do like your Western hospitality," I said.

"Okay, sailor, you'll find food through there," the bartender said, pointing to another heavy wooden door. He didn't seem too pleased. There were all the passengers, filling the restaurant's booths and counter. I saved the seven cartwheels to give to Dad.

After lunch we took our seats and waited for the new passengers to board –a group of American Indians. There weren't enough seats, but since they were traveling together, the driver let them on. The young boys and older men sat, and made two women stand. The sailor and I looked at each other.

Nebraska seemed flat and endless. As the bus droned on, past fields of corn, wheat and other grasses, I looked at the squaws. They seemed old and tired. I looked at the sailor. He nodded and said, "Let's do it."

We got up and invited the Indian women to take our seats. At first they refused and looked at their men, who just stared straight ahead. But finally the women gave in and sat down. I felt good. I'd been taught to treat women with respect, to hold doors open for them, offer them my seat in a crowded bus or trolley, and to remove my hat in their presence. This time I did not act like a Pushmondon. I nodded hello to the Indian men. Only one nodded in return. They never lost that stone-faced expression. We removed our sea bags from the rack and sat on them.

"Next stop, Omaha," shouted the driver. Thank goodness!

When the bus pulled into the depot, some of the passengers, including the Indians, left. As they were leaving, the two Indian women smiled. I said farewell to the sailor, went inside the depot, and sat in a booth. It felt good to sit and stretch my legs.

When it was time to board the bus, the driver opened the door and said, "Just a minute, folks.

Hey sailor," he said, pointing at me. "Come over here." I walked up to him and he said, "Folks, this sailor gets on first. Some of you already know he gave his seat to an Indian squaw and stood all the way from Cheyenne to Omaha. Okay sailor, get on, pick any seat, and don't you dare give it up to anyone!"

I boarded the bus, deeply embarrassed. We rode through Iowa, past tiny towns and vast acres of corn, wheat and other tall grass crops. In Illinois, we began to pass industrialized cities and the homes seemed closer together. We stopped in Chicago to change drivers, and then continued on through the flatlands of Indiana and Ohio.

"Pennsylvania up ahead," shouted the driver.

Crossing into Pennsylvania felt magical. All at once, I saw rolling green hills and pastures, picturesque three-story white farmhouses and well-kept red and white barns. On the horizon loomed the forested Allegheny Mountains. I never realized that my home state was so beautiful. As we drove through a dense forest, I heard a passenger say that we were in the Blue Ridge Mountains. I kept looking to the right, then left, then straight ahead. I didn't want to miss any part of it.

"We'll stop at York for a half-hour lunch break," said our driver. The bus station was like a country inn, clean and bright, with a beautiful Pennsylvania Dutch charm. Even the waitresses had a pink fresh glow.

Back on the road, we wove through the hills before descending onto a main highway. The highway sign read, PENNA 30. That's the street I live on! Another hour, and I should be home.

As we rode along Route 30, Lancaster Pike, familiar sights and landmarks came into view.

We passed the golf course where now stands the Radnor Inn and office complex, and were quickly approaching Villanova College. I walked up to the bus driver.

"Sir, can you make an unscheduled stop?"

"Sorry, sailor, my next stop is Philadelphia." He looked at me and asked, "Are you sick?" "No sir, I live just a few blocks up the road."

He slowed the bus and said aloud. "Folks, I'm making a quick, unscheduled stop. This sailor lives just up ahead and we're taking him home." Everyone in the bus cheered.

"Okay sailor, point out your home." "There it is. That tailor shop on the right."

He stopped directly in front of my home. I hurried to my seat for my sea bag and duffel bag and almost ran to the open door.

"I really appreciate it. Thanks a lot."

"Glad to, sailor. You know, I've always wanted one of those sailor hats."

I took off my hat and handed it to him. "I hope you don't mind a used one." He took off his visored cap and put on my hat, much to the amusement of the passengers. As I left, they all shouted and waved goodbye.

When I entered the store, the bell above the screen door jingled. "It's okay. It's only me!"

STATE TEA   RS COL EGE, W   ESTER, A

The Navy offered me four years of college
on the G.I. Bill. But could I cut it? To find out,
I enrolled in summer courses at West Chester
State Teachers College. The long trolley ride
from 69th St. Terminal became my study hall.

CHAPTER 48

HIGHER EDUCATION

Growing up in a small town, in close communion with family, friends, and the folks you work with, life has a special continuity. With the coming of World War II, that gentle flow stopped. Now, almost three years later, most of my friends and classmates had moved, married or entered college. Merchants greeted me with a certain aloofness. They didn't know what to say to me. All I wanted to hear was the same "hello" and small chat I left behind. But everyone, including my brothers and sisters, were too busy putting their lives back in order. There was no time to relax or to listen. I felt alone.

My time in the Navy earned me four years of college on the G.I.Bill. There was little future without it. I was very apprehensive. I didn't know if I had the ability, but I had to find out. After recuperating from scarlet fever in the summer of 1946, I applied for summer courses at West Chester State Teachers College. The registrar, a stern-looking woman asked, "You wish to attend our summer program?"

"Yes ma'am."

"What level do you plan to teach?" "I'm not going to be a teacher."

"Mr. Shamlian, this is a college for those who wish to enter the teaching profession. We cannot accept anyone not wishing to teach."

"Ma'am, I only want to attend summer school. If you will please listen, I'll tell you why." "Please go on."

"For nearly three years in the Navy, I read very little. The English I spoke was not the English I was taught. After spending most of my time on duty, in barracks and saloons, I don't know if I'm capable of earning a college degree. I thought if I could attend West Chester for the summer, I'd see if I have what it takes."

"Please admit him," said a voice behind me. I turned to face a dignified gray-haired lady. She extended her hand. "How do you do, young man? My name is Dr. Denworth. I teach Psychology, which you will take along with English and Medieval History. We will see if you have what it takes."

Three times a week, I made the long trolley ride from 69th Street Terminal in Upper Darby to West Chester. It was a single-track route. The trolley would pull onto the sidings to allow an oncoming trolley to pass. A few years later, buses replaced the trolley line and West Chester Pike was widened to accommodate the increasing auto traffic.

Study was difficult. I had to learn how to concentrate. I discovered that the best time to study was at night, when all were in bed.

The trolley ride became my study period. I could review my homework or complete reading assignments. The frequent and unannounced review quizzes demanded constant reading and completion of assignments. At the end of the summer session, I averaged a B grade. I went to say goodbye to Dr. Denworth and to thank her for her support.

"Frederick, you could have had all A's. You must apply yourself harder. But you did prove one thing: you have what it takes. I wish you the very best." I was told by one professor that Denworth Hall at Radcliffe College was named in her honor.

All of my efforts to enroll in a college were futile. Every school was booked to capacity with waiting lists of ex-servicemen like myself. Fortunately, Ben Gile, who had gone through Bryn Mawr Grammar School and Lower Merion High with me, told me about American International College in Springfield, Mass. We both applied and were accepted at once.

When we arrived, we were informed that the school, being new, had no dormitories.

Through the help of the Masonic Lodge, of which Ben was a member, we found a room in the home of Mr. and Mrs. Green, who lived with their daughter and granddaughter. Rent was twenty dollars a week. Our room was small, and no food was allowed, but we managed to make instant coffee to keep us studying into the early hours of the morning. We could walk to the school, and along the way, we passed the Indian Motorcycle Company.

Unfortunately, our GI papers were lost in transit. We were accepted by showing our Honorable Discharge I.D cards, in the hope that the records would soon be found and the school reimbursed. Without our papers, we would not receive the seventy-five dollar monthly GI check to cover our room and board.

With our meager funds just about exhausted, we placed an ad in the local paper... HOUSES, CELLARS CLEANED. LAWN CARE. There were few jobs at first, mostly cleaning kitchens, some of which I don't think saw a scrub brush in years.

One evening we were called to a large manor home in Forest Park. The owners wanted their cellar cleaned. Ben and I descended the stairs, but stopped halfway. The place was infested with fleas.

"It's not much of a job," said the husband. "We just want it tidied up," said the wife.

"It will cost one-hundred dollars," I said, hoping Ben wouldn't lower the price. "One-hundred dollars! For that much, I'll do it myself," said the husband.

"Sir, you don't need your cellar cleaned. You need an exterminator," I said.

We left the place breathing a sign of relief. We scratched all the way home, hoping that we and Ben's car were not infested with fleas.

We stopped at Gus' Restaurant near the Springfield Armory. The cafeteria was clean, and empty. We both ordered the fifty-cent spaghetti dinner. Gus's became our every night dinner spot.

One evening Gus came to our table. "Mind if I sit with you?" We all introduced ourselves. Our conversation soon turned to AIC, lost GI papers and housecleaning. "When the Armory was producing arms for the war, this was a busy place. Now most of it's been shut down. Pretty soon it will close for good."

"What will you do, Gus?"

"Right now, my wife is expecting our first child. After the baby comes, I must make plans for our future."

One afternoon, Ben and I had just entered the cafeteria when Gus said, "I'm glad you're here. The baby's coming! Will you run the place until I get back?" He didn't wait for an answer.

Ben and I took our places behind the counter and waited for customers. That night, we served only four people. It was after nine when Gus returned.

"It's a boy. They're both fine!" he shouted. We congratulated him. When he calmed down, we told him what we served the customers and what we charged. Gus gave Ben and I the biggest spaghetti dinner we had in months. The next day we took a bouquet of flowers to Gus to give his wife.

"No. You give them to her. I've told her about the two college boys who helped me and who would not accept money."

Gus's wife was a beautiful dark-haired, dark-eyed girl. She thanked us for the flowers, and for helping Gus. He wouldn't let us leave the hospital until we saw his son.

A few weeks later, Ben and I dropped in for our usual spaghetti dinner. Gus said, "Tonight, you are my guests for our farewell dinner."

"You're closing?"

"With the help of relatives, I'm moving my family to Washington, DC, where I'm opening a restaurant." That night, we feasted on steak, baked potatoes, vegetables, hot buns, ice cream and coffee. When we said farewell to Gus, he gave each of us a bear hug and a kiss on the cheek. "Come to Washington. Your first dinner will be on Gus," he said.

We took a job cleaning a donut shop after hours. Everything was caked in dough. We had to scrape the tile floor, the huge vats and stirring paddles, and the worktables encrusted with thick, hard dough, which must have been there for days. It took until midnight to get the place clean. The owner left us a large bag filled with leftover and broken donuts, which we kept in the trunk of Ben's car. We managed to sneak some into our room to have with the instant coffee.

Though we needed the money, our grades suffered. We decided to find a college closer to home. With the help of my sister Newert, who was teaching Spanish at Juniata College, I was accepted there. Ben was accepted at West Chester State Teachers College.

In February, 1947, I arrived at Juniata.

JUNIATA COLLEGE LIBRARY

JUNIATA COLLEGE,

HUNTINGDON, PA.

Thanks to Newert, who taught Spanish at Juniata, I was able to transfer from American International College, arriving in Huntington in February, 1947.

CHAPTER 49

GIANTS

The railroad station in Huntingdon, Pennsylvania was like every other gray stone station along the way. I asked the ticket agent for directions, then took the local jitney to Juniata College at the north end of town. The main building was an old red brick structure with a tall fire tower. There were a few other buildings nearby, and then, rolling hills. It was February, 1947. For the next three and a half years, this would be my home.

In my sophomore year, I learned that there were two types of teachers: those who know a little and speak with bombastic authority on all subjects, and wise and learned men and women who constantly strive for deeper truths. Though they speak with humility, you can feel their breadth of knowledge. They go beyond facts and test grades to teach us that respect for all things is acquired through a love of learning. I met two such professors at Juniata.

It was spring, and my biochemistry class was walking through a field of yellow buttercups, blue violets and a rainbow of other wildflowers when Dr. Will ordered, "Everyone, please freeze in your tracks."

As we stood motionless, Dr. Homer C. Will walked around us, searching the ground. "Please step back," he asked a classmate. He knelt where she had stood. "Come here, everyone. We've made an important discovery today." He pointed to a tiny flower about two inches tall. "Can anyone tell me what plant this is?" No one answered.

"This is a wild orchid, very rare in Pennsylvania. We must protect it from harm." We surrounded the plant with a circle of twigs pushed into the dirt. They stood high enough to be seen above the grass.

Dr. Will was a conservationist long before the world recognized the need to preserve our threatened planet. Though he never spoke of his work with the Pennsylvania Conservation Committees for the preservation and reclamation of our lakes, streams and rivers, I read his biography in the College Directory, and learned more about him from others who knew of his work. He was acutely attuned to the sights and sounds of woodland life, and had dedicated his life to protecting the natural world, and all living things.

A long walk from the college was Trough Creek Park, also known as Paradise Furnace. This large woodland park, with hiking trails and hand-hewn log bridges over pristine streams, was a haven for deer, raccoon, pheasant, wild turkey, quail and dozens of other birds.

I sat by a crystal clear stream memorizing Chaucer for my comprehensive examinations. When I tired of reading, I watched the trout. The water was frigid. Little did I know that within decades, pollution would make the speckled trout all but extinct.

When it comes to conservation, our government gives lip service to preserving our natural lands, even as it opens vast tracks of national forests to mining, clear-cutting, and other lobbying interests. And while states talk of cleaning our rivers and reforesting our parks, toxins from industry and large-scale farms continue to pollute our precious waterways.

The beauty of Trough Creek Park and the thousands of parks like it can be attributed to the Civilian Conservation Corps (CCC), the Works Progress Administration (WPA) and the Public Works

Administration (PWA). They were established during the Depression of the thirties to provide work for the unemployed.

The family-owned companies that took pride in their work have largely disappeared. Succeeding generations focused on The Bottom Line have sold out to foreign interests and entrepreneurs who move production overseas, regardless of the detrimental effects on their fellow Americans. Instead of welfare for the physically and mentally able, why not reinstate the CCC, WPA and PWA? Welfare may put clothes on a man's back, but meaningful work would restore pride and hope, and help save the environment. I think Homer Will would approve.

Professor Dubbel taught Early English Literature, Modern English Literature and Poetry.

One day, he recited two lines of poetry and surprised me with a question. "Freddy, who is the author of that poem?"

"Professor, I've never read those lines, but the style sounds like Shelley."

"By Jove, you've got it! If you had answered incorrectly, I would have picked you up and thrown you out the window!"

With probing questions about the style and philosophy of each book or poem, Professor Dubbel constantly encouraged us to think beyond our assignments. He taught us that the arts represent man's desire to express the beauty of the human soul. His love of literature and life had a profound effect on everyone he taught.

"How's your studying for your comprehensives coming along?" he asked me one day. "Not too well," I replied. "With the radios, record players and constant interruptions, it's hard to concentrate in the dormitory."

He thought for a minute, then replied, "Meet me in the library at three o'clock."

When I arrived, the Professor beckoned me to follow him into the basement. At the foot of the stairs was a small clean room with a few bookshelves. In the center of the room, under a single hanging light, stood a spartan wooden table and chair.

"Freddy, I had the library put this table and chair in here. You can study in this room. Review every chapter in every subject from the past four years, as well as every subject you're taking now. Think, and absorb. Do not fail me." Professor Dubbel gave me a key to the outside cellar door and left. I went to my dorm, lugged all my notes and books back to the cellar, and did not tell anyone where I was going. For the next six months, this would be my secret workshop.

Harry Frye asked me to be the best man at his wedding. Professor Dubbel, a lay minister, was asked to officiate. The ceremony in the United Brethren Church next to the college was one of beautiful simplicity. The reception was held in a room at the back of the church. After a toast of fruit punch and the cutting of the cake, the Bride and Groom left for a short honeymoon.

"A beautiful service, Professor," I said. "How long have you been a minister?"

"Many years, Freddy. Trust me when I tell you, what made this wedding beautiful was not the words, but the love the bride and groom share." Then he shared something he said he had never told anyone: "Freddy, if I could live my life over, I would be a Catholic."

"Why Catholic, Professor?"

"It's the purest religion, beautiful and philosophical, and it was founded by Jesus Christ. What could be better?"

My comprehensives lasted six grueling hours, starting with two hours of oral examinations. Until the moment of my oral test, I had no idea who was on the examination board. On exam day, I walked into the classroom alone to face Professor Dubbel, Dr. Will and Dr. Binkley. Their questions demanded deep concentration. Once the ordeal was over, there was no discussion of how poorly or how well I did. The written tests were just as hard. Two days after my last written test, a letter from the college informed me that I had passed.

Before leaving Juniata, I went to visit the Professor and Mrs. Dubbel at their home. We talked of my future, and of books. "Freddy, I need a book to complete my collection of the works of Anthony Trollope. If you should find a copy, please purchase it for me. I will reimburse you."

About a year later, in a second-hand bookshop, I found that very novel by Trollope and mailed it to the Professor as a gift. We wrote at least twice a year. He inquired about every phase of my life. Then one Christmas, my card and letter were returned. I had lost a dear friend.

Though small in stature, and though childhood meningitis left him with a high-pitched voice, to me, he will always stand ten feet tall.

CHAPTER 50

ON THE COURT

We called our intramural basketball team the Shmoos after the lovable character created by cartoonist Al Capp. There were six of us, mostly ex-servicemen. Our bright red tee shirts, with SHMOOS printed in bold white letters, took every cent we could save. On the back of the shirts were our names: Boo-Boo, Coo-Coo, Doo-Doo, Goo-Goo and Woo-Woo. Our numbers were 7- 5/8, 11-3/4, 15-5/16, 6-7/8, and 11-3/16. I was 1-3/8. Never having played basketball, our twisted logic dictated that my name should be Choo-Choo Trainer.

Our team center was about five feet, four inches tall. The stub of his rum-soaked stogie never left his mouth. Whenever we played, the gym was crowded with cheering students. Each game was a fun-filled disaster.

I vividly remember the final game of our season. We had yet to win; in fact, we hardly ever scored. We were going to win this game! For the first period, the Shmoos ran and tripped over each other to the delight of the crowd, but still managed enough points to tie our opponents.

Near the end of the game, Boo-Boo hurt his knee. I had to take his place. I took off my glasses and handed them to Boo-Boo. It was my very first time on the court. I could barely see where I was going.

I blocked and tried to get the ball to pass to a teammate. Thank God they were wearing red. With just seconds to go, Woo-Woo grabbed the ball from an opponent and raced down court, amid yells and cheers from the stands. Not seeing too well, I watched in amazement as he ran unopposed to the end of the court. The ball sailed through the hoop, just as time ran out.

There was pandemonium in the stands. Our Center was on his back, laughing so hard I thought he would swallow his cigar. My other teammates were in a fit of uncontrolled laughing. The crowd left the stands and congratulated us on a great game.

In June, three SHMOOS graduated and the team disbanded. But I'll never forget how Woo-Woo took the ball down court and scored the winning points for the other team.

May 18, 1951

Ah. Yes.....

(Manufacturers have been ordered to cut back on material in bathing costumes in order to conserve cloth—News Item.)

Her bathing suit is something
rare —
a beauty of creation.
It's made of just a thread or two –
and my imagination.
—FS

Why did my Public Speaking professor choose *me* to announce the Ladies' Homecoming Fashion Show? Was he having a good laugh? Believe me, all my classmates did. So did the audience.

CHAPTER 51

PERMANENTLY CLOSED

"Helen Wilson is wearing a tailored suit of light brown worsted wool. Notice the flair to the jacket and the straight, non-pleated skirt for that professional look." There I was, before a packed auditorium on Juniata's Homecoming Day, describing women's fashions.

I had taken Public Speaking to help further my journalistic career. I wanted to learn how to speak before a large group without having my knees shake like Aspen leaves in the breeze.

Professor Doyle announced our assignments. "Frederick, you will narrate the Annual Fashion Show." Everyone in the class laughed.

"Professor, I don't know a thing about women's fashions. I'll look like an idiot up there."

"Either you do it or fail the course."

After a week of tortuous rehearsals, with my manhood at stake, the moment arrived. I stepped out on stage, introduced myself, and announced the great event. Looking out at the audience, I saw hundreds of beaming mothers, aunts and sisters – and as many bored fathers, uncles and brothers. As the houselights dimmed,

I decided to have some fun describing each outfit. I relaxed into my role, the men did not fall asleep, and the evening proceeded smoothly.

The climax of the show was a new fashion innovation: a permanently pleated skirt. As the final model approached center stage, I was eager to end the ordeal and announced:

"Tonight's last fashion is a skirt with a new, modern feature you parents will surely appreciate. It's PERMANENTLY CLOSED!"

I couldn't believe I'd said it. I saw visions of being ejected from Juniata and drummed out of the world. The girl just stood there glaring at me. Light giggles turned into a roar of laughter and applause.

"Excuse me, I meant permanently PLEATED! Thank you and good night." I left the stage with the model amid waves of laughter. I could not speak to her, for nothing I could think of would appease her anger, or my embarrassment.

I borrowed fifty cents from Bill Hansen, a G.I. classmate, and went to the American Legion Club to drown my stupidity in three fifteen-cent bottles of beer.

The next morning I found three notes in my mailbox. From President Ellis, it read, "Well done."

From Professor Dubbel, "Thank you for turning a dull evening into a memorable event." From Professor Doyle, "You passed."

BOTTLED BY
ENGELS AND KRUDWIG WINE CO.
SANDUSKY, OHIO
E and K
American
Muscatel
ALCOHOL 20%   BY VOLUME

L·S
LONE STAR
CALIFORNIA
MUSCATEL WINE
ALCOHOL 19% TO 21% BY VOLUME
WITHDRAWN FROM TAX PAID CONTAINER
BOTTLED BY
O. DEL PAPA & SONS · GALVESTON, TEXAS

OLD 48
BRAND
CALIFORNIA
MUSCATEL
ALCOHOL 20% BY VOLUME
BOTTLED BY · ASSOCIATED WINERIES · NEW HAVEN, CT.

THE HOUSE OF FINE WINE
PIO
100% Pure California
MUSCATEL
ALC. 20% BY VOL.
BOTTLED BY Bartolomeo Pio, Inc., PHILA., PA.

"The Sterno Gang" is what we kids called the local
band of World War One veterans. Whenever one
received a disability check, they all headed to the
liquor store to score a bottle of muscatel.

CHAPTER 52

STERNO GANG

They walked single file, like a ten-legged centipede. Their unshaven faces were full of great expectations as they snaked their way to the State Liquor Store. This sorry band of World War I veterans had suffered from shell shock, mustard gas or battle wounds, and never readjusted to society. When one of them received his disability or welfare check, the entourage would immediately head to the liquor store.

From outside the store, his followers watched his every move. When he emerged with a bottle of cheap muscatel, held tightly lest it be jostled out of his arms, they all laughed and licked their lips.

In their hideaway near the railroad underpass, they passed the magic elixir until, one by one, they settled into a misty neverland. This ritual was repeated month after month, year after year, until cheap booze, sickness and old age claimed them all. Their passing went unnoticed. They had become castaways in their own hometown.

Besides the Winos – or as we kids called them, the Sterno Gang – Bryn Mawr had all types of drinkers, including our town drunks, most memorably Olaf and Harry.

Olaf was a long, lean, blue-eyed Swede. When I first met him, he was helping Dad and Warren repair our car. Olaf was a first class mechanic when sober. Dad would never give Olaf any money until the repair was completed. Once, Dad paid him before the work was done, and Warren had to finish the repair.

Many men become loud, obscene or troublesome when they drink. Not Olaf. He was always soft-spoken and cordial. Even at his most inebriated, I never heard him swear. Where he lived, or if he was married, we never knew.

Our home became Olaf's refuge. In the room where Dad did his pressing was a large, unused showcase. Dad removed the sliding glass doors and added an old mattress and blanket for Olaf to sleep on. Though he was gone before we woke, we could always tell when Olaf slept there; the room smelled of stale beer.

We had a Chow dog named Tippie. We tried leaving him in the yard without a leash, but he attacked anyone who ventured near the house. Tippie broke every rope. Eventually we had to chain him when we put him out. Olaf was the only person who could pet him. We always knew when Olaf was nearby, because Tippie would whine, stand on his hind legs and pull at the chain, greeting Olaf with barks and tail wagging.

Olaf would unhook the chain and say, "Come, we go for a walk." He petted the dog as they walked side by side. The bond between them was deep.

One Sunday morning, Tippie broke loose and raced across the street to greet Olaf. He didn't see the truck that killed him. Olaf carried him to our backyard and cried unashamedly as he explained what happened. Dad and Mother asked him in for coffee, but Olaf was too ashamed to enter our house. With hat in hand and tear-stained face, he gave Tippie one last look and walked away. We wrapped Tippie in a sheet and buried him in the backyard.

Olaf continued to come to our pressing room and, when needed, to work on our car. His hands worked on a motor as if they felt the life within. His respect for the machine was great.

One day, Olaf came to say goodbye and announced that he was going home. We never saw him again.

"Some men drink to become what they cannot be sober. When a man cannot live sober, something is troubling him," Dad said as we watched the police remove a few rowdies from the saloon.

I never saw Harry sober. But, though he was the brunt of kids' jokes and catcalls, he never caused any trouble. One day, during college summer break, I was in the store with Dad and said, "I haven't seen Harry since I got home."

After awhile Dad replied, "I never told you this, but many times when I opened the store, Harry would be asleep on our doorstep. I would take him to the kitchen, make him drink coffee and eat something, and send him home."

For a long moment, Dad just stared out at the street. "Last month," he continued, "Harry walked in. He was without drink. He sat down in that chair (pointing to a wicker chair in the corner) and said nothing. After many minutes he looked up and told me his story."

"Mr. Victor, he said, I wish to tell you why I drink. When I married, I wanted a son to carry my name when I am gone. No one knows that I have a son. No one. He was born an idiot, a vegetable who would never know his father. He lives in an asylum. I asked God what I did wrong. I began to drink to hide my shame. Everyday I grew worse, until being drunk was the only way I could face living."

"'Why are you telling me this?' I asked him.

"In this whole town, you are the only one who did not laugh at me or hide from me when I passed by. When you found me on your doorstep, you took me in and fed me. Your doorstep became my haven. But now, my time has come. Tonight, I will die. Before I die, I wanted you to know why I am a drunkard."

248

"That night," said Dad, "Harry went to bed in his own home for the first time in years and quietly passed away in his sleep."

Neither of us said a word. We just stared out at the street remembering Harry.

CHAPTER 53

THE MAGIC MOUNTAIN

"Hello, this is Fred from 'Turntable Terrace' overlooking the beautiful rolling hills of Huntingdon. Kick off your shoes, sit back and relax while your dinner is cooking and the kids play outside. Here's some music to dream along with."

My half-hour radio program on WHUN aired every Thursday afternoon at four. As Christmas approached, the station manager asked me to read letters to Santa Claus from the children of nearby towns. Most asked for a multitude of toys, but some of the letters were charming, sad and heartwarming.

A few days before Christmas break, I was asked to wear a Santa outfit, and children were invited to the station to hear Santa read their letters. Instead of the plastic boots that came with the suit, I wore a pair of black Wellington boots my brother John lent me. The station was wall-to-wall with children. I must have read every letter ever written to St. Nick.

On the jitney back to campus, I sat facing a mother and son. I was still wearing the boots.

"Did you like Santa?" she asked her son.

"Oh yes. He was the REAL Santa."

"How do you know that?"

"Because he had real boots, and his hands were clean." Thank God my trousers covered the boots.

As I sat alone in the dorm bemoaning my finances, I recalled another of Dad's folktales from Armenia – the story of The Magic Mountain.

"One day, the people in my father's village were told of a magic mountain. If one laid his troubles at the foot of the mountain, they would disappear. Naturally, everyone carried their troubles on their backs to the mountain. Along the way, they passed multitudes of other men and women like themselves, bent over and straining beneath their heavy burdens.

When they reached the base of the mountain, everyone laid down their troubles and stepped back to watch them disappear. They looked at their own troubles, then scanned the small mountain of troubles deposited by their neighbors. Gradually, their own bundles seemed to shrink, until they seemed very small indeed. Silently, one by one, they picked up their bundles, which now seemed remarkably light and, walking erect, carried them home again."

My trouble was, my father didn't make enough to send money. The four dollars I earned each week barely paid for my laundry, cigarettes and other sundries the G.I. Bill didn't cover – leaving me just fifty cents a week. I couldn't ask a girl out. I couldn't buy Christmas gifts. All I could do was tote my troubles to the American Legion Club, buy three bottles of beer, and put a nickel in the slot machine. I was wallowing in self-pity when I was told to report to the Dean's office.

The Seniors – a status I achieved by sheer luck – were each asked to become a "big brother" to a child of a needy family, take them to lunch, and then to a store to select a Christmas gift. We received five dollars each to pay for lunch and the gift.

My little brother was about ten years old. Pete wore a worn wool coat much too small for him and a wool stocking cap. At the local diner, he ordered a hamburger, fries and a Coke. He was quiet as his lunch disappeared like magic. He looked down at his empty plate.

"I don't know about you," I said, "but one burger is never enough for me." "Yeah, me too. We don't get them much at our house."

"Miss, would you please bring my friend another hamburger, fries and Coke?" Pete's eyes lit up.

"We can't go shopping hungry, can we?" I said.

"Gee, no. Thanks. This is the best food I've eaten in a long time." He paused, looked at me, then asked hesitantly, "If I can't finish everything, do you think maybe I can take it home?"

"Eat what you can. I'll ask the waitress." I got up and asked the girl to add an extra hamburger and fries to his bag.

"Are you from the college? Is he your little brother for the day?"

"Yes to both questions," I answered.

As we were getting ready to leave, she handed Pete a very large bag. "How much do I owe you?"

"Let's see. That was two burgers, two fries, two cokes and a coffee. That will be one dollar and seventy-five cents, plus tax."

"What about the extras?" I quietly reminder her.

"There were no extras," she replied. Such a generous, warm and beautiful smile! I thought I had seen an angel.

Pete carried his treasure tightly in his hand as we walked to the store. After a thoughtful search, he chose a game, which neatly exhausted the five dollars, plus a few cents of mine. As we were walking out, Pete spied a toy truck on the counter. He turned it around slowly, admiring it.

"My brother would like this for Christmas. He doesn't believe in Santa. He never gets what he wants."

That was the longest speech I heard him make. The price tag read two dollars and twenty-five cents. I asked the clerk to Christmas wrap it.

"What do I tell my brother if he asks who bought it?"

"Tell him one of Santa's helpers found out what he wanted."

We walked back to his home near the edge of town, a small clapboard house badly in need of paint. His mother invited me in and thanked me profusely. I put the gifts on the table. The place was furnished with the barest of necessities. Everything looked clean, old and worn. Pete still held onto the bag from the diner. I felt that he wanted me to go so he could share his treasure with his mother and brother. I said my goodbyes and left with very little money in my pocket, yet I felt like the richest man in the world.

I, too, had been to the Magic Mountain.

CHAPTER 54

THE LETTER

"I say, guv'ner, does this train stop at Paoli?" I asked the conductor as I boarded the train. He walked to the front of the car to another conductor, and with a hitchhiker's thumb pointing in my direction, whispered loud enough for me to hear.

"There's a limey up there. Wants to know if we stop at Paoli."

They turned to stare at me, whispered some more and left the coach. My suitcase, on the seat next to me, was decorated with a large red, white and blue sticker which read ROYAL PHILHARMONIC ON TOUR. My brother John gave me the sticker when his orchestra was touring the United States. I was wearing the only suit I owned, a dark gray worsted wool with a white shirt and navy blue tie with polka dots. I must have looked like an Englishman to them. Soon, the conductor re-entered the car and walked towards me.

"Paoli is not a scheduled stop, but since you are a guest in our country, we'll make the stop for you."

For the good of all, I continued the charade. "Jolly good. Thank you veddy much." I vowed to keep my mouth shut for the rest of the trip. As I watched the countryside glide by, I dreamed about the last time I saw Shirley.

It was the eve of our Easter break. We sat in the theater holding hands, watching "Battleground." Every so often I would steal a glance at her. The picture of beauty, with olive complexion and brown eyes, she wore very little makeup. Her lipstick accented the full, graceful curve of her lips. She raised my hand to her lips and kissed it. "I'll always love you," she whispered. I was totally, helplessly in love.

After the movie, we walked slowly back to school. I loved the way she walked; straight with slim feminine grace. With each step, her auburn hair with its soft waves would catch the light. We stopped at a local soda fountain away from the college. As we talked, Shirley looked at me with those intelligent probing eyes, seeing things in me that I did not or could not see. Her voice was soft and low, not sultry, but like warm music. When we kissed good night, she held me close for a long time. She did not answer when I said I'd call her at home. All I knew and wanted to know was that she loved me.

I arrived home late Thursday evening. We now lived across the street from the old three-story home, which seemed so forlorn. It was being used by Hobson & Owens to store furniture and rugs. In a few years, the place would be torn down.

Friday morning, I walked to the drugstore to call Shirley. "Hello. May I please speak with Shirley?"

"Who's calling?" a woman asked.

"Fred Shamlian."

"Shirley is not home." The phone was immediately hung up. I called twice more, and received the same chilly answer. Saturday morning I tried again, and was told, "Do not call here again. Shirley is not at home to you!" This time the receiver was slammed down.

I was stunned. What did I do wrong? I was never forward or unkind. I never hurt her. My parents knew little about Shirley, and I didn't tell them about being shut out. I was still the kid with the wisecracks and puns. But inside, I hurt terribly. It was the longest weekend I ever spent at home.

As soon as I returned to Juniata, I called her dormitory and asked for her. Her roommate came to the phone, and said she was out. I was sick at heart. I knew her roommates well, but this time, the friendly banter was gone. I called again and again. Each time, the same awful reply.

The next day, I got a break. Her roommate called me. "Can I meet you somewhere – off campus?" she said.

"I'm leaving for the radio station." "I'll meet you halfway."

Even from a distance, she looked troubled.

"What's wrong?" I asked.

"Before I tell you, you must promise to never repeat what I'm going to say. If you do, I will lose a dear friend. Promise me."

I had never seen her dark, intent eyes so serious. "I promise. Cross my heart, I will not repeat a word you tell me."

"There was a letter," she said. "The Dean of Women wrote to Shirley's parents."

"What??"

"She told them she should not go out with you. She said you are an ex-sailor, which doesn't speak well for your character, and that your father is a foreigner whose income doesn't meet their standards."

I must have looked as sick as I felt.

"She said you take up too much of Shirley's time, so she doesn't have a chance to meet young men of better character from more suitable backgrounds. Shirley's parents told her that if she sees you again, they'll transfer her to another college."

I never felt so alone and so betrayed in my life.

"I'm sorry, I'm so sorry," her roommate said, and hurried away.

With one letter I was accused, tried and convicted. But I couldn't go to the Dean. I couldn't tell anyone. I had made a promise. The sickness bottled up inside me.

Not long after, I saw Shirley across campus. It was the last time I ever saw her. She left Juniata that weekend. I wrote to her almost daily, but every letter was returned. I never found out where she went.

I despised Juniata, and lost all interest in my classes. I was warned that if I didn't maintain my grades, I'd lose my G.I. privileges. My only recourse was to bury myself in my work, with one goal: get my degree, get the heck out of Juniata, and never come back.

The train is slowing down, and the conductor is approaching me. "Sir, we are coming into Paoli."

With a jolt, I tried to resume my jolly British facade. "Oh, goodo!" As I stepped off the train, I thanked the conductor "veddy much." He waved goodbye to this foreigner. "Cheerio!" I said.

Now what? I stood on the platform a long time, glad to be out of Huntington, but feeling too wounded and pitiful to go home. Where is she? Were there other reasons? Was there really a letter?

Why didn't she write?

CHAPTER 55

PARVIN'S PHARMACY

"Why do they have to come here for ice cream when they have everything they need at school?" said Mrs. Horn, who was watching the girls from the Baldwin School. Their conversations and laughter filled the store.

"They're not hungry, Mrs. Horn. It's just their escape from studies. Some women buy hats. Some men drink beer. We all have our diversions."

She gave me a quizzical look, then handed me a list of items to be picked up in an hour. On the way out, she paused to look at the girls, then turned to me with a hint of a smile.

Parvin's Pharmacy was next to the Bryn Mawr train station. Unlike Liggett's Drug Store down Lancaster Avenue, Parvin's catered to students from the Agnes Irwin School, the Baldwin School, Harcum Junior College and Bryn Mawr College. Many of the customers were listed in the Social Register.

I watched as a very pretty Harcum girl, slim with golden-red hair and brown eyes, approached the counter. A frequent visitor to the store, she would occasionally stop to chat with me.

"I'd like some lipstick. Here," she said, reaching into her purse, "is the color I need."

"It's the wrong color," I said without looking at the lipstick. I took a tube from the display and handed it to her. "Try this color."

She removed the cover, looked at the lipstick and said, "You want me to wear this?"

"If you don't like it, I'll return your dollar. And, if you don't mind me saying, your earrings are too big. Thin gold ones would suit you better. And get rid of those braids."

She dropped a dollar bill on the counter and walked out without saying a word. I wondered if she would ever return.

Two weeks later, she did return, and walked straight to the counter where I was standing.

She was wearing the lipstick I sold her, thin golden earrings, and her hair was long and wavy. All I could do was stare.

"What's wrong this time?"

"Nothing," I said. "Don't change a thing."

In a whisper, she said, "My boyfriend thinks so too. I came to thank you." As she walked towards the door, everyone in the store turned to look at her.

Another Harcum girl whom I chatted with came in and sat in a booth. She looked as if she'd been crying. I brought her a Coke.

"Can you take me someplace where we can talk?" she asked. "Will you come to the school at seven?"

We sat in a booth in a small restaurant away from the school. I'd never seen a girl so tense. After a few sips of coffee, she relaxed a little. She spoke for a long time. I just listened, nodding occasionally. When she finished her story, she let out a long sigh. We bundled up

259

and walked silently back to Harcum, our heads bent against the cold December wind.

"I can't thank you enough for listening, and for your help. Goodnight."

Walking home, I wondered why she asked me. Then it hit me. I was twenty-six. To a nineteen-year-old, I was her proxy big brother and father confessor. She could bare her innermost thoughts without fear of recrimination.

On Christmas morning, there was a knock on our door. It was a Special Delivery – for me.

Everyone was eager to know who would send me a package on Christmas Day. So was I. I tore off the wrappings. It was a beautiful pair of loafers, and a second pair of dress shoes.

"What does the card say?" asked Dad. "Read it to us," said Mother.

I read aloud, "Dear Fred, thank you for your help. I hope these are the right size. Signed, A." "Who is "A"?" asked mother and dad in unison.

"A girl from Harcum who needed someone to talk to. All I did was listen." "Sometimes," said Dad, "listening is the best help."

After Christmas vacation, she came to the drug store. "Thank you for the shoes," I said. "They are so fine – and they fit perfectly! How did you know my size?"

"You told me," she said, laughing. It was the first time I saw her laugh. "I told you?"

"You were tying your shoelace. I said, my aren't they big. What size are they? You said 12C. You said the Navy didn't need more ships to win a war. They just had to launch your shoes."

After her graduation, one of her classmates told me her father owned a shoe company.

Though I spoke with and teased many of the college girls, I never asked them out. Why? I'm not sure. Finances, no doubt. Or maybe they did not fit the vision of my dream girl who, very soon, was to come into the drug store, and into my life.

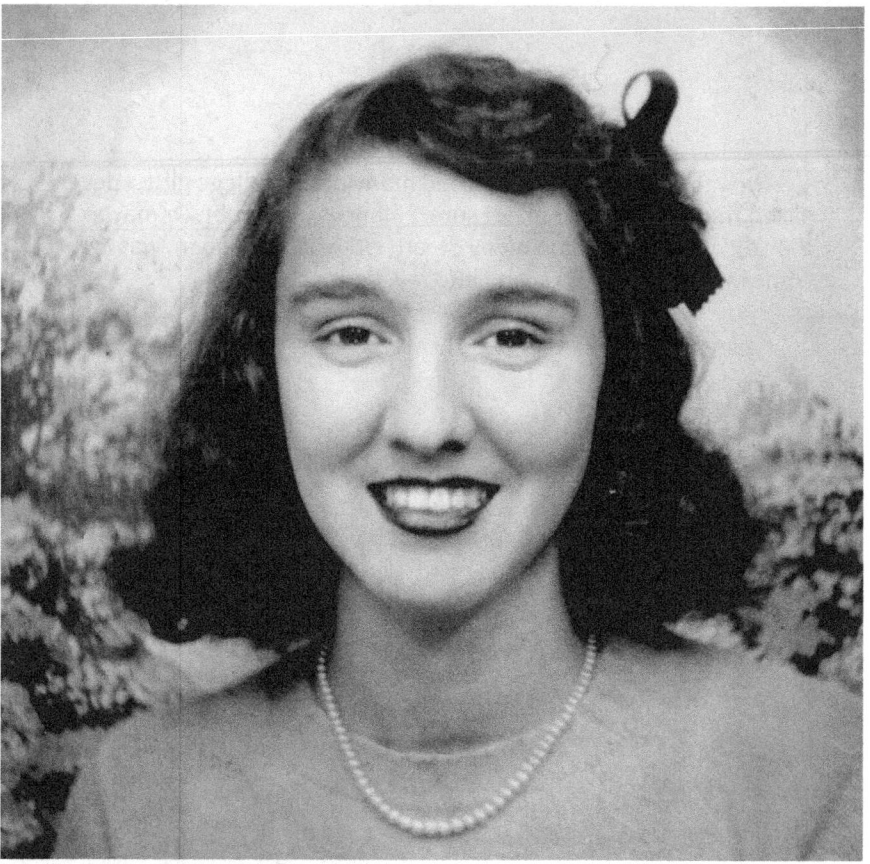

Come noontime at Parvin's Pharmacy, I'd position myself behind the tobacco counter to watch for Gerry. Gigi, her friends sometimes called her.

CHAPTER 56

GERRY

The fountain at Parvin's was always crowded at noontime. When there were more customers than Thelma and Jane could handle, Doc Parvin would ask me to assist.

One afternoon, I was bent over the sink washing glasses when three girls sat down directly in front of me. When I straightened up, their faces were hidden behind menus. Then she looked up. Her sparkling brown eyes lit up her exquisite face. I knew I was staring, but I didn't stop. I finally managed to speak.

"May I help you?" I asked.

"I'd like cream cheese and olives on white toast, and a cup of coffee." Her voice was soft, her smile warm. Where did she come from? As I waited on other customers, I would steal glances at her. Once our eyes met, and she smiled. It felt like a million dollar tip. After she and her friends left, I thought of nothing but that lovely face.

The next day, I kept looking at the clock, hoping she'd return. I was just putting on an apron and walking to the counter where she had sat when she and her friends walked in.

As I waited on them, she asked me questions. Why couldn't I respond intelligently? Why is it I can tell a girl I don't know what lipstick to use, but when I meet someone special, I'm tongue-tied?

Each day, just before noon, I would stand behind the tobacco counter at the front of the store where I could watch for her. When I spied her, my insides would leap. I had lost some of my shyness. Her name was Gerry. Sometimes her friends called her Gigi. Her full name, Germaine Elizabeth Gardiner, sounded like music.

I didn't know it, but Doc Parvin had been watching me. The look on my face must have telegraphed her approach, for at that very moment he would step from behind the pharmacy and say, "Fred, Thelma and Jane need your help." I didn't have to be told twice. Thelma or Jane would tell me to man the counter where Gerry sat. And I thought I was being so secretive!

One afternoon, I added a hard-boiled egg with Gerry's sandwich. She looked at her plate, then at me, and was about to speak. I just smiled. From then on, I always added something extra; a dip of ice cream on her pie, or a dessert if she didn't order one. When it was time to pay, I stood directly in front of the register on the back counter, so no one could see the amount. I made sure Gerry's charge was the middle one, so it wouldn't show on the register. I kept her lunch tab very small, and paid Thelma the difference.

When it came time to leave, Gerry would let her friends Mary and Kay precede her, then turn and say goodbye with that beautiful smile. I watched them until they were out of sight. When I turned to resume my work, Thelma and Jane would be looking at me, each wearing a great big grin. I grinned back.

At her holiday party, Gerry was such a magnet
for her friends, I had to wait till the guests
had gone to spend time with her.

CHAPTER 57

HAPPY NEW YEAR

It was right after Christmas when Gerry invited me to a pre-New Year's Eve party. Of course, I said Yes. The next few days, I was worse than a child waiting for Christmas. The day before the party, I said to Dad, "Please don't turn off the pressing machine. I want to press my suit. I've been invited to a party tomorrow."

"Is it someone's birthday?" asked Dad. Mother was sitting close by, listening. "It's a pre-New Year's Eve party. In Drexel Hill."

"What's her name? Will we get to meet her?" asked Mother.

"Her name is Germaine Gardiner. I hope you'll meet her soon. You'll like her."

Mother and Dad just looked at each other, wondering what this Pushmondon is getting into now.

I didn't own a winter coat. Dad gave me one left by a customer over a year ago – a heavy black six-button Benny that hung down almost to my ankles. It looked like a great coat from World War I. I was embarrassed to wear it, but the weather was frigid.

Before I rang the doorbell at 2455 Marshall Road, I draped the coat over my arm. A guest opened the door. Someone took my coat and another handed me a drink. I hoped that the person who took my coat didn't get a broken arm carrying it.

Gerry came over, took my arm, and introduced me to her friends and parents, who were warm and sincere. Gerry was so lovely and spirited, her friends demanded her attention, and I had little chance to be with her. I waited until all the guests had gone so I could speak with her. "I really like your friends and your parents. Thanks for inviting me."

"I'm glad you came. You better hurry. The last bus is due in a few minutes." She handed me my coat. "Can I see you again?" I asked bravely.

"I'd like that," she said with that beautiful smile. I waited until I was outside to put on my coat. I floated all the way home.

CHAPTER 58

FIRST DATE

After giving Mother and Dad a portion of my pay, and paying off a hundred and fifty dollar college debt, little was left of my thirty dollar a week salary. I started saving every penny so I could ask Gerry out.

For our first date, I took Gerry to the Academy of Music to hear the Philadelphia Orchestra.

We rode the elevated to City Hall, then walked to the Academy at Broad and Locust Streets.

As the orchestra took the stage, I pointed out my brother John in the bassoon section. Benny Goodman performed Mozart's Clarinet Concerto and William Warfield sang "Ole Man River." The thrill of the evening for Gerry was Andre Kostlanetz conducting Ravel's 'Bolero.' When the program ended, I took her backstage to meet my brother. It was her first time backstage after a concert.

Gerry held my arm as we strolled to the Drake Hotel on Spruce Street. The Sir Francis Drake Lounge was a cozy room with a welcoming blaze in the stone fireplace, a dark mahogany bar, and large overstuffed leather chairs. Soft lights set the mood.

Once our drinks were served, Gerry nestled her feet under her, snuggled deeper into the chair and said, "Tell me all about yourself." What a beautiful picture she made.

We chatted quietly and sipped our drinks. I marveled at how comfortable I felt with her. Finally, it was time to leave. I asked our waiter his name.

"Ray."

"Ray, we'll be back next Saturday. Could you save the two big chairs by the fireplace for us?" He looked at Gerry, then me and nodded yes.

Whether it was an opera, concert or movie, we would end our evenings at the Sir Francis Drake. One Saturday, Ray came to us carrying a tray with Gerry's favorite Grasshopper in a king-size glass, and a whiskey & soda for me.

"What fantastic service," said Gerry.

"For old friends...who I will miss." "Are you quitting?" Gerry asked.

"No Miss. The Drake has been sold. The new owners are hiring only waitresses. Everything is being changed."

"In what way?" I asked.

"They're adding chrome, indirect lighting and a piano. And these armchairs will be replaced by small tables and chairs.

"Our favorite chairs?" asked Gerry. Ray nodded. "When?" I asked.

"The room will close after tonight."

We lingered over our drinks, in the same chairs we sat in for our first date. I left Ray the largest tip I could. We said our farewells and left the Sir Francis Drake, never to return.

CHAPTER 59

PROPOSAL

My first attempts to find a job with a future were with a one-man ad agency with one client, and the two man advertising department of a wholesale plumbing supply firm sliding into bankruptcy.

My third attempt began at nine p.m. on April 15, 1953 with Meyer Barr, President of Barr's Jewelers & Silversmiths. After a ninety minute interview in his office above the store at 1112-14 Chestnut Street, Mr. Barr showed me the advertising department. Another one-man operation. At least they had a Baltimore agency to handle the creative work.

Somehow, despite my utter lack of experience, I exited the store onto the now dark and nearly deserted Chestnut Street as the new Advertising Manager. Had I realized how that late hour would foreshadow my long workdays for the next 12 years, I might have been less elated. My role would focus on production. Over time, my responsibilities would expand to include creative too.

Earl Schloss, our agency Account Executive, became my mentor. I spent countless hours in newspaper art and production departments, and in letterset, offset and rotogravure printing plants and typesetting houses. Many nights, I'd arrive home close to midnight. Come Friday, I couldn't wait to see Gerry.

I was always rushing out of her door to catch the last bus home. Most of the time, I was the only passenger. I sat up front and talked with the bus driver during the ten-minute ride to the terminal, where I took the high-speed trolley to Bryn Mawr. I became such a regular, if I wasn't outside to meet the bus, the driver would stop across from Gerry's home, beep the horn and wait for me. I made it a point to tell him when I'd be calling on Gerry, so he wouldn't beep in vain.

Between work and dating, I spent very few evenings at home. One evening, as I was getting ready to visit Gerry, Dad asked, "Why don't you date an Armenian girl?"

"I don't like an Armenian girl. I like the girl I'm going with."

"How much do you like her?"

"Very much."

As I walked to the trolley, I thought, Dad, why do you have to object to the girls John and Warren married, and to the girl I love? I'd often daydream of coming home to her, and to our own little place.

Growing up, my family never openly expressed our feelings for one another. Maybe that's why I couldn't say all the wonderful things I thought and felt about Gerry. So when I finally proposed on her living room sofa, I said quietly, "I love you, Gerry. Will you marry me?"

Gerry hugged me tightly, kissed me and whispered, "Yes." We held each other a long time, savoring our joy.

Then it hit me. "I wonder if your parents will object."

She kissed me and said, "All you have to do is ask them. You'll have to ask Roger, too."

Her brother John was called Roger by family and friends. His sister Blanche gave him the nickname. Though the office of his

271

accounting firm at 15th and Market was just a few blocks away, I couldn't get time off the next day to visit him. I couldn't even go to lunch. So I phoned him.

"Roger, it's Fred. I wanted to see you in person, but I can't get off and this can't wait."

"What can't wait?"

"I want to marry Gerry and would like your okay."

"I was beginning to worry about your intentions. Did you ask her?"

"Last night. She said yes."

"Then it's okay by me. You better be damn good to her."

That night, from beneath my bed, I took the cigar box where I'd been saving as much as I could from my weekly salary. I dumped the bills on the bed and began counting. There was over three hundred dollars. I put the cash in an envelope under my pillow.

The next morning, I knocked on Mr. Barr's office door. He was dictating to his secretary. "Come in, Fred," he said.

I entered and stood there, hoping his secretary would leave. "Is there a problem?" he asked.

"I have something personal to discuss."

Mr. Barr excused his secretary, who discreetly shut the door.

"Mr. Barr, I'd like to buy an engagement ring. I've saved three hundred dollars. I'll pay the balance from my weekly salary."

"The girl you intend to marry...how long have you known her?"

"Nearly two years. I love her very much."

"Wait here." He left the room. A few minutes later he returned with three blue tissue packets and lined them up in front of me. In each was a beautiful stone.

"Pick the one you like best," he said.

"Mr. Barr, I'd prefer if you'd tell me which one I should buy."

"That's odd. My other employees all seem to be diamond experts."

"I couldn't tell a diamond from a piece of glass."

"Good. Take this one," he said, pointing to a three-quarter carat diamond. "What kind of setting would she like?"

"A simple four-prong Tiffany mounting in white gold. How much will the ring cost?"

"Exactly three hundred dollars. That includes his and her wedding bands."

I handed him the envelope. "I'd like to pay you now."

He stood up, shook my hand and said, "I'd like to meet your bride-to-be."

"Thank you sir. You'll get to meet her. You'll like her, too."

That went well! Yet at my desk, I was filled with worry. I still had to ask her mother and dad for their blessing. And what will *my* Mother and Dad say?

Gerry's parents at home with Gerry, Fred and Blanche.

"Mr. Gardiner, I said, "I would like to marry Gerry.
I love her very much." He studied me through
thick lenses. "Fred, you may marry my Pupetta.
Now let's drink some wine." As we clinked glasses,
Gerry walked in. "Having a party without me?"

CHAPTER 60

ASK PAPA

Two days ago, I asked Gerry to marry me. Tonight, I had to ask her parents.

Gerry's mother answered the door. "Come in, Fred. Gerry is upstairs dressing. She'll be down soon."

"Hello, Mrs. Gardiner. I'm glad she's upstairs. I have something I must ask you and Mr. Gardiner."

"Papa is outside with the neighbors. Can I help you?" I followed her into the breakfast room, and we sat across from each other at the small table. There was always a twinkle in her eye. It was there when she smiled and asked, "Now what is it that you must ask me?"

"Mrs. Gardiner, I love Gerry. I would like your permission to marry her." My hands shook as I tried to light a cigarette.

"I know you love my Gerry. I know you will take good care of her. Yes, I would like that very much."

I took her hand in mine and whispered, "Thank you."

"Remember, you must ask Papa, too," she said. At that instant, the back door opened and Gerry's father came in. She rose and said, "Papa, Fred has something to ask you."

He looked at me through his thick glasses, sat down across from me and said, "You have something to ask me?" His eyes stared directly into mine. I was really shaking now.

"Mr. Gardiner, I would like your permission to marry Gerry. I promise I will always love her and take good care of her." I took a deep breath. I felt as if I had talked for an hour. He continued to stare at me through those thick glasses.

"You love my Pupetta?"

"With all my heart."

He smiled. "Yes, I would like it if you marry my Pupetta. Now we will drink some wine." From a cupboard he took a bottle of wine and two glasses. When the drinks were poured he raised his glass and said, "To my Pupetta and Fred."

We clinked glasses and drank the wine. At that moment Gerry walked in. "Having a party without me?"

"Your father and I were sampling his special homemade wine." I rose and helped her with her coat. "Come home early," her father said.

The door closed behind us. The porch light was off. I held her in my arms, kissed her and said, "They said yes. They said yes!"

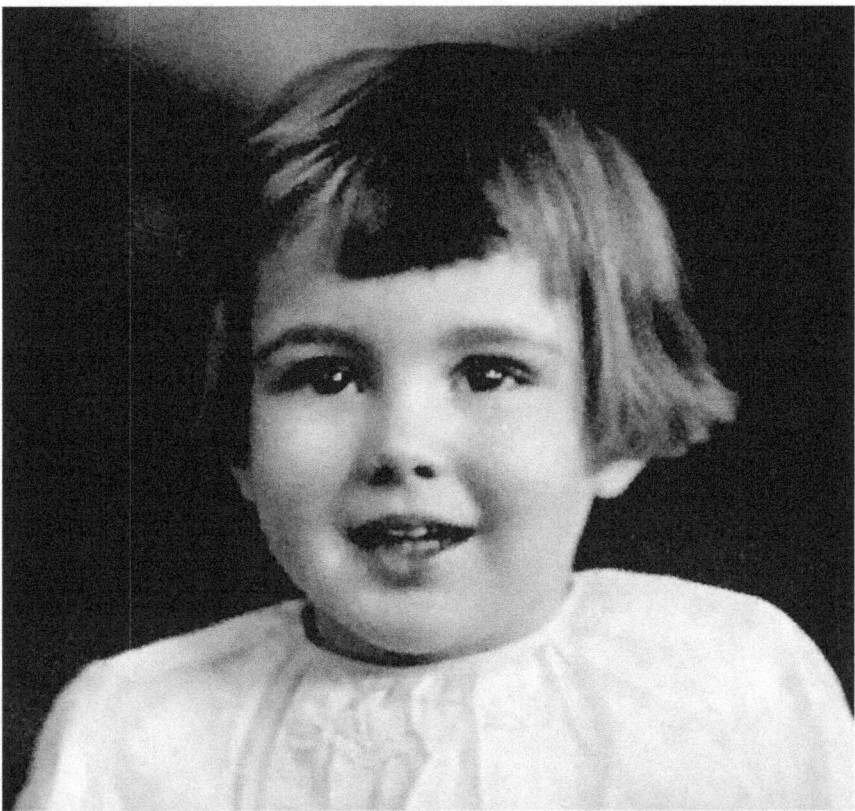

Germaine Elizabeth Gardiner

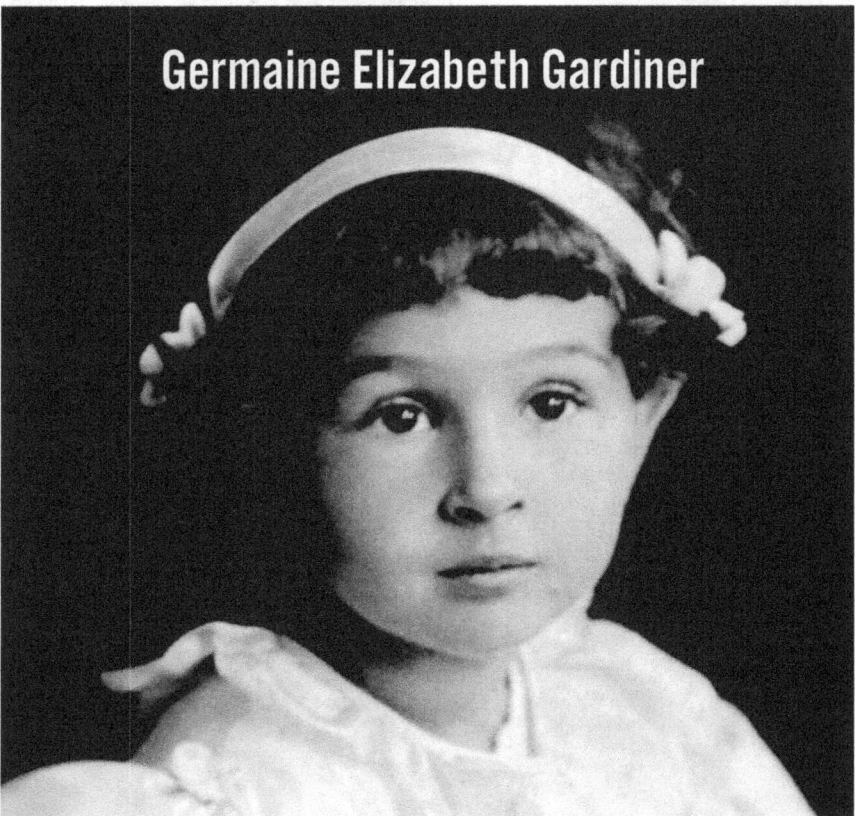

The Baronis,
Gerry's
grandparents,
lived in the
ancient walled
city of Lucca
in Tuscany.

Born in Italy, Germana Baroni and Silvino Giardinelli married in 1904 in Philadelphia and raised 4 children.

While a reporter in Chicago, Silvino was picked up in a limo and delivered to the gangster Al Capone. "When I kill two men," Capone told him, "you say I killed two men. From now on, when I kill someone, you'll know first." Silvino moved to Philly, changed his last name, and became a real estate investor.

Silvino became an American citizen at age 56.

PRESENT THIS PASSPORT WITH YOUR APPLICATION FOR A NEW PASSPORT

IMPORTANT

The person to whom this passport is issued must sign his name on page three immediately on its receipt. The passport is NOT VALID unless it has been signed.

The bearer should also fill in blanks below as indicated.

Germana Baroni Giardinelli
Signature of bearer
2316 S. Croskey St
Bearer's address in the United States
Phila., Pa.
Lucca Italia Toscana
Bearer's foreign address

IN CASE OF DEATH OR ACCIDENT NOTIFY
Miss Blanche Giardinelli
Name of person to be notified
2327 S. Bouvier St
Exact address
Phila., Pa.

CAUTION

This passport is a valuable document. It should not be altered in any way. Due care should be taken to see that it does not pass into the possession of an unauthorized person. If it is lost or destroyed the fact and circumstances of the loss should be immediately reported to the Passport Division, Department of State, or to the nearest American Consulate, or, in an outlying possession of the United States, to the chief executive thereof, and to the local police authorities. New passports in such cases can be issued only after exhaustive inquiry.   1—1107

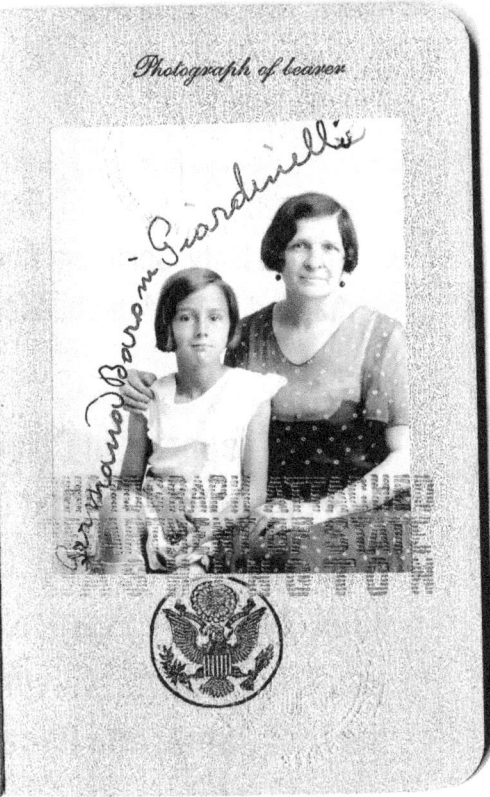

Photograph of bearer

Gerry and her mother.

Brother John
(AKA Jack or Roger)

Gerry   Janet

Gerry, Blanche and Janet

Gerry and best friend Kay Naughton.

SPARS
APPLY NEAREST COAST GUARD OFFICE

When WWII broke out, Gerry and Blanche volunteered for the newly created Coast Guard Women's Reserve – known as the SPARs, from the motto "Semper Paratus."

My sister Minnie joined the Navy Waves, serving in San Diego as a Radioman.

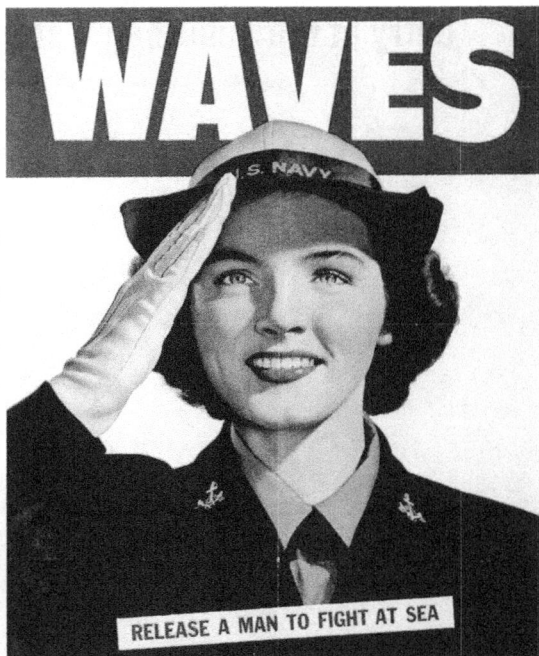

WAVES
U.S. NAVY
RELEASE A MAN TO FIGHT AT SEA

Gerry at the Suburban Water Company's Annual Banquet.

Gerry, John, Germana and Bee at their Marshall Rd home.

Jack and Blanche grew up during the Roaring Twenties and knew the good life: fine clothes, trips to Europe, a chauffered Packard limousine.

Gerry was five when the Crash of 1929 ushered in the Depression. She did not recall their once lavish lifestyle.

An elegant lady who loved riding horses, Blanche endured an unhappy marriage to Arthur Frost.

Their home in Landsowne was just blocks from ours. She, Jack and Julie often dropped in for coffee and cake.

Bee with son Arthur ("Skippy") and her mother.

John J. Gardiner,
a tall man who
lived large.

During Prohibition,
Jack owned a
speakeasy and
sold bathtub gin.

His Oldsmobile
Ninety-Eight was
nearly 19 ft long.

with brother-in-law "Butch" Cole (right)

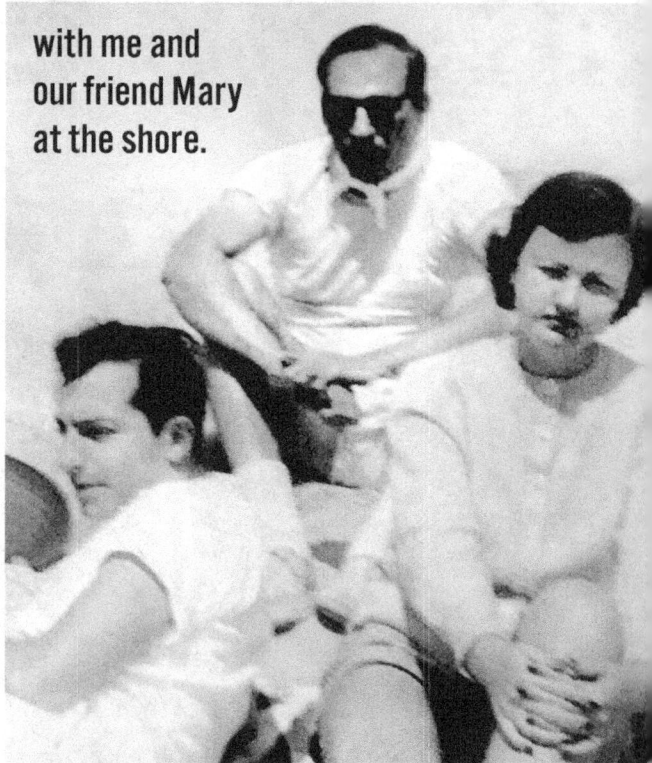

with me and
our friend Mary
at the shore.

with Ricky, 1957

A dapper man who favored cologne, French cuffs and 13 AAA Italian shoes, Jack founded the accounting firm of Gardiner & Goines, and lived a life of service:

President (1965), National Society of Accountants

Treasurer, National Health Council (1975-76)

Phila. Chapter President and national Treasurer, Muscular Distrophy Assn.

Julie & Jack Gardiner, 1984

The daughter of fashion designer Alice Testardi, Julie shared his love of painting and opera.

Silvino's brother, center, with Germana behind him,
flanked by Gerry's cousins Minnie Maroni and Virgie
Skillogi. That's Janet far right (top), and below.

Butch and Janet with son Jay, whose IQ placed him in the top 0.1% of students across America.

Cuz & Janet's husband Jack

in Korea with the Signal Corps

Jay, Jan and Butch Cole

Fear kept Gerry from telling anyone about
the lump in her breast until it was too late.

Janet & Gerry

Gerry's Cousin Ed Toti – "Buz."

Buz's sister Carina – "Cuz."

A top salesman and avid sailor, Buz and Betty Toti lived near Detroit with daughters April and Jamie.

Cuz married Jim Mulligan, a civil engineer. They lived outside Chicago.

Cuz's sons – Jay, Jack and Pete.

Uncle Alexander, Gerry's father's brother, was the personal tailor of General "Blackjack" Pershing during WWI.

Aline Baroni, Germana's sister, married chef Peter Toti and raised Corrin and Edward ("Cuz" and "Buz") in South Philly. A brilliant seamstress, "Aunt Lena" made Gerry's wedding dress, and later altered it for our daughter.

CHAPTER 62

THE CONVERT

One Sunday I accompanied Gerry to church. I was struck by her quiet reverence as she listened to the Priest, responded to the litany and knelt to pray after communion.

Whenever I attended Mass with her, that reverence was there. It was the same with her entire family. In her home, religion was never spoken of, but they lived their faith everyday. It felt wholesome and sincere – something I had never experienced.

As a child, I attended the Episcopal Church of The Good Shepherd. I even sang in the choir until my voice began to change. Mother and Dad never joined us, and only rarely attended the Armenian Church. Later, when the drug store required Sunday hours, I really never missed going to church. I thought about that, and about Gerry and her family. Even on vacation, they never missed Sunday Mass.

Though the Catholic Mass was similar to the Episcopal service, I sensed something different, deeper. I never discussed it with Gerry, but it was beautiful, and often in my thoughts.

The living room light through the screen door lent a soft glow to the porch. We were alone. "Gerry, how do I become a Catholic?"

She looked at me with those dark eyes. "Really? Do you mean it?"

"I've thought of nothing else for weeks. I've never known anyone who lives their faith like you. If we share one faith, think what it will mean for our children, and for us. I mean it, with all my heart."

Gerry held my hands tightly. We sat there without talking, each with our own thoughts.

I dared not tell Mother and Dad about becoming Catholic. When I told them I had asked Gerry to marry me, Dad said, "She is not right for you. You should marry an Armenian girl."

"Dad, I don't love an Armenian girl. I love Gerry. And we are getting married!" Mother stared at Dad with a pained expression, then left the room. I hoped she understood how I felt.

It was long after we were married that I told Gerry what Dad said.

To prepare for my Confirmation, I immersed myself in evening classes and studying. I also needed to choose a middle name, typically the name of a Saint. My brother John's middle name is Victor. Newert's is Victoria. One night, Gerry and I were trying out the names of family members. "Frederick John Shamlian. Frederick Anthony Shamlian." And so on, until she came to "Frederick Alexander Shamlian."

"That sounds great," I said. "I like it too," said Gerry.

"Gerry, who's Alexander?"

"He was a distinguished uncle of mine."

At last I was ready to be confirmed. With Gerry's brother Roger as my sponsor, I became Frederick Alexander Shamlian. Fate must have guided our selection, because Gerry's Uncle Alexander was a tailor, just like my father. In fact, he made the uniforms for General Pershing in World War I.

During the ceremony, a rite of solemn joy and beauty, I thought that when we were married, Gerry and I would become one with God.

Knowing how much Dad wanted me to marry an Armenian girl, I never brought Gerry home during our courtship. He and Mother did come to our wedding, but they looked sad.

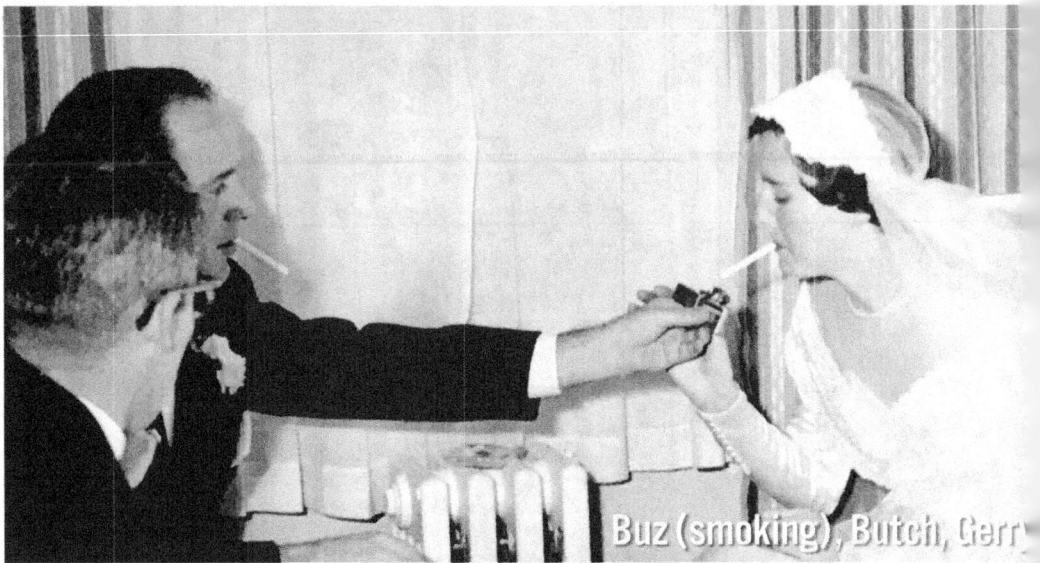
Buz (smoking), Butch, Gerr

Germaine Gardiner Of DH Is Wed To Frederick Shamlian

The marriage of Miss Germaine Elizabeth G a r d i n e r, daughter of Mr. and Mrs. John S. Gardiner of Drexel Hill, to Mr. Frederick A. Shamlian, son of Mr. and Mrs. Victor Shamlian of Bryn Mawr, took place Jan. 8 at St. Charles Borromeo Church in Oakview.

The bride, given in marriage by h riage by h sheath gow with an off of velvet an lusion neckl held by a h pearl applic

Mr. Warr brother of t Washington,

man and Mrs. James Mulligan of Fairview, N. J., was matron of honor..

Mr. John J. Gardiner, brother of the bride, senior partner of the accounting firm of Gardiner & Gaines, was usher, and Miss Mary Katherine Burke of Philadelphia was bridesmaid.

A reception at the Drexel Hill home of the bride followed the ceremony, with the sisters of the bride, Mrs. Arthur Frost 2d of Lansdowne, and Mrs. Jack Newcomb Cole of San Antonio, Tex. as nostesses.

Wedding Day
January 8, 1955

The SHOREHAM
Connecticut Avenue at Calvert Street
Washington 8, D. C.
December 20, 1954.

Mr. Frederick Shamlian
1003 Lancaster Avenue,
Bryn Mawr, Pennsylvania.

Dear Mr. Shamlian:

In reply to your request, we wish to advise that our rate for a double-bedded room and bath is $14.00 per day, a double-bedded one-room suite is $15.00 per day, a parlor, bedroom and bath is $20.00 per day.

Awaiting your further advices and hoping to have the pleasure of entertaining you and your bride at The Shoreham, I am

LGM:R

Honeymoon!

CHAPTER 63

THE WEDDING

Father Donahue, Warren and I are standing at the foot of the altar in Saint Charles Borromeo Church in Drexel Hill. It's Saturday morning, January 8th, 1955, and the church is crowded. Gerry's mother gives me a warm smile. Despite his threat, Dad did come with Mother and Minnie, but Mother and Dad look sad.

Knowing how Dad objected to my dating her, I never brought Gerry home to meet them during our courtship. I felt Dad's mind was made up, and I was afraid he'd say something to break us up. I wish they knew Gerry as I know her. They would love her too.

The Wedding March begins and everyone stands. The Bridesmaid, Mary Katherine Burke, accompanied by Gerry's brother John, is first through the alcove. Then comes the Matron of Honor, Gerry's cousin, Carina Toti Mulligan, known to one and all as "Cuz." Gerry and her Father follow slowly down the aisle. I take a deep breath. How beautiful she looks; so slim, so graceful. Her aunt, Aline Toti, made her gown. Thirty-two years later, our daughter Germaine will wear the same gown in this same church.

Gerry is holding her father's arm. He looks nervous. I wonder if I look the same to him. As he places her hand in mine, he looks at me as if to say, "Please take good care of my Pupetta." My hands shake as I lift the veil and look into those magnificent eyes. Hand in hand, we stand before our Priest and before God.

After the vows and the exchange of rings, Cuz hands Gerry a small bouquet of flowers.

Gerry walks to the statue of the Blessed Mother, kneels, and lays the flowers at Mary's feet. As she prays, the soloist sings "Ave Maria." I watch from a distance, deeply moved by her reverence. The beauty of that moment will remain with me always.

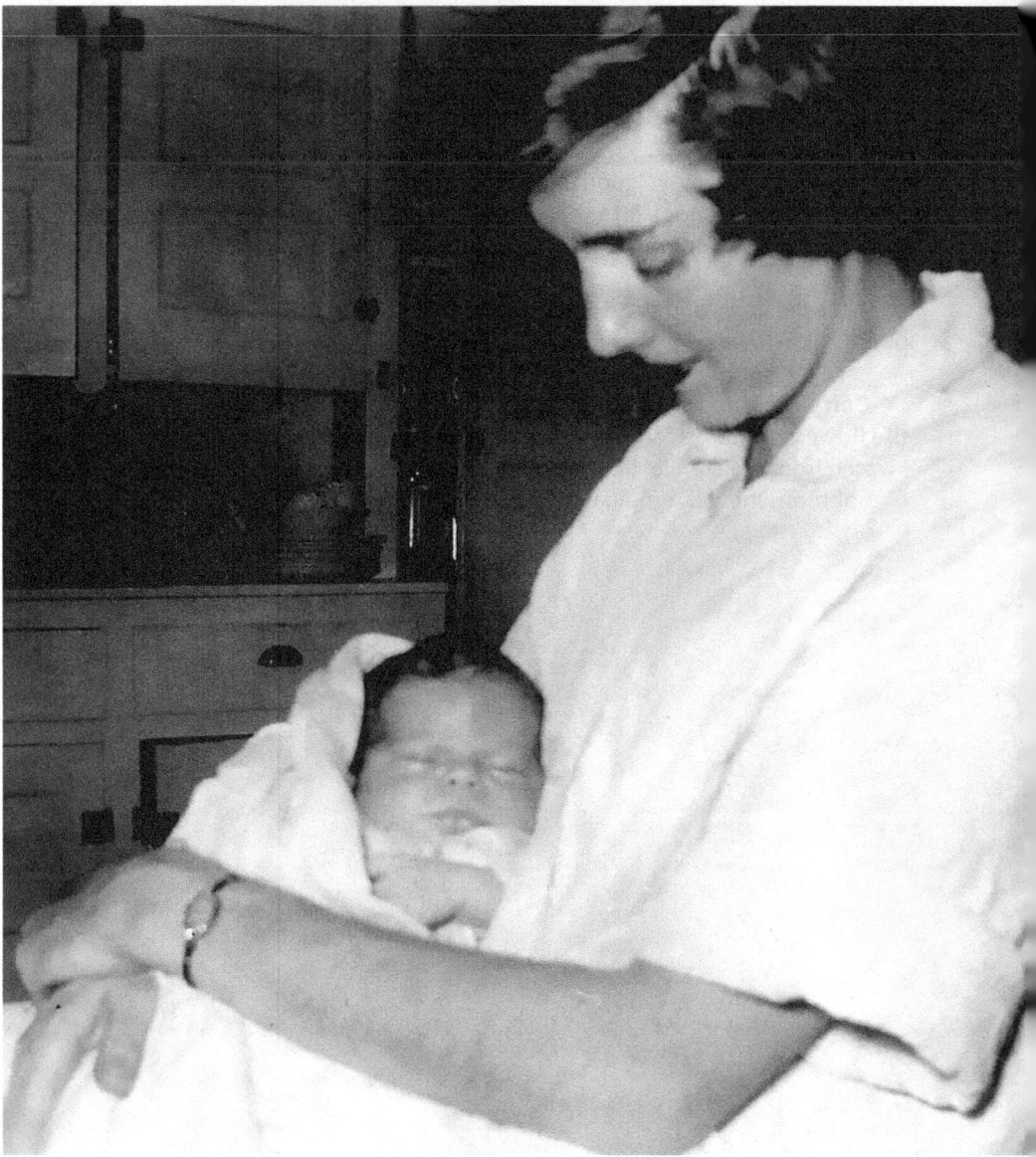

I was pacing and smoking in the waiting room when Dr. McCarron entered. "It'll be hours yet, Mr. Shamlian. Go home." The call came that night at eleven: "Fred, you have a fine healthy son."

CHAPTER 64

107 EAST GREENWOOD AVENUE

The town of Lansdowne boasts many grand Victorian homes where three generations once lived under one roof. Exactly five weeks before our wedding day, Gerry and I rented an apartment in such a house on Greenwood Avenue. The rent was perfect for my sixty-five dollars a week salary, and we could furnish our new home before we were married.

Mr. and Mrs. Wright, who lived on the first floor, had converted the second and third floors into apartments. Mr. Wright, a photographer, also conducted his business on the first floor.

Our apartment had a screened-in porch that had been damaged by Hurricane Hazel the previous September. It was still under repair when we moved in. The living room and kitchen were so large, our few pieces of furniture were lost in them, while the bedroom barely accommodated our bed, dresser and nightstands.

We didn't own a television or a washing machine. Gerry washed our clothes in the bathtub using an old fashioned scrubbing board. Mrs. Wright found Gerry doing just that one afternoon when she came to visit.

"That's a disgrace. No woman should have to work like that. You will use my washing machine in the basement. That's final!"

Though our apartment lacked furniture, the bathroom was tiny, and we were not allowed to paint the burgundy walls in the living room, we were happy in our second floor palace.

Knowing Gerry would be there with a smile, a hug and a kiss made my long workdays bearable. Working for Barr's meant never knowing when I'd get home. Thursdays were the longest days, when Barr's sponsored a weekly television movie hosted by the not yet famous Dick Clark, a warm and sincere person. Later, Barr's sponsored *The Weather Show* with Judy Lee, a beautiful woman who died too young.

Despite my late arrivals, a hot dinner was always waiting. Gerry would tell me of her visits with the neighbors, or her walk to her parents' home about a mile away. We couldn't afford a car, so we either walked or took public transportation.

If she bought something for the apartment, she couldn't wait to show me, and watched breathlessly as I opened her precious purchase. It might be a lampshade, a picture frame, or curtains for one of the rooms.

"Boy, this is pretty," I would declare.

"You really like it? You're not just saying it to please me?"

"I do like it, very much."

With the few cents Gerry put aside each week, she transformed our apartment into a welcoming home. The glow which radiated from her, and her joy in each small improvement, made our life together even more beautiful.

Spring came early in 1955. The crocuses and forsythia were already in bloom when Gerry told me I was going to be a father.

The Wrights, much to our relief, were happy to hear the news. Mrs. Wright was like a mother hen, checking in on Gerry almost daily.

In her eighth month, Gerry placed my hand on her belly. I felt our child move. "Doesn't it hurt?"

"Sometimes. It's a good kind of hurt. It means the baby is well."

The birth, according to Dr. Daniel McCarron, was expected around October 20th.

The day came and went without a sign. More days followed. Finally, Dr. McCarron decided that for the sake of mother and child, they would induce labor. At seven forty-five Tuesday morning, November 1st, I accompanied Gerry to Fitzgerald Mercy Hospital. Relegated to the waiting room, I paced, smoked, and waited. It was almost noon when Dr. McCarron told me to go home. "Mr. Shamlian, Gerry's been given a needle to induce labor. I'll have the nurse call you when it's time for you to come."

"Why can't I wait here?"

"It will be some time before she begins to dilate. There's nothing you can do here."

"Gerry's okay, isn't she?"

"She's fine, believe me. Just go home. You'll do better there."

I followed the doctor's orders. At home, I paced, smoked, and waited. Gerry's sister Blanche came to keep me company. Every hour I called the hospital, and each time I was informed that Mrs. Shamlian was in labor. At eleven o'clock, the doctor called.

"Mr. Shamlian, you have a fine healthy son. He was born at ten forty-five this evening. He weights eight pounds, fourteen ounces and is twenty-one inches long."

"A son! I have a son! Is Gerry okay?"

"Other than being tired, she's fine. It's been a long day."

"Thank you, doctor. May I see her now?"

"Just for a brief visit. She needs her rest."

Blanche and I raced to the hospital. A Sister of Mercy took us to the nursery window. "Such a healthy, beautiful baby," said the nun.

"Are they all that red?" I asked.

"By tomorrow, he will look natural. Let's go see your lovely wife.

Gerry seemed to be sleeping. "Remember," said the sister, "only a few minutes."

When I kissed her cheek, Gerry opened her eyes and said, "Did you see him? How does he look?"

"Beautiful. He has almost as much hair as I do."

"Is he all right?"

"He's perfect in every way."

"I told Dr. McCarron that his name is Frederick Alexander." She smiled at me, and closed her eyes.

"You better say good night," said the nun.

I kissed Gerry and whispered, "I love you." She was fast asleep.

It was our first Christmas Eve with Ricky,
a festive evening with family and friends.
I still carry this photo of Gerry in my wallet.

CHAPTER 65

CHRISTMAS, 1955

Six days later, I brought Gerry and our son Ricky home. To avoid confusion, Gerry split the name Frederick in two. I was Fred, and our six-day old son would be Rick.

There was hardly a day or night when we did not have family and friends stopping by. Those few evenings when we were alone, Gerry and I planned our first Christmas.

Gerry missed having a large house with folks dropping in. She craved the happy din of eight or more at the dinner table. So before Christmas, we purchased a solid cherry, double drop-leaf table with matching chairs from John Wanamaker, which we placed in front of the living room window. Now our guests didn't have to eat in the kitchen. I was grateful that the table could only seat four; we only had four place settings of china and crystal.

Gerry loved decorating for Christmas. Each day, she added something new to brighten the holidays. She loved candles; we had lots of them. Our first Christmas tree stood seven feet tall. Our meager decorations and lights were lost in its branches, but we thought it was the prettiest tree in the world. We couldn't afford an angel for the top. In its place was a gold, steeple-shaped glass ornament; it looked like one of the points of the Christmas star.

On Christmas Eve, the apartment was made ready for company, and we both dressed for the occasion. Gerry looked beautiful in a white silk blouse and long black velvet skirt. As I put the gifts beneath the tree, Gerry brought out trays of snacks. The glowing candles gave our home a festive look.

Being a host was a new experience for me, but I managed to get through the evening without blackening the family name. It was after midnight when Gerry's family left. Ricky was awake, dressed in bright red Doctor Dentons (long johns with stocking feet, but without the back flap). Gerry brought him into the living room to see the tree and gave Ricky his bottle.

"This was a wonderful Christmas Eve," she said. Do you know what I wished for tonight?"

"I wish I knew. I would have bought it for you."

"You will, someday. I wished for a house. Our own house. On Christmas morning, when we hear the children waking, we'll put on our bathrobes and hurry downstairs to see their faces when they see the tree and gifts. You'll take lots of pictures."

"We'll have our own home, I promise. Only I can't tell you when." It was to come sooner than expected.

The Gardiner family moved to 2455 Marshall Road in 1939. Gerry was 15. That's her mother on the porch. After her parents died, we moved in, and eventually purchased the home from her brother and sisters.

CHAPTER 66

THE FAMILY HOMESTEAD

At one-forty A.M. on April 23, 1956, Gerry's mother died. What had started as severe pain proved to be cancer of the pancreas. It spread rapidly. After several excruciating days, she slipped into a coma, and never awoke.

Because of her love, gentle wisdom and wonderful sense of humor, Gerry's mother was the magnet who drew family and friends together. She would have been a wonderful grandmother. Her passing left a great void, and Mr. Gardiner was lost without her.

Gerry and her sister Blanche took turns each day to see to their father's needs. With Ricky in his carriage, Gerry walked the mile to and from his home on Marshall Road to clean, wash and cook. I never heard her complain, and never saw anyone as radiant as she was with our son. There was always time for family members, friends or neighbors who came to visit.

When I came home each evening, I never knew whom I'd find at the dinner table. That special magnetism had passed from mother to daughter, and our home became a gathering place.

Less than six months later, on October third, Gerry's dad suffered a massive stroke. It left him completely paralyzed and unable to speak. His condition did not improve, and he was transferred from Hahnemann Hospital to Community Hospital at Tenth and Carpenter.

Something else was troubling Gerry. At dinner, if I asked a question, her reply was curt. She seemed withdrawn and agitated. "I don't know why you've been angry with me," I said. "Please tell me what's wrong." She stared into space as if trying to find the courage.

"I'm sorry. It's not you. It's Roger and Blanche. They want us to give up our apartment and move back to Marshall Road."

She paused, looking around the room. "I'm happy here. I like the Wrights and our neighbors."

"I like this apartment, too. You've made it a real home."

"They said it isn't good to leave a house empty. And we won't have to pay rent, just keep the house in good shape. Should we move?"

"When did they talk to you about moving?"

"When Dad was transferred to Community Hospital. They said he would be there a long time, so you and I should move. One or the other calls me almost everyday. I don't know what to do. I love that house, but I love it here."

I said we should stay. But my decision did not make it easier for Gerry. She seemed more nervous than ever. I spent my lunch hours on a bench in Washington Square, thinking of Gerry and the home she grew up in. My youth was spent living above or behind our store. Gerry was raised in a home with a front lawn, a porch and a backyard. I knew what had to be done.

When I arrived home, I kissed Gerry, took her hand and said, "We're moving to Marshall Road. We'll be just as happy there."

"You're sure?" Her eyes were wide, and searching.

"If we have another child, we'll have to move anyway. And deep down, I think this is what you really want. It's the right thing to do."

There were tears in her eyes when she kissed me. "Dinner will be ready in a minute. You play with Ricky." Gerry was back.

We moved to Marshall Road at the end of October. We spent our spare time plastering and painting. By Thanksgiving, the downstairs was in pretty fair shape.

I think there were ten at our Thanksgiving table. It was a happy group, with two or three conversations going at once. Gerry's eyes sparkled. It was my first time hosting so many guests, but no one succumbed due to lack of food or drink.

Some folks are slow to recognize the needs of others, especially those near to them. Though I phoned each day at lunch, Gerry still had to face each day practically alone. One evening she asked, "Is there anything special you'd like to do for Easter?"

"I haven't given it a thought."

"Do you think we can go to Mass at St. Patrick's Cathedral? And maybe have brunch in a nice restaurant or hotel?"

We were expecting our second child in July. I was about to say that public transit might be uncomfortable in her condition, but the look in her eyes told me to say, "Yes."

"Sure. We'll put on our Sunday best and make a day of it in town."

It was a warm Easter Sunday. Gerry looked radiant in a white silk blouse with the gray worsted suit and Lady Stetson hat she wore on our honeymoon. She dressed Ricky in an Eton-type suit, with short pants, a light wool coat and matching Eton cap.

After Mass, and brunch in a nearby restaurant, we strolled through Rittenhouse Square, then went window-shopping on Walnut and Chestnut Streets before heading home.

"We spent much more than we planned," Gerry said. "Did you have a good time?"

"Wonderful. I can't remember the last time I was in the city."

"Let's not wait a whole year before we go out again."

It was just plain ignorance that I did not see the signs. Working every day at home, with only an infant to talk to and a trip to the market to break up the routine... I'm sure Gerry would have been twice as happy if I had suggested the trip. If my Dad knew how thoughtless I was, he surely would have called me a Pushmondon.

We made it a point to have breakfast after Mass at least once a month. Each week, Gerry put a tiny sum aside for entertainment. When our savings permitted, she'd invite family and friends for a 'no reason' party. The old house would shine, and Gerry glowed.

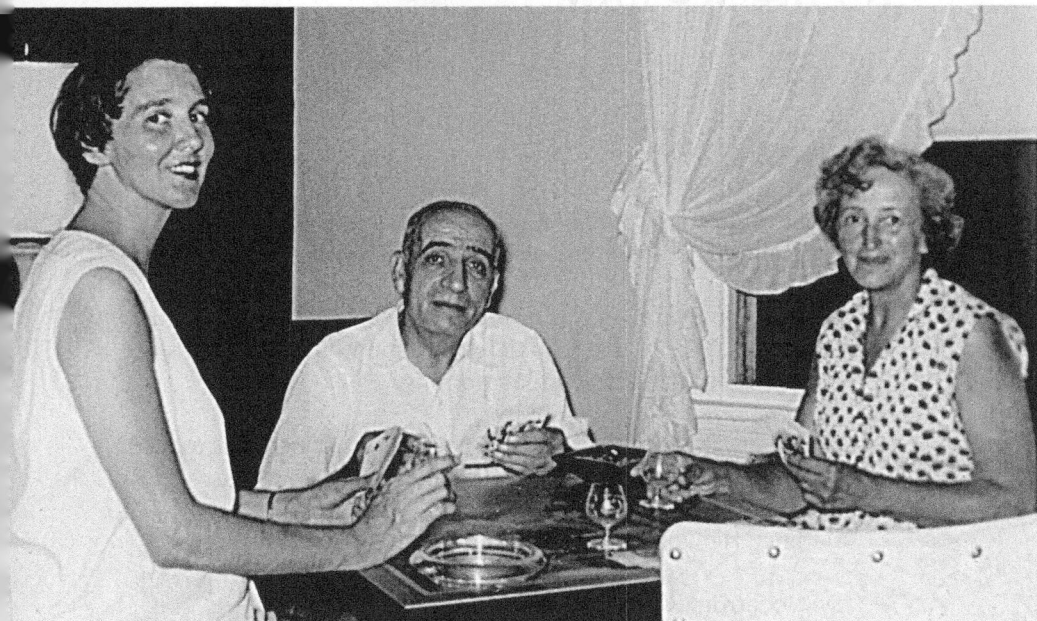

The coveted Seal of Approval!

One Sunday about six months after their first visit to our apartment, Dad lit his cigar, leaned forward and said, "I must tell you, I was wrong about your Gerry. She is a fine woman."

CHAPTER 67

A FINE WOMAN

The Sister of Mercy put her forefinger to her lips. "Only a few minutes," she whispered. "Your wife has had a trying day."

John Warren Shamlian was born at Fitzgerald Mercy at 8:30 pm on Wednesday, July 24, 1957, but it felt as if months had passed since I brought Gerry to the hospital that morning.

I nodded to the Nun, and sat in a chair by Gerry's bed. She looked pale in the dim light. When I kissed her, she opened her eyes.

"Darling." Her voice sounded distant from the anesthesia.

"Dr. McCarron just called."

"Did you see our son? Is he all right?"

"Ten pounds, eight ounces! Doc says he's healthy as an ox."

"Really? Ten pounds?" She squeezed my hand and held it as she fell asleep. The Nun tapped me on the shoulder. It was time to leave.

Six days later I brought Gerry and John home. Soon after that, on a Sunday morning, my parents came to visit! I was as surprised and nervous as Gerry, knowing how much Dad had opposed our marriage. But Mother and Dad were warm and cordial, and insisted on holding and rocking Ricky and John like happy grandparents. I stayed with them while Gerry made breakfast, but as far as my parents were concerned, I wasn't there at all.

Gerry returned, beaming. "Let's eat," she announced as she laid John in his bassinet. I took Ricky from Dad and put him in his playpen.

"We did not come to eat," said Dad.

"We haven't had breakfast. Please join us," Gerry replied. "There's plenty for everyone." The dining room table was laden with sausage, scrambled eggs, hot coffee and buttered toast. There was also Dad's favorite rye bread, sweet butter and 'strombelly' preserves. Later, Gerry told me that she'd left by the kitchen door and walked to the delicatessen.

My Mother, now very hard of hearing, had become suspicious of those who did not speak loud enough for her to hear when conversing with others. Gerry and I practically yelled to make her feel at ease. Still, according to Mother, Gerry was unworthy of me. But then, Warren and John's wives were not good enough for them, either. Neither was Newert's husband. I hoped more visits would change her mind.

Mother and Dad visited almost every Sunday morning. They never called ahead; the telephone was for business and emergencies only. Growing up, I don't remember ever using the phone to make a call.

Not knowing if they were coming, Gerry set places for them every Sunday. With each visit, they seemed more at home, and more relaxed with Gerry. They loved holding the boys, and were always disappointed when it was time for their naps. Eventually they stayed so long, Gerry asked them to stay for dinner.

One Sunday, about six months after Mother and Dad's first visit, Dad and I were sitting on the porch. He lit his cigar, leaned forward and said, "I must tell you this. I was wrong about your Gerry. She is a fine woman. When I come here I see that she is a good wife and mother. Your Mother thinks the same."

"Thanks Dad, I'm really glad you feel that way," I said, trying not to sound amazed.

"But I warn you."

"What's that, Dad?"

"You be good to her and to your sons. You treat her with respect. Be a man, not a Pushmondon." Dad settled back in his chair and smoked his cigar. I said nothing. I was too happy.

My Gerry had just received the coveted Vahan and Sophia Seal of Approval.

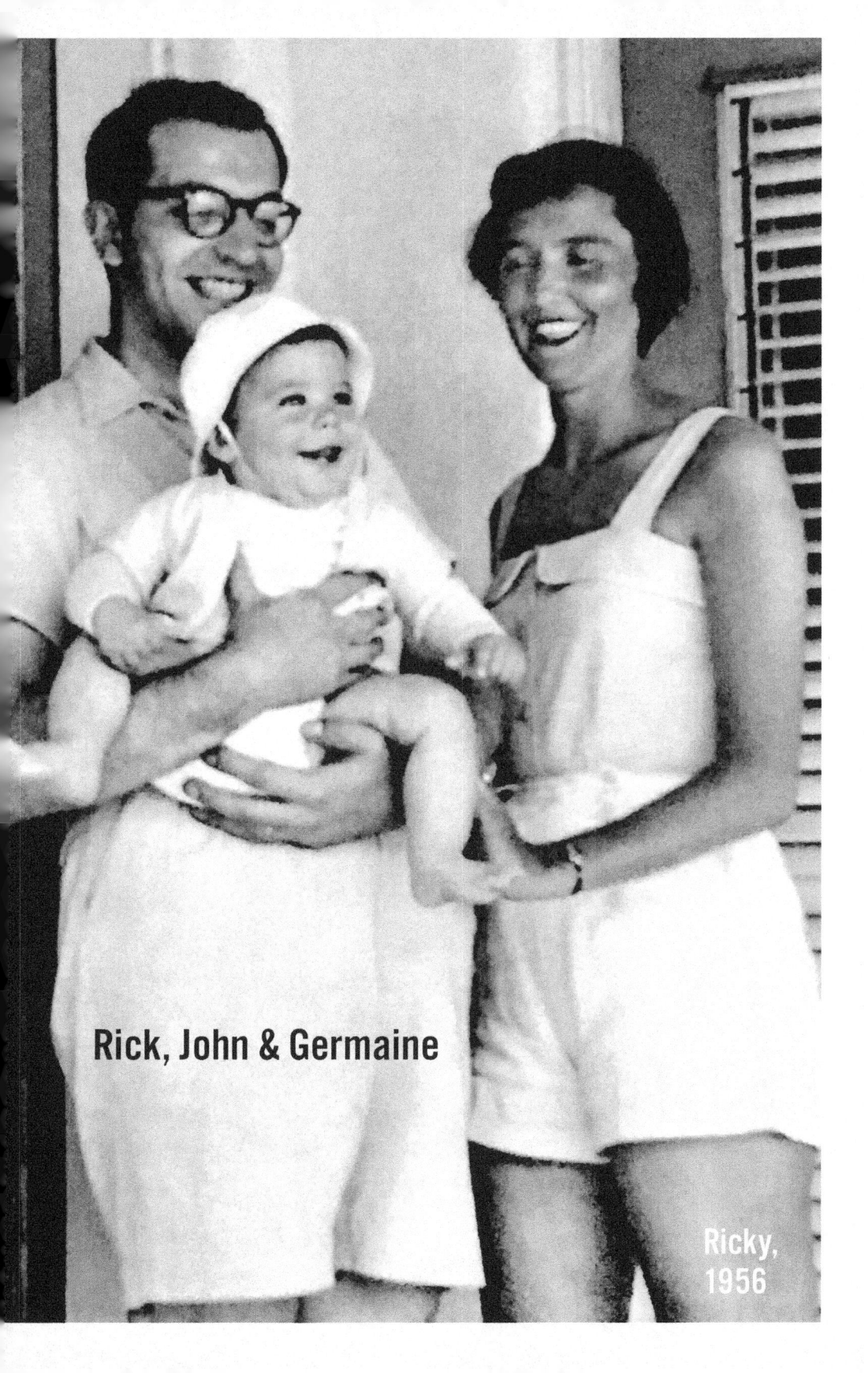

Rick, John & Germaine

Ricky, 1956

Ricky
Nov 1 1955

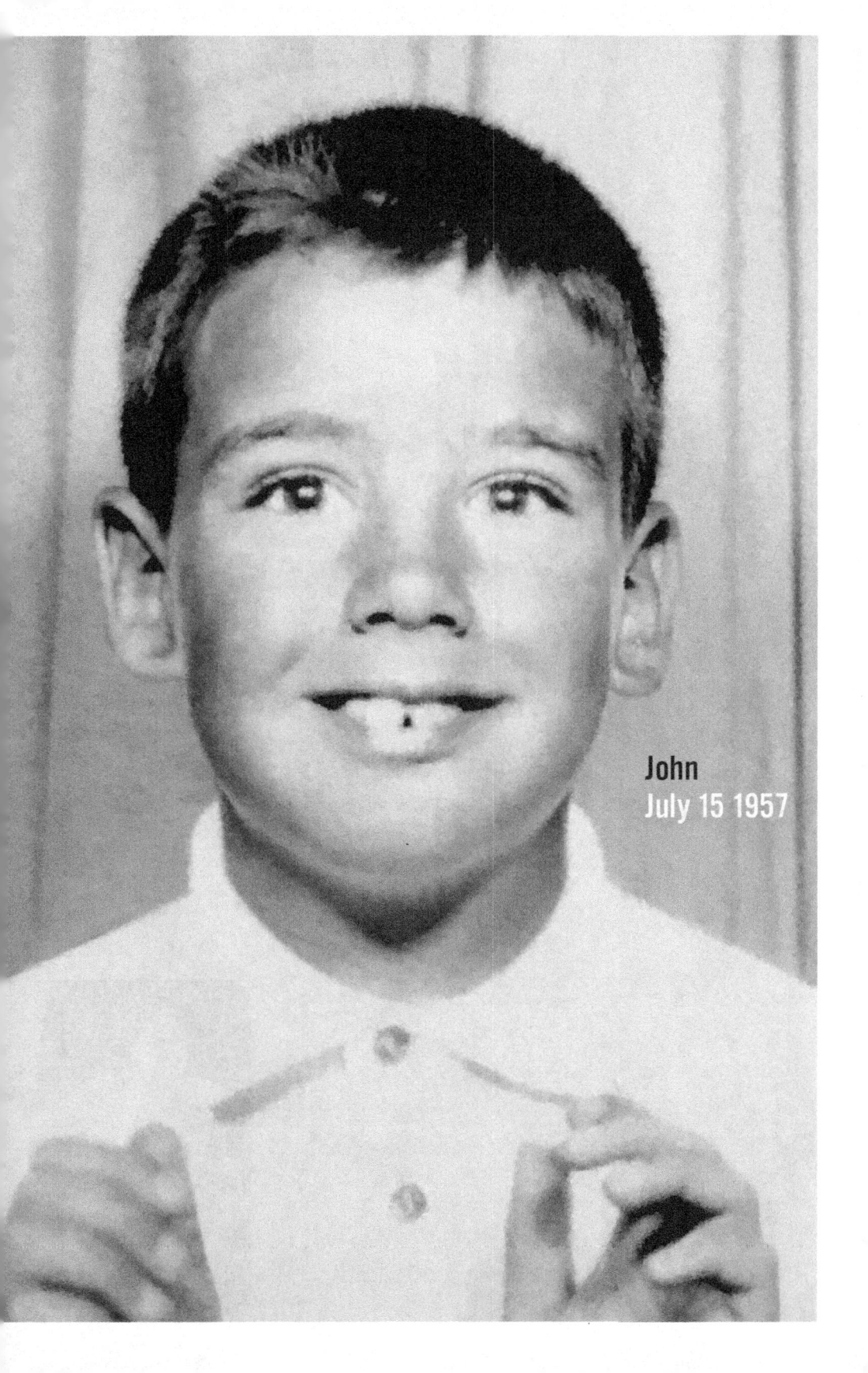

John
July 15 1957

Germaine
March 16 196

I remember so many great vacations at The Dolphin Apartments in Ocean City. Here's our kids in front of the Ocean Rest.

In front of our AMC Rambler, dressed for Sunday mass. Rick is wearing his choir boy cassock.

John, Germaine and Rick, 1964

Dear Rick + John,
You are the greatest brothers I have ever had in my entire life.
Love
Germaine

Gerry and I were blessed with three happy, bright and very wonderful kids. Rick says our early days mirrored the TV shows of the 60's, like *My Three Sons*, *Ozzie & Harriet* and *Leave it to Beaver*.

CHAPTER 69

HOMEOWNERS

On July 2, 1959, Gerry's father passed away in his sleep. For nearly three years, he lay unable to move or speak. Gerry felt his loss deeply. I saw it in her meditative look when holding the boys. She had no mother or father to love her sons. Rick and John would never know her parents.

In October of the following year, Gerry's brother and sisters came to our house to discuss its fate. I sat in the living room with Jeanette's husband, Colonel Jack Cole, called Butch by the family. It was strictly a family affair, and we had no part of it.

The meeting droned on with no sign of coming to an end. Gerry looked tense. The Colonel noticed my agitation and said, "Let's go for a beer." We walked a block to Stewart's Saloon. It was my first time there since moving to Drexel Hill.

"You looked like you were ready to interfere," said the Colonel. "It's none of our business."

"You're right, Butch. But Gerry looked so nervous. I wanted her to know I'm here."

"She knows."

Just two days ago, Gerry told me she was pregnant. After the meeting, she planned to tell her family the good news. With the baby due in mid-March, I couldn't let them sell the house. We drank our beer in silence.

When we returned, Gerry seemed on the verge of tears. I had to speak up.

"Sorry to interrupt, but I have something to say. Forget about past promises of giving us the house. Let's have this house appraised, and we'll buy it at that price, less Gerry's share of the inheritance. I hope this is agreeable to you all."

As I turned to leave, I gave Gerry a wink. She returned it with a million dollar smile.

Everyone agreed. Gerry's brother helped us get a low interest mortgage and a down payment to match our meager savings. In January, 1961, we became the owners of Gerry's beloved home.

My bosses had rejected 14 straight ads for the new Barr's Jewelers campaign, including some of my best work. Despairing, I submitted one more layout. "Fresh! Bold! Exciting!" they proclaimed. It was an exact copy of their ad from 20 years ago.

CHAPTER 70

BIRTH AND REBIRTH

"What we want is a new look to our advertising. A look that will attract new customers."

As Meyer Barr spoke, his father and brother nodded in agreement. All I could think was more unpaid overtime. "Mr. Barr," I said, "between ad scheduling, working with newspaper art departments and printers, plus the hundreds of details involved in ad production, I don't have time to create new ad styles. We have an ad agency. Give them the job."

A look passed between the triumvirate. "We feel you can do it just as well. You can work at night."

Of course have me do it. They would have to pay the agency for time and talent, while I was on salary.

Each new layout I presented was turned down. What was I doing wrong? I showed Earl Schloss, our agency account executive, three more layouts I was going to present. He looked them over carefully, suggested a few changes, and placed them in order of preference.

All three were turned down. "They're good, but not what we're looking for."

I was at my wit's end. They didn't know what they wanted, and Gerry was in her last month of pregnancy. I wanted to be home with her and the boys. At any moment, I could receive the call that the baby was coming. I had made arrangements well in advance to take a week's vacation the day Gerry went into the hospital.

It was late when I arrived home. Gerry greeted me with a kiss. "You look tired. Did you have dinner?"

"I had a hot dog at Nedick's."

"I've saved dinner for you. Come into the breakfast room and I'll tell you the news."

"The boys all right?"

"They're fine. I just got off the phone with Blanche and Roger. Dr. McCarron wants me at Fitz by seven thirty in the morning to induce labor. Blanche will watch the boys while Roger drives us to the hospital."

Once again, Dr. McCarron told me to go home. I protested, to no avail. As with Ricky and John, I expected to spend all day pacing, waiting for his call. Instead, he called at noon on March 16, 1961. "Congratulations, Mr. Shamlian. You have a beautiful daughter."

"Daughter!" I had no sooner said the word when Blanche yelled, "IT'S A GIRL!!"

"Your baby girl was born at eleven twenty-two. Six pounds, fifteen ounces, and eighteen and a half inches."

"Are they both okay? Can I see them now?"

"Come. Gerry and your daughter are both fine."

Through the nursery window, I read the nameplate on her crib: GERMAINE ELIZABETH SHAMLIAN. Her thick hair was jet black.

Gerry was awake when I arrived. "Fred, we have a daughter!! The first girl in my family since I was born."

No wonder Blanche was so excited. "Your sister was on the phone as I was leaving. By the time I get home, half the world will know."

I called Meyer Barr and told him I was starting my vacation. His secretary had a status report on all ad projects. He seemed pleased and wished Gerry and I much happiness.

A week later, I brought Gerry and our daughter home. The boys watched as their mother fed her the bottle of formula. Ricky and John took turns holding the bottle for their sister. How proud they looked. How much they had grown! How much I had missed! I promised myself never to work five nights a week again. Maybe it was time to look for work with a small manufacturing company or a large corporation.

Back behind Barr's, I resumed trying to create the ad that would satisfy three bosses. I revisited all the layouts I'd done. There were a few I was very proud of. Then I started digging through dusty scrap books of Barr's Jewelers ads created well before my time.

At about eight that evening, I submitted my latest concept.

Meyer Barr said, "This is what we're looking for." "I think you nailed it," said his father.

"It's new and will attract customers," said the brother.

I arrived home, all smiles. "Guess what? No more five nights a week." "They liked your layout? Is it a nice ad?"

"They wanted a brand new approach. And after rejecting fourteen ideas, including some of the best ads I've done, they agreed that my new layout is completely fresh, exciting and bold."

"Fred, I'm so proud of you!"

"I just hope they never find out that their 'brand new look' is an exact copy of their ad from twenty years ago."

The doctor said Dad passed away at 2 a.m.
"That's when I woke up," my mother replied.
"I thought I heard Victor calling me."

CHAPTER 71

THE PUSHMONDON

"Please go home," the doctor implored, looking at Mother. "Victor has had a massive cerebral hemorrhage. There's nothing we can do but wait. We will call you if there is any change."

As we left Dad's hospital room, I looked at him lying there. Despite the tracheotomy, his breathing was labored. Could this be the same man who once roamed the Middle East, journeyed to America, became a merchant, and raised a family? The same Dad who shouted and banged his fist on the table when playing pinochle, who loved classical violin, and who was secretly proud when his children were recognized for extraordinary work?

Only a few hours ago, Minnie had called to say that Dad was at Bryn Mawr Hospital for a minor heart problem. He was sitting up in bed when I arrived. His eyes looked so sad, I felt like hugging him and giving him a kiss. I didn't.

"Hi Dad. What did the doctor say?"

"Your father is going home tomorrow," said Mother. "The doctor said he will be fine."

"That's great, Dad."

"Are you alone, son?"

"Gerry's in the lobby with the kids. I'll go down soon and let her come up and visit. Dad, is there anything I can do for you?"

"I'm fine. It's getting late for the children. Go now and let your Gerry come up."

I kissed Mother and said, "Goodbye Dad. I'll call you at home tomorrow." Driving home, all I could think of was those sad eyes.

The next morning the hospital called and said come at once. By the time Gerry and I arrived, Mother and Minnie were already there. John, his wife Peg, and our sister Newert arrived soon after.

As the doctor approached Mother, the look on his face told us what we dreaded to hear. "Mrs. Shamlian, despite our efforts, Mr. Shamlian passed away this morning at approximately two o'clock."

"That's when I awoke. I thought I heard Victor calling me," said Mother. The doctor failed to get the significance of what she said.

"The hemorrhage was too massive," he continued. "He went peacefully. We are truly sorry." He turned to John and me. "You are the sons?" We nodded. "You will make the arrangements?" Again, we nodded.

At the funeral home, John and I felt as if we were buying a car. We selected a nice casket, not too fancy, which wouldn't take too much of Dad's insurance. We couldn't wait to leave.

A few years before I was married, I was riding with Dad to King of Prussia. As we passed Valley Forge Memorial Gardens, Dad said, "When I die, I want to be buried there. It looks like a park."

When we lived at 1008 Lancaster Avenue, Dad would sometimes walk around our backyard. When Mother asked what he was doing, he replied, "Just walking around the estate." With Mother's permission, John and I went to the Valley Forge Memorial Gardens and selected a spot on a knoll near a shade tree.

"Dad would like this place," I said to John. "From here, he can see his entire estate."

The funeral service was held in Saints Sahag-Mesrob Armenian Church in Wynnewood. After a short prayer at the grave, we filed away to the waiting limousines. Sick at heart, I felt like the lowest Pushmondon on earth.

I never kissed my father.

FREDERICK SHAMLIAN

ASSISTANT ADVERTISING MANAGER
JOHN B. STETSON COMPANY
PHILADELPHIA

(215) 676-9100

Frederick Shamlian
Advertising Manager

The Bunting Company, Inc.

1771 TOMLINSON ROAD, PHILADELPHIA, PENNSYLVANIA 19116

ARTHUR H. THOMAS COMPANY
Scientific Apparatus and Reagents

FREDERICK A. SHAMLIAN
Advertising Manager

Vine Street at 3rd • Philadelphia, Pa. 19106 • 215-574-4500

After twelve years of late nights, I left Barr's in 1964 to become Asst. Advertising Manager at the John B. Stetson Company. I did some of my best creative work there. And to Gerry's delight, I arrived home every evening at 5:30.

CHAPTER 72

WHAT I'VE LEARNED

It's been forty-eight years since Dad died in 1967. Not long after, my Mother and Minnie moved to an apartment in Bryn Mawr. They were frequent visitors to our home; Gerry invited them for dinner all the time. No one, not even Mother, knew of the colon cancer that would take her life eight years later.

After graduating from Juniata in 1951, I was hired by Barrs Jewelers as their Advertising Manager. There was so much to learn! I worked hard honing my craft. The position brought all sorts of temptations, notably the Kickback. Working sixty hours a week and getting paid for forty made the temptation very real.

One day a salesman dropped by to thank me for a big printing job, and left me a fancy memo pad. I noticed an envelope sticking out of it, and took it to my boss, Meyer Barr.

"What's in it?" he asked. "I don't know."

"Why didn't you open it?"

"If there's money inside, you'd always wonder if I took some."

339

"Open it." Inside was two hundred and fifty dollars.

"What should I do with it?" I was hoping he would say, "Keep it."

"Give it to the Treasurer. Have him credit it to Advertising Income."

Mr. Barr never said another word, but as I marveled at my next paycheck, which included a twenty-five dollar raise, Dad's words resounded in my brain: "I hate liars, cheats and teeves."

In 1963, our son Rick joined the Cub Scouts, so I pitched in, first as Treasurer, then Webelos Den Leader, and later as an assistant to the Scoutmaster, Wilford Allen. Will did a great job leading and teaching his scouts. I learned so much from him that when Will resigned to move back home to West Virginia, I became Scoutmaster of Troop 266, St Charles Borromeo, Valley Forge Council.

After twelve years of late nights and lost hours with Gerry and the kids, I left Barr's in 1964 to become the Assistant Advertising Manager at the John B. Stetson Company. There was joy when I arrived home every evening at five-thirty. I did some of my best creative work at Stetson, where I was privileged to work for the finest boss of my professional career. Thomas E. Thompson knew every facet of advertising. Regrettably, his superiors were another story.

One day I asked Mr. Thompson if Stetson's designers were working on new hats suited to the modern generation of low-slung cars, like the Mustang. He took me to see the Vice President of Marketing. Stetson's Chief Marketing and Innovation Executive pointed to a display of Stetson hats and said, "We've always done it this way!" As we left his office, Tom shook his head and said, "That kind of thinking spells an end to any company."

In the spring of 1969, after one hundred and four years, the John B. Stetson Company closed its doors. Mr. Thompson opened his own successful advertising agency.

The Bunting Company, founded in 1827, was the home of the Bunting Glider and other sturdy metal furniture seen on porches across America. In my first month as Ad Manager, I hired photographer George Gelernt, whom I had worked with at Stetson. Together, we created the first full color catalog in Bunting's history. Every furniture set was displayed on the patio or lawn of a magnificent Main Line home, and every photo filled the entire page. The response was fantastic.

In 1972, the company was sold to new owners, who instituted many changes for the worse. With declining product quality came lost sales, reduced ad spending, a deeply demoralized staff – and my two-year search for a new employer.

The day I gave my notice, the President's secretary resigned too. In a foul temper and filthy language, he called us both traitors, handed us our money and barked at us to leave. I firmly believed the company would fail in three years. I was wrong. Four years later, after 150 years, the Bunting Company closed its doors forever.

The Arthur H. Thomas Company, founded in 1900, produced the first major catalog of medical and scientific equipment, and their clients included laboratories from around the world. I joined the firm in 1974, the year the Executive Officers declared that business was so good, they could eliminate both national advertising and the 1976 catalog. It did not take long before sales began to slide.

When the Advertising Manager died, I was promoted. I called my staff together and announced that we would bring the "Bible of the Industry" into the modern age. I told our Production Manager to replace every woodcut with photos, retouched to show the fine details. The Catalog Editor and her three scientific writers brought new life to over two thousand pages of product descriptions. Thanks to their creativity and dedicated efforts, the 1980 Thomas Catalog won the first national design award in the company's history, and became an indispensable reference for scientists and lab technicians the world over.

Another of Dad's sayings was "Do not do half a job. Do not be half a man." When I did something stupid, especially after graduating from college, Dad would say, "Don't be an educated jackass." His advice went with me everywhere I worked, and I never did half a job on a marketing project. I also discovered that, while there are educated jackasses in every firm, I could succeed by finding the dedicated people and nurturing their talents.

The President of Arthur H. Thomas was the son of one of the founders. When he passed away, his son took over the business. It was around this time that I remembered Dad's other career advice: "You will be surprised how much you can learn about a person when you keep your ears open and your mouth shut."

Somehow, I managed to convince the new President that a national ad campaign was vital, and turned to the McKinney Agency, which had served the firm well for many years. In my strategy session with their Account Manager, I added one unusual request. I told him to pad the budget with two hundred and fifty thousand dollars worth of useless junk.

After a brilliant presentation by the Agency, our new President said, "If you can cut the budget by $250,000, I'll approve it."

"How did you know??" the incredulous Account Rep asked me.

"That man has no idea how an ad department works. To show his leadership, I knew he would ask to cut the budget."

With little knowledge of the business, and no desire to shoulder responsibility, the new President appointed a Vice President as Executive Officer, who gradually replaced knowledgeable managers with family members. Nepotism reared its ugly head, and once again, I was witness to a slow and steady decline in sales and morale caused by small-minded men. I fought the battles I could fight, seeking better lighting, seating and salaries for my staff who, like me, were underpaid and unappreciated.

During this time, I found satisfaction and purpose as Scoutmaster. With each meeting and camping trip, I learned the need for patient mentoring, constant vigilance, and leading by example. I'm proud to say that our happy troop was always welcome in the state parks and scout camps of Pennsylvania and Maryland. I was even prouder to see four of my Scouts achieve the rank of Eagle Scout. Two of them eventually became Catholic Priests.

In July, 1990, I turned 65. After nearly eighteen years at Thomas Scientific, the new company name I suggested, I tendered my resignation, and left in January. I also resigned as Scoutmaster. Gerry was struggling with the effects of the chemo and radiation therapy for her cancer, and she needed me. Despite the sometimes terrible pain, Gerry maintained her good spirits. Her courage taught our family the real meaning of character.

My Gerry passed away in our home on March 20, 1994. On a cold winter night, the receiving line at her wake extended far into the street. It took almost three hours for the roughly 400 visitors to say their farewells. There were women from the St. Charles Ladies Auxiliary, where Gerry contributed her time. Former members of the St. Charles girl's basketball team came to remember their volunteer coach. All of our neighbors and friends were there, reminiscing about her warmth, kindness and sense of humor. Her co-workers from JRP Surveys recalled the joy and professionalism that enabled her to entice complete strangers to answer long, detailed surveys. Even her fellow volunteers at the Delaware County Hospital and St. John's

Hospice came to pay their respects. At times, the outpouring of love left me speechless.

Gerry was buried in the Saints Peter and Paul Cemetery on Sproul Road in Springfield. She was the catalyst who brought our family together. Her passing marked the end of a wonderful part of our lives. There isn't a day when I don't think of her.

I was alone in a house filled with memories of Gerry. I tried to busy myself with home improvements, reading and television, but the quiet was deafening.

One day my son John and his family visited from Syracuse. John asked me to tell his young son and daughter one of the Archibald and Murgatroyd stories I used to tell at bedtime. I sat Jarrett and Quinn on my lap and, just like I used to with their dad, invented a story point blank. When I described how Windy, the West Wind, saved the day, their wide eyes rekindled my passion for writing.

To date, I've written nearly sixty Archibald and Murgatroyd adventures, as well as other stories for young adults about the way life was before World War II. Many of the people and events that shaped my life have made it into my stories. Sometimes I recall a much younger me sitting beside a creek with pad and pencil. In many ways, that romantic young man still lives in me – and in the boundless optimism and goodness of Archibald and Murgatroyd.

On July 15, 2015, I turned 90. All my children all married now. So are Jarrett and Quinn. The youngest of my nine grandchildren is eighteen. In a few weeks, my son Rick turns 60. I'm proud of my sons and daughter for who they are, and for the way they are passing on to their children all of the love their mother gave them.

Despite the loss of many loved ones, including dear Minnie, the last of my four brothers and sisters, I'm blessed with a large circle of friends. I enjoy cooking for the people I love, and look forward to

Wednesday dinners at my apartment in Media with Rick, Germaine and, sometimes, their sons. I cook their favorite dishes: spaghetti and homemade meatballs, beef stew, pot roast, and chicken cutlets. My chili is Rick's favorite. I also make stuffed cabbage and stuffed peppers the way Dad used to – with a few special touches of my own. And every April and October, I get to visit and cook for my son John and his family at his beautiful farmhouse outside of Syracuse.

On my wedding day, the Priest asked, "Do you take this woman for better or worse, in sickness and health, for richer or poorer, forsaking all others?" I said Yes. And I meant it. My work for Bunting took me to Chicago, New York and Greensboro, North Carolina, where there were many beautiful girls. I was always true to Gerry. Tom Gilroy, my friend for over fifty years, put it best: "There is no pillow as soft as a clear conscience."

My nearly forty years with Gerry had its trials, but what we shared most was love. During the summer, our family would picnic at the Brandywine Battlefield, playing ball, flying balsa wood airplanes, and emptying a picnic basket full of Gerry's good cooking.

Every summer, to Gerry's delight, we spent two carefree weeks at Ocean City, New Jersey. Each day brought new guests. Janet and Butch lived ten minutes away in Marmora, NJ. They visited every day. Janet would come very early with sticky buns and head to the beach with Gerry, while Butch arrived later, and we sat on the porch sipping beers and playing pinochle. From our second floor perch on the corner of 31st and Central, we could look across the street past the Ocean Rest to the ocean.

That apartment was always filled with laughter – and people! In later years, Jack and Julie bought a condo at 5th Street on the boardwalk, and their visits were as regular as next door neighbors. We always looked forward to our days with our dear friends the Kellys and the Tremoglies. And our kids always had at least one friend come and stay. One time I awoke to find Rick's best friend Tommy Purcell sleeping on the dining room table.

Bee and Minnie were frequent guests too. They loved the beach, and would literally glow from hourly applications of Coppertone sun-tanning oil, SPF O. Gerry always achieved a lovely tan, but Bee, Jan and Min took tanning to whole new level. Once, when Ricky was very young, he asked me "Daddy, is Aunt Bee a negro?"

Next to our Summer vacations, I cherished Christmas most. Christmas day, our children would hurry down the stairs in flannel pajamas and robes to find their presents beneath a glittering tree, decorated with real lead tinsel by Santa. In the evenings, we drank hot chocolate by the fireplace, then Rick, John and Germaine would stand in front of the tree, one by one, and sing Christmas carols.

What I've learned from a lifetime of true friends, four generations of loving family, and a few misguided bosses, is that there are three keys to a happy life: a warm hug, a kiss, and the spoken words "I love you." Steve Stefankowitz, who drove with me to Bunting each workday, summed it up this way, "You've got to do a lot of loving if you want to do a lot of living."

The End

Knot Tying

My introduction to Scouting began in 1963, when Rick became a Cub Scout. As Scoutmaster from '77 to '92, Troop 266 awarded 4 boys the rank of Eagle.

In 30 years of surfcasting, I've caught one flounder,
two blues, sandsharks, blowfish, seaweed – and a boot.

While conducting the enthusiastic Thomas Scientific Choir,
I dreamed that my co-workers called me "Maestro."

Aunt Minnie's 88th Birthday , September 4, 2010.

Front, L to R: Joe Rickards Jr., Me, Germaine Rickards, Minnie, Lynn Shamlian, daughter Lauren, and Chase Shamlian (Rick's son). Back: David Shamlian, son Daniel, Joe Rickards and son Cole. Below: with my son John at his Avalon home, his first wife Roz, and the kids (L to R): Wesley, Rory, Jarrett, Haley and Quinn.

In my study, filled with books, music and memories.

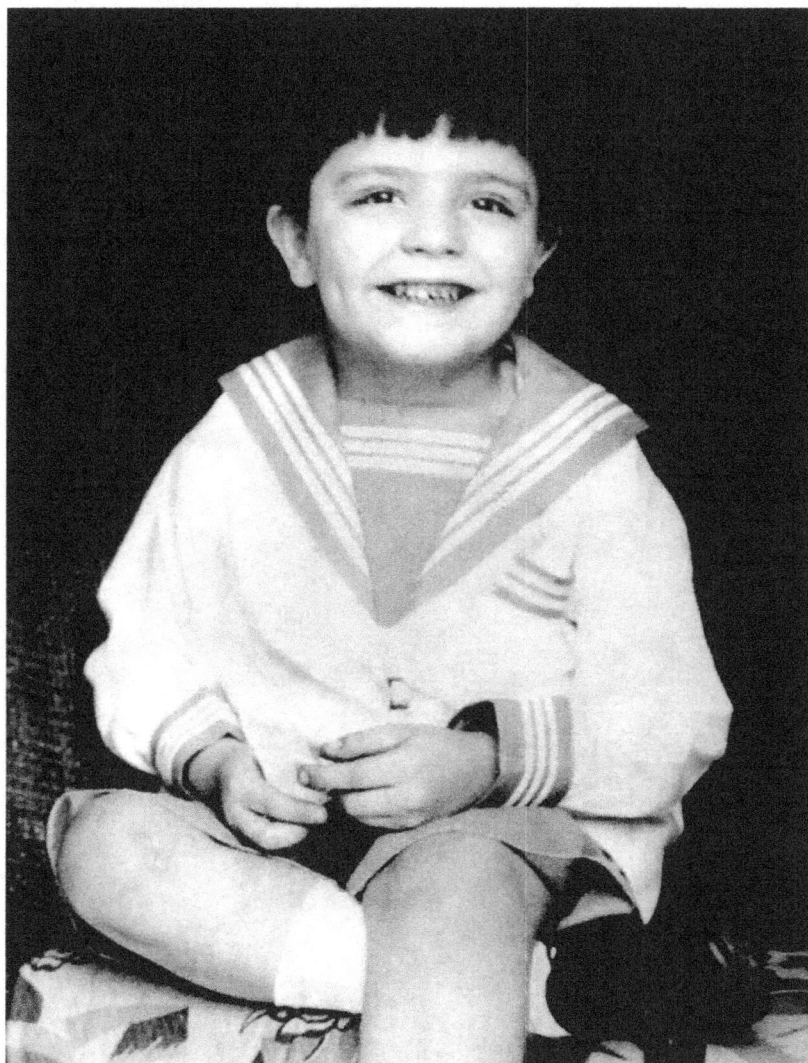

Made in the USA
Las Vegas, NV
07 November 2023